The County Books Series

GENERAL EDITOR: BRIAN VESEY-FITZGERALD

HIGHLANDS OF SCOTLAND

THE COUNTY BOOKS SERIES

A Series comprising 57 Volumes. It covers every county in England and there will be five books on Scotland, two on Ireland, two on the Hebrides, and one each on Orkney, Shetland, Wales, the Isle of Man and the Channel Islands

THE FOLLOWING FORTY-EIGHT VOLUMES
HAVE NOW BEEN PUBLISHED

PLEASE WRITE TO THE PUBLISHERS
FOR FULL DESCRIPTIVE PROSPECTUS

HIGHLANDS
OF
SCOTLAND

by

SETON GORDON

Illustrated and with a Map

London
Robert Hale Limited
63 Old Brompton Road, S.W.7

Some books by the same Author

Highways and Byways in the Western Highlands
Highways and Byways in the Central Highlands
A Highland Year
Thirty Years of Nature Photography
Wild Birds in Britain
The Charm of the Hills
Afoot in the Hebrides

First published 1951

Printed in Great Britain by
Billing and Sons Ltd., Guildford and Esher
G 2551

TO

FRANCIS CAMERON-HEAD

OF INVERAILORT

CONTENTS

ILLUSTRATIONS

ix

Present-day difficulties do not permit of a comprehensive map of the area being included in this book. For more detailed information readers are referred to the respective Ordnance Survey sheets.

ACKNOWLEDGMENTS

The illustrations above, numbered 1, 16, 17, 18, 19, 20, 21, 22, 23, 24, 25 and 26 are reproduced from photographs supplied by Mr. Robert M. Adam of Kingussie; the remaining thirty-seven from photographs supplied by Mr. G. Douglas Bolton of Shipley.

INTRODUCTION

So far as I can discover, the word "Highlands" is an English-coined word, and was originally applied to high-lying country in the northern part of the British Isles. The area *now* classed as Highland is greater than it was, and the country right down to the tide in the west and north-west districts at the present time is usually considered as belonging to the Highlands.

In the east the matter is rather different. The Aberdeenshire coast, for example, is usually classed as Lowland territory. When I was a boy living on Deeside it was commonly said that the Dinnet burn, which crosses the main Deeside road on the north side of the river Dee, about a mile east of Dinnet, was the dividing line in that district. I never saw any written confirmation of that saying, and it may have been a myth, like the old belief among anglers (they may hold it still) that when the Dee in fine weather rose unaccountably with strong south-west wind it was because that wind was blowing the water out of Loch Muich on the Balmoral forest. The actual reason was very different: with a south-west wind from the Atlantic there was often heavy rain on the Cairngorms and the White Mount massif, when dry weather prevailed lower down the Dee valley. A little reflection will show that for a loch of inconsiderable size like Loch Muich to cause even a small spate in a river the size of the Dee a tremendous hurricane would have to blow.

In the south, Colonel David Stewart of Garth in his *Sketches* gives the Highland boundary as the small burn of Loch Ewan below the bridge of Dunkeld, and says the inhabitants on either side present perfect characteristics of the Saxons and Celts. In the north, Caithness is generally considered without the Highland boundary.

The earliest race in the Highlands, as elsewhere in Britain, was probably a people of the Iberian type, small, dark-skinned and curly-haired. They were followed by the Celts, one branch of which race, according to Skene, was named by the Romans Picts or Painted People. These were a fair-skinned, large-limbed, red-haired race, sometimes named Tuatha De Danann by the people of Eire. The

11

other branch of the Celts was early named the Milesians, and, after the fourth century, the Scots. They were also a fair-skinned people, with brown hair. The Celtic race was followed by a Teutonic people, from the low-lying country along the north coast of Germany. They did not penetrate far into the Highlands, but their descendants can be recognised in the eastern fringe of the Highlands at the present day. In St. Columba's time the northern Picts, whom some authorities believe to have been purely Celtic, both in race and in language, inhabited and held sway over the whole of the northern Highlands.

The population of Argyll was of unusual interest. Here was the kingdom of Dalriada, founded by Scots from Irish Dalriada at the end of the fifth century, who took with them the name of their Irish home. The capital of this kingdom was Dunadd, a small fortified hill near the Crinan Canal. There is some ground for believing that at the time Columba arrived on Iona from Eire Iona stood exactly on the boundary which separated the kingdom of Dalriada from the kingdom of the Picts.

The western Highlands, and more especially the Hebrides, at a later date were much influenced by the Norse, who for some centuries colonised the Hebrides and made their presence felt also along the western seaboard of the mainland. Many place-names commemorate them.

The true Highlander is an aristocrat, with a veneration for old families and old traditions and customs: these characteristics he retains despite two world wars. There is socialism in the towns, but you will find little socialism in the remote country districts.

Clansmen are loyal and devoted subjects to their chief; in their eyes he is second only to the king of the realm.

The title of Highland chief usually passes from father to son, although there are instances when a person not of the direct line has been appointed by the people. The right of the chief of a Highland clan to wear three flight feathers of an eagle in his bonnet is well known. This custom, like many other old customs, is gradually falling into disuse, and the imposing feathers have now given place to three symbolic silver feathers in the silver crest worn in the bonnet.

The origin of the wearing of the kilt is lost in the mists of antiquity, nor is much known concerning the evolution of tartans. It is, however, known that there were at one time certain tartans, known as District Tartans, which were worn by the clans living in a particular district.

The Huntly district tartan, for example, was worn by Gordons, Forbeses and Brodies. In the old red Huntly tartan there is a vertical yellow stripe and a vertical white stripe running through the sett close to one another. The only difference between the modern Gordon tartan and the modern Forbes tartan is that the yellow stripe in the Gordon is replaced by the white stripe in the Forbes, and I have often thought that when the modern Gordon tartan, which is really a regimental one and was evolved on the raising of the Gordon Highlanders in 1793, was decided on, the yellow stripe in the Huntly tartan was chosen for the new Gordon tartan, while the Forbeses for their new and very similar tartan chose the white stripe.

The Highland chief was not only a leader in war; he was the father of his people, interesting himself in their lives, in their hopes and their sorrows, and settling their disputes. When on some warlike foray he shared the hardships of his men. The Highlanders were so inured to hardship that it is said they could with difficulty be persuaded to sleep in tents during the campaign of 1745.

The old story, often told, of the Highlander who was expelled with ignominy from the clan because, when sleeping out in the open in the snow, he fashioned a pillow of snow for his head, illustrates the contempt in which the people of the Highlands held comforts. The tartan plaid, which they almost invariably carried, acted as a shield against rain and snow alike, and also as a blanket in which to sleep. Its use at night is well illustrated in the English translation of the Gaelic word *plaid*, which means a blanket. It is perhaps a sign of the times that the carrying of the plaid is now very rare, except on some special occasion, as a Highland ball, gathering, wedding or funeral. At a dance, or even on full-dress occasions during the day, some plaids are now little heavier than ladies' scarves.

A change is also seen in the colour of the Highland bonnets now worn. These bonnets were usually blue; this earlier and pleasing colour has now been superseded by a blue so dark that it is almost black. The earlier colour is recalled in the title of the old song, "The Blue Bonnets are over the water." Had the bonnets been of the modern colour it is clear they would not have been commemorated thus.

A Highland chief in the old days had his bard, his harper, and his piper. There is said to have been a harper's window in Duntuilm Castle in the Isle of Skye! The office of harper has long died. One of the last of the harpers was Murdo MacDonald, harper to Maclean of Coll until 1734. He had received his musical tuition from that famous harper Roderick Morrison, commonly named Ruaraidh Dall, Blind Rory, he who was MacLeod's harper. It is likely that there was considerable rivalry between a chief's harper and his piper, for the music of the piper in volume of sound must have been supreme, nor can the soft music of the harp have been heard with pleasure after the shrill strains of the bagpipe.

Among pipers the illustrious family of MacCrimmon, hereditary pipers to the MacLeods of Dunvegan for centuries, were most renowned. Among other piping families of fame were the MacKays, pipers to the MacKenzies of Gairloch, and the Macintyres, pipers to the MacDonalds of Kinlochmoidart.

All the great piping families were proficient in the classical music of the bagpipe, the Big Music (Ceòl Mór) or Piobaireachd. It is remarkable that so many of these old tunes should have come down to us through the centuries untouched, or almost so, in form. They were handed down not by staff notation but by a form of singing or chanting known as Canntaireach. They are all, or almost all, older than a hundred years; so old indeed that the original name of many of them has been lost. These old tunes of Ceòl Mór are mostly slow and stately in their measure, and it is therefore commonly supposed that they are all laments, but this is not so. A Piobaireachd (Anglice Pibroch) may be a Salute, a Welcome, a tune composed for a chief's rowers to keep time to while rowing their master's galley, a Taunt, a March, a Lament.

The chief was head of his clan. His Highland title was usually different from the name by which he was ordinarily known amongst English speakers. Thus the Duke of Argyll, chief of the Campbells, is in Gaelic styled MacCailein Mór, which in English is Son of Great Colin. The title of some chiefs is taken from a place-name in their territory—for instance, Cameron of Lochiel is always known in the Highlands as Lochiel. Here it should be mentioned that an innovation which has sometimes appeared in the press of recent years is entirely wrong; I refer to the prefixing of the word 'The' before the title of a Highland chief. As an example, MacLeod of MacLeod, chief of his clan, is sometimes referred to in the press as The MacLeod. I recall the remark of a distinguished authority on Highland customs and etiquette: he said to me, "There are only three persons who have the right to the definite article before their names—the Chisholm,

14

the Pope and the Devil." The Chisholm is the chief of the clan Chisholm.

Superficially, it would perhaps appear that the second world war has brought few changes to the Highlands, yet deeper knowledge shows that the change has penetrated to the most remote corner. With very few exceptions, the head of a Highland family is no longer able to keep up his ancestral residence. Few people can now afford to rent or staff the shooting lodges, and the result is that these houses have been transformed into hotels, or into Youth Hostels to accommodate the increasing number of visitors to the Highlands. National Parks are being organised, and it is probable that before long the whole of the great mountain area of the Cairngorms will become a National Park.

What of the hydro-electric schemes which have in recent years aroused so much controversy? These undertakings are of two sorts. The great schemes—that, for example, of Loch Sloy near Loch Lomond—are intended to provide electricity not for the Highlands but for the Lowlands and industrial areas. Lesser schemes, as, for example, those at Mallaig, Kyle of Lochalsh and the Isle of Skye, provide light and power for the local inhabitants. Yet many of the crofters of the western Highlands, who are still without roads or running water, would prefer either of these two luxuries (perhaps they might indeed be termed necessities) to electric light in their houses.

Will these hydro-electric schemes repopulate the Highland glens? I do not think they will. There is a more promising outlook in the various forestry schemes set on foot by the Government in different parts of the Highlands. Hillsides which were formerly bare are gradually supporting a population of thriving trees, mostly coniferous. One sees the thin, upright and bright green *Pinus contorta* growing in certain sites more vigorously than the native Scots pine. In damp situations the hardy and quick-growing Menzies or Sitka spruce withstands the strongest winds of ocean, and where the soil is richer the Japanese larch with reddish-brown bark grows faster than the better-known European larch, but is less resistant to frost.

Forestry may bring back a population to the glens, and indeed afforestation is now a more pressing problem for the Highlands than ever before. During the years 1939-45 tremendous areas of old forest were felled. This is seen in Upper Deeside and on Strathspey.

In both districts large areas of some of the finest naturally grown Scots fir (*Pinus sylvestris*) were felled—the remains of the ancient Caledonian Forest which at one time covered the Highlands from Ardgour, Loch Arkaig and Loch Maree in the west to the lower reaches of Dee and Spey. During war it is the devil who drives. The trees were felled hastily, for the matter was of extreme urgency. Had time permitted, it might have been better in the long run to have left certain mother trees from which natural regeneration might later arise. In a few, but only a very few, places was this done, and even here, unless fencing was run up as a protection against deer, seedlings will have little prospect of survival. A private landowner has now no money for such things as fencing on a large scale; unless it is done by the Government or under the new Dedication Scheme with Government assistance, it is not done at all.

What of the fishing industry in the west Highlands?

Here the crofters engage in fishing only during certain times of the year. There are few whole-time fishermen, such as one finds along the north-east coast of Scotland, at Peterhead and Fraserburgh, Buckie, Banff and other places. The boats of the west are usually small and, until recently, depended on sail. The white fishing, carried on chiefly in the early spring months, has greatly deteriorated. For this the large steam trawlers are blamed, and during the war years they certainly fished with impunity within the three-mile limit, working right inside some of the Highland sea lochs. The fishery cruisers being engaged on war duties, there was nothing to check this illegal fishing, nor would it perhaps have been popular had it been checked, for the trawlers were kept to inshore waters by the depredations of enemy submarines. But now, in the post-war years, the fishery cruisers are active and illegal trawling has been largely checked. The harm done by illegal trawling in west Highland lochs during the early spring months of the year is two-fold—the fish are taken on the spawning beds, and in addition the ova and young fish are trawled up, caught in the nets and, although thrown overboard later, are destroyed. There is, too, considerable risk that the long lines set legitimately by the local crofter-fishermen may be fouled and broken by the trawl, for trawlers which work mainly at night when trawling illegally are unable to see the buoys marking either end of a long line. Indeed, in one district I know the local fishermen gave up setting their long lines because of the damage done to them.

16

Herring Fisher Girls at Tarbert, Loch Fyne

It is not difficult to check illegal trawling, but there is another problem which has arisen in certain districts and which is not so easily solved. Lobster fishing is in the west Highlands of more importance locally than white or even herring fishing. There is an unwritten law that the skerries and reefs of their neighbourhood belong to the local fishermen. Of late years large motor-boats from comparatively distant ports have been fishing lobsters on the local fishermen's grounds. These boats are able to be at sea and to lift their lobster creels when the conditions are too stormy for the local boats, and the local lobster fishermen see their livelihood being taken from them, apparently without means of redress. They themselves perhaps have not sufficient capital to obtain these larger vessels.

Herring fishing is carried on from several west Highland centres. The most important centre, at Stornoway, being in the Hebrides is without the scope of this book. At Oban, at Mallaig, at Kyle of Lochalsh, at Gairloch and Ullapool, large quantities of herrings are landed and are sent south, by rail or by road. A new fishing base for vessels operating in the northern Minch has recently been opened at Kinlochbervie, on the north-west coast of Sutherland a few miles south of Cape Wrath. Unlike the lobster fishing, which is engaged in chiefly by local boats, the herring fishing is carried on mainly by the larger east coast boats. Herring are at their best in June, July and August, when they are full-fed and fat. The herring is of the tribe of the salmon and the sea trout, which are protected by law during their spawning season, but the herring has no close time, and is caught in early spring, when it is thin and tasteless. I have sometimes thought that a close time for herring fishing (that close time varying in different districts, according to the habits of the fish) would benefit the industry as a whole.

Foreigners do not interfere with the herring fishing, but the fishing of lobsters was influenced before the 1939-45 war in an unexpected way. Large sailing smacks—I hear they were old Dundee whalers, built in the days of sail—from Camaret in Brittany appeared in Scottish waters and, their crews being skilled fishermen, soon accounted for great numbers of lobsters and crayfish, which they kept alive for three weeks or a month in their wells before sailing back to Brittany. Being foreigners, they were not entitled to fish, even for lobsters, inside the three-mile limit, and several were caught by the fishery cruisers, one of them just as she was about to sail for

17   B

Kilchurn Castle on Loch Awe

Brittany, and her large catch of lobsters confiscated. These Camaret smacks were able to keep at sea in all weathers.

What is the future of the grouse moors and deer forests of the Highlands? During the war years the enemies of the red grouse preyed upon the birds unchecked, and the moors besides were frequently disturbed by the exercises of British and Allied troops. The result was that at the close of the war the stock of grouse on Highland moors was perhaps the smallest in living memory. A remarkable increase in most districts was recorded in the summer of 1948, and it is possible that this sport, if financial times improve, will regain something like its former popularity. The prospects of the deer forests are more doubtful. Some of the largest of these forests have not been stalked over since the war, except by the keepers. Much of their land is now pastured by sheep and Highland cattle. Times have changed when one hears of a well-known peer of over three-score and ten years, unassisted, loading his stag on to the pony at the end of an arduous stalk, and then at the close of the day walking home many miles, there to sleep the dreamless slumber of the hillman.

Yet though times have altered the Highlander is at heart a Conservative, although he may call his politics Liberal or even Labour. More than most of the British race he holds to the old values; his lonely and often isolated life causes him to think for himself, and thus he remains unswayed by popular movements which more easily influence the dwellers in city or town. His loyalty, as I have said, towards the old families of the Highland aristocracy remains unaltered, and when they have of necessity parted with their lands he greets them with joy and affection should they return to visit their ancient patrimony.

The people of the west Highlands—I am now thinking of the seaboard and especially the north-west seaboard—are notably co-operative. A crofter always helps his neighbour, whenever his help is needed, knowing that he in turn will be helped in the same way. In this respect the people of the west differ from those of the central Highlands, who are more self-contained, and are perhaps, although there are of course exceptions, less obviously friendly and hospitable. The people of the western seaboard live largely on salt fish and dried saithe, as the young of the coal fish are named. These saithe they catch in great numbers with rod and line, usually on a white fly, in the

autumn and early winter of the year, the fishing being generally
from boats, and the time of fishing being from sunset to dusk. Lythe
or pollack are also caught, but are usually eaten fresh. Salt herrings
are greatly relished. Few people have gardens, so that vegetables are
rarely grown or eaten, and no fruit. The seaweed known as carageen
is gathered from the rocks at low tide, is spread out on the grass to
dry, and when it has been bleached by the action of sun and wind
is used for puddings, being boiled with milk. Limpets are also eaten,
and near the houses of the crofters are usually to be seen limpet heaps.
Whelks are laboriously gathered and are sent in sacks to the markets
of the south. The population is decreasing almost everywhere; the
language is still Gaelic in the more remote districts, yet this is being
superseded by English.

At a time when much discussion has arisen as to the manner of
keeping the people on the land, and bringing back to the land those
who have gone to the towns and cities, it is perhaps worth recalling
the suggestion which was made about forty years ago of making
Fort William a Transatlantic port. The project is mentioned in
Lochaber in War and Peace, a book written by Wm. T. Kilgour
and published in 1908. At the time the book was written this ambitious
project was evidently much in men's minds, but came to nothing.
The author mentions that from Quebec to Fort William is a straight
passage of about 2,083 miles, as against 2,625 miles from Quebec to
Liverpool. He states that Loch Linnhe at its shallowest is 8 fathoms,
that is, 48 feet-deep, at the narrows at Corran, so that the largest
liners could make the passage. He reckoned that a gain in time of
1 day three hours would result if Fort William and not Liverpool
was used on the journey between Quebec and London. He concludes:
"All points considered, the project is one worthy of the fullest consideration, and indeed it would be difficult to find within the three
kingdoms another port possessed of greater natural advantages for
the development of a shipping terminus such as Canada would find
in the basin described." I put forward the suggestion that this scheme
should be reconsidered, for it would bring employment to the whole
of the West Highlands in a way that no other project could.

The five Crofter Counties are Argyll, Inverness, Ross, Sutherland
and Caithness. In these counties most of the people are crofters
holding their land under the Crofters Act of 1886, by which they
have security of tenure and other advantages. Much of the Crofter

Counties area is now owned by the Department of Agriculture for Scotland.

The tweed industry, because of purchase tax, is in a bad way. This industry grew from each district having its weaver and all the women being spinners. Native dyes were used from plants to colour the tweed. The industry has now entered a new phase, and mills have largely taken the place of the old hand loom.

Agriculture is going back in the west Highlands. This is partly due to lack of labour for drainage, and long years of cultivation without enough being put back into the soil. Almost all the crofts are in need of a liberal application of lime. Rushes are everywhere increasing.

The west Highlands suffer from a lack of water supplies and roads to the more remote townships, and from a lack of accommodation for visitors. There is also a considerable loss, as I have said, through the absence of shooting tenants, owing to increased taxation. The shooting lodges are either empty or have been turned into hotels.

PART I

THE ANCIENT KINGDOM OF DALRIADA IN THE WEST HIGHLANDS AS IT IS AT THE PRESENT DAY

CHAPTER I

DUNADD TO LOCH FYNE

ABOUT the year 500 a migration of Scots from Northern Ireland founded the kingdom of Dalriada.

According to the historian Skene, the kingdom of Dalriada extended northwards from the Mull of Kintyre to Loch Leven near the head of Loch Linnhe, the present boundary between the counties of Argyll and Inverness. It embraced the islands of Bute, Islay, Jura and Colonsay, and half of the Isle of Mull, crossing the Sound of Mull to take in the southern fringe of the mountainous district of Morvern. Eastward it extended to the shore of Loch Long and Loch Lomond, thence northward along the eastern fringes of the great hill range of Drumalban which forms the watershed of the Highlands, but embracing the hills of Loch Etive and the Blackmount Forest. To the east of this imaginary line was the kingdom of the Picts. The capital of Dalriada was Dunadd, pronounced Doonatt, near Crinan, of which more anon. The Pictish king of the day in 736 laid waste Dalriada and took possession of its fortified capital. From this attack the kingdom of Dalriada seems never to have recovered.

Before describing the present-day confines of the old kingdom, a short account of Dunadd as it appears at the present time may be interesting. It was a day of golden autumn sunshine when I visited the old fortress, which stands near the Crinan Canal, not far from the main road between Oban and Ardrishaig. There is now little left to show the importance of the place in early times, for, so far as is known, it has never been inhabited nor rebuilt since King Angus of the Picts captured the stronghold and bound in chains the two sons of Selbach, the Dalriadan king. On a level surface of rock surrounded by short green grass is a footprint; beside it a wild boar has been incised in the rock, and near the figure of the boar is a circular hollow, apparently made by hand. The footprint of the man is rather small and delicately shaped. It is the print not of a bare foot, but one covered by a *cuaran* or stocking. Celtic scholars are inclined to believe that the kings of Dalriada were crowned as they stood with the left foot forward and placed in the footmark, and were anointed with holy water taken from the hollow in the rock. It is claimed that the people who colonised and named the kingdom of Dalriada were Scots, their name taken from Scotia, which was then the name of a district of Northern Ireland. Where did they first set foot on the land to which they have given their name—Scotland? If they landed on Kintyre, they chose the district nearest to their native country, yet separated from it by that stretch of twenty miles of stormy ocean known as the Moyle, where the tides of the Irish Sea contend with those of the Atlantic, so that the water is often turbulent and wild and a danger to small craft. It is more likely that they sailed in their galleys up the Firth of Clyde and landed on some of the sea lochs of Cowall, a district which they colonised and which is said to have received its name from one of their nobles, Comgall by name. Cowall, a land of hill and glen and of deep sea lochs sheltered from the Atlantic swell, lies on the north side of the Firth of Clyde, and is in actual distance near to the busy Clyde ports, but is a lonely country even at the present day, a land that has changed little since the days when it was colonised by men from Ireland and since the days when the Lamonds, predecessors of the great ducal family of Argyll, held sway here.

The Lamonds claimed to be of royal race, descended from the kings of Ulster. Documents of early times refer to their chief as "The Great Lamond of Cowall." The Highland chief has always been renowned for his hospitality and his generosity. The following incident, which occurred about the year 1440, is an example of this magnanimity. The son of Sir Duncan Campbell, Black Knight of Lochow, died while being educated in the Lowlands of Scotland. The burial-ground of the Campbells was on the shore of Loch Awe (or Lochow, to give it its early spelling); there was deep snow on the ground, and the Black Knight professed that it was impossible to carry the body hither across the hill passes. He therefore requested permission to bury his son at Kilmun on the Holy Loch, at that time in Lamond territory. He received permission in the following words: "I, the Great Lamond of all Cowall, do give unto thee, Black Knight of Lochow, the grave of flags wherein to bury thy son in thy distress." Kilmun has ever since that time been the burial-place of the Campbells.

At the entrance to Loch Striven in Cowall stand the ruins of

Castle Toward, ancestral home of the Lamond chiefs. The castle has been deserted since the year 1646, when the Lamonds were besieged by a strong Campbell force, and on surrendering were treated in a manner more barbarous than that meted out to the unfortunate MacDonalds at the Massacre of Glencoe. Even allowing for exaggeration, this massacre seems to have been unusually infamous. The "new" Statistical Account written about 1830 has something to say of it. It accuses the Marquis of Argyle of having violated the terms of the capitulation, on which the surrender of the castle was made, in that he—

> did most treacherously, perfidiously, and traitorously fetter and bind the hands of near 200 persons of those who were comprehended within the said capitulation, detaining them prisoners with a guard, their hands being bound behind their backs like thieves within the said Sir James' (Lamond's) house . . . and most cruelly, traitorously, and perfidiously, cause hang upon one tree near the number of thirty-six persons, most of them being SPECIAL GENTLEMEN of the name of Lamond and vassals of the said Sir James.

From that fatal day centuries ago the Lamonds never recovered, yet their name lives in the traditions of the country, and at least one noble family of the old name, the Lamonds of Knockdow, remains here.

The port of Cowall is Dunoon, at which steamers frequently call and give a quick passage across the Firth to Greenock. The castle of Dunoon (there is little remaining now of its ruins) is beside the pier. This castle appears to have been a royal fortress as early as the fourteenth century. From about the year 1440 the Argyll family were keepers of the castle.

Sandbank, beside Dunoon, is the winter quarters of yachts. Here is a safe and sheltered anchorage.

Near Dunoon, on the shore of the Holy Loch, is the old chapel of Kilmun; not far from the loch is Glen Masan, associated with Deirdre, highest type of Celtic womanhood. She is the heroine of one of the Three Sorrows of Story Telling, the Tale of the Sons of Uisneach. The tale recalls the love of Deirdre for Naoise of the royal Irish race, and the sorrow and tragedy which followed that love.

The road from Dunoon to Loch Fyne and Inveraray travels through the hills. The country is now a National Park, and Benmore, with its stately trees and magnificent rhododendrons, is a forestry centre. I passed that way on an early May morning. There had been frost in the night, but the sun was warm and the sky of unusual clearness, with white cumulus clouds floating in the blue vault of heaven. The rhododendrons—some of them *Rhododendron arboreum*, approaching 30 feet in height—which line the avenue to Benmore were laden with rose-coloured blossoms. When I reached the shore of Loch Eck that fresh-water loch was without wind. Even on this cold May morning after a night frost trout were on the move, and the rings of rising fish were travelling over the glass-like surface. Above the shallows, and on the pebbly shore, sandpipers were courting, their recent long flight over sea and land from Africa now forgotten in the joy of life and of their love affairs. The sandpiper, more than any bird, adds charm, beauty and music to many a Highland loch. Its flight, too, possesses a singular delicacy and airiness; it flies low over the water, its wings moving at tremendous speed, in marked rhythmic intervals. The actual speed may be slow, for the wings are used as much to lift the bird as to drive it forward. The birches beside the loch were filmed in green: high in the air sailed a peregrine falcon, and at a great height above the loch a golden eagle flew westward. The extensive plantations in the district are altering the appearance of the bare hillsides, for the Forestry Commission have of recent years planted large areas, chiefly with conifers such as the Sitka and Norway spruce. The high rainfall does not inconvenience those trees, for they thrive in the moist Atlantic climate of the district.

After leaving Loch Eck, the road descends to Strachur beside the waters of Loch Fyne. This long sea loch has its opening between Bute and Arran, and its head waters near Inveraray. The Gaelic name of this loch is Loch Fine, and it is celebrated for the size and quality of its herrings.

At Strachur the road from Dunoon reaches Loch Fyne; a few miles down the loch is the ancestral seat of the MacLachlans, Castle Lachlan. The MacLachlans of MacLachlan are an ancient race, whose origin is lost in the mists of the past. They fought in the crusades, and during one of the crusades MacLachlan of Strathlachlan and MacLachlan of Strachur, who were neighbours and close friends, made a compact that if one of them should be slain the survivor should accompany his body home and see it laid in the family burial-place. This close association between the two families remained unbroken for centuries. The MacLachlans are believed to have owned the lands of Strathlachlan since the eleventh century. MacLachlan was a close friend of Robert the Bruce and there is a tradition that he and the king used to fish on the river Add. The chief received a charter from Robert the Bruce, and sat in the first parliament of the Bruce at St. Andrews. The chief of the time led a regiment of foot under the leadership of the Great Montrose; he was taken prisoner after the battle of Philliphaugh and executed by his enemies.

Like other old Highland families, the MacLachlans had their Brownie, a friendly elf to those with whom he lived, as all Brownies are. But he had his own ideas on the arranging of furniture, and sometimes after the servants had tidied the rooms in the evening they would find them in the morning in a state of confusion— Brownie's idea of tidiness. One cold winter it was decided to make Brownie a pair of trousers. He would not permit his measure to be taken, so a pair was made and hung on the back of a kitchen chair. The Brownie came in. He lifted up the trousers; he turned them round and round, and then exclaimed, "Oh, oh! Breeches about his backside without his measure; it is time Munn was going" (Munn was the Brownie's name). But he did apparently take to the trousers in the end, for it is said that he was accustomed to wear them back to front, and also to have sported a red waistcoat. On one occasion, when he did not approve of the husband-to-be of one of Mac-Lachlan's daughters, he is said to have caused the wedding feast, all set out, to vanish.

It says much for the independent spirit of the chief of the Mac-Lachlans at the time of the 'Forty-five that, although living near that great noble and staunch Hanoverian MacCailein Mór, Duke of Argyll, he raised his clan and marched to join the Prince. He crossed Loch Fyne by boat with his men. At Crarae Point, on the farther shore, when he mounted his horse the animal turned round thrice widdershins—that is, against the sun. MacLachlan addressed his men: "It is likely you will return, but I myself will not return." His fine qualities were recognised by Prince Charlie, who made him his A.D.C. He was killed on the field of Culloden, and thus escaped the tragic years of those who had supported the Prince and, escaping

27

with their lives, were obliged to fly to a foreign land, their estates confiscated. It is said that the dun-coloured horse on which Mac-Lachlan was riding when he was slain at Culloden made its way alone back to Castle Lachlan, its arrival being the first portent of the tragedy. The castle was a little later bombarded from the sea.

CHAPTER II

INVERARAY TO CRUACHAN

BEFORE travelling to Inveraray at the head of Loch Fyne, let us
continue on our way down the shore of the loch. At Otter Ferry
Loch Fyne is no more than a mile across. I suspect that the word
"Otter" in the place-name is from the Gaelic Oitir, a Shoal, for the
loch here is shallow off-shore, and in spring when I passed that way
I was cheered by the gannets in their white plumage which were
diving for fish in these waters. These were Ailsa Craig birds, for the
flight thence is one of little distance for a bird of the wing power of
a solan, as the gannet is usually named in Scotland. From Otter Ferry
the road goes by Kilfinan, thence over high ground to Ardlamond
Point, there swinging southward along the shore of the Kyles of
Bute and Loch Riddon to the Clachan of Glendaruel, the home for
many years of a great Highland lady, Mrs. Burnley-Campbell of
Ormidale.

Glendaruel, of which the Gaelic spelling is Gleann Dà Ruail,
may be the Glen Dà Ruadh mentioned in Deirdre's lament on leaving
Alba, although it has been suggested that a side glen in the country
of Loch Etive was at one time known as Glen Dà Ruadh. The road
crosses over to Loch Fyne from Glendaruel, passing near Ardkinglas,
rounds the head of the loch and, bending now westward, passes the
ancient castle of Dundarave, an ancestral stronghold of the Mac-
Nachtans, at one time a great and powerful clan in these parts. The
name Dundarave is a curious one, for as it stands it apparently means
Dùn dà Ramh—Dun or Fort of the Two Oars. But the earlier
form seems to have been Dùn dà Rudha—Point of the Two Head-
lands.

Dundarave is surrounded by old beech trees, which are a soft and
very beautiful green in early summer and in autumn gold as the seaweed on the shore: they lessen the austerity of the old castle. One
looks from it across Loch Fyne to Ardkinglas, and perhaps recalls
that the earlier Campbell residence at Ardkinglas was associated with
the Massacre of Glencoe, for it was the home at that time of Sir
Colin Campbell, Sheriff of Argyll. Thither hurried, his time running

29

short, MacIain, chieftain of the MacDonalds of Glencoe, to swear allegiance to the Crown. The tragic sequel will be heard in a later chapter. The ghostly drummer of Ardkinglas was said to have heralded the departure of the old family of Campbell with loud muffled sound; I have not heard that his drums have sounded since. The present Ardkinglas is the third house of the name. Its architect was Sir Robert Lorimer.

Writing of Dundarave reminds me of the interesting tradition concerning the wedding of the son of MacNachtan of Dundarave, sheriff of Argyllshire, in the year 1685. The son was engaged to be married to a daughter of Campbell of Ardkinglas. The wedding was performed with befitting ceremony. It was customary in those days for the bride and bridesmaids to have their faces veiled at a wedding. The marriage took place in the evening, the bridal couple remaining until midnight at the dance which followed. The brides-maids then put the bride to bed, and the best man put the bridegroom to bed, afterwards carrying away the candle. The bride's eldest sister impersonated the bride (with or without the latter's connivance we are not told) and MacNachtan was ignorant until daylight of the true identity of his bedfellow. At breakfast next morning, he said he feared that a mistake had been made, but Ardkinglas said that it was customary for the eldest girl to marry first, and she would make as good a wife as her sister. MacNachtan apparently agreed to the *fait accompli*. When the time drew near for his wife to be confined, her sister (whom he had intended to marry) came to look after her. A son and heir arrived on the scene, and all was apparently harmonious for some months, when it became apparent that the younger daughter also was in the family way. MacNachtan was suspected and apparently admitted the affair. He was imprisoned in the old tower of Inveraray, but his unofficial wife helped him to escape, and they sailed over the sea to Eire, where they were married, and did not again return to the country of Loch Fyne.

It is not known whether the MacNachtons (or less correctly the MacNaughtons) built their castle on the site of an ancient dun. They certainly inhabited it from a very early time. The family traces its descent from Nachtan, a son of the family of Lochow, before ever that family assumed the surname of Campbell. Mac-Nachtan of Dundarave accompanied the Earl of Argyle to the battle of Flodden, and met his death there. Before the castle was rebuilt, there is said to have been a curious stone figure above the door. The figure, seated with legs crossed, was playing a pipe chanter, the nose of the figure being prolonged to form the chanter.

The second world war completely changed the face of Inveraray, yet the old atmosphere of the place remains, and the proud castle of MacCailein Mór has come unscathed through the war years, during which it welcomed many of our allies from overseas.

It was at Inveraray that the prince of Highland writers, Neil Munro, was born. The beauty and simplicity of Neil Munro's prose is matched only by his deep knowledge of the Highland subjects on which he has written. It is indeed doubtful whether anyone will in future be able to write of the Highlands as he has done, for the old customs which he so vividly describes are dying. He wrote, for example, of the Ceòl Mór or Piobaireachd of the Highland bagpipe, as one having inner knowledge. Neil Gunn is another Highland author who saw the soul of the ancient classical music of the bagpipe. I hope he will forgive me if I quote here an exquisite passage taken from his book *Morning Tide*:

> Every note was clear and distinct. The grace notes were like tiny golden sparks. The drones sent a waving flame ascending among the rafters; it grew solid, a beaten wave, reverberating near and far, insistent; against it the theme, slowly, so slow that every note became freighted unbearably, every phrase a piece of sorrow set in eternity, so that no time could conquer it.

Inveraray has been for long the capital of the Loch Fyne country. Indeed, at one period the county families of Argyll had their town houses in Inveraray, and instead of travelling to Edinburgh or London, wintered in Inveraray. They perhaps attended the parish church, then divided into two parts so that a Gaelic service for the more humble folk and an English service for the gentry might be conducted at the same time. It is not recorded whether a preacher with unusually powerful lungs ever unwittingly sent his voice through the partition.

A building with old associations is the courthouse where that unhappy man, James Stewart of the Glen (Sheumas a' Ghlinne), was tried for the murder of the Red Fox, Campbell of Glenure. He had little chance of acquittal, for he was tried by a Campbell judge and a Campbell jury, in a Campbell stronghold, was sentenced to death, and was hanged at Ballachulish, where the murder had taken

31

place. Perhaps no Highland trial has caused, and still causes, more controversy. It is generally believed that James Stewart was innocent, and indeed it is said that the identity of the murderer has been handed down in secrecy by the few families who know the facts of the case.

The room in which the trial was held is surprisingly small, and must have been uncomfortably crowded during the proceedings. One of the small windows has the following words incised in the glass, perhaps with a diamond, "Inveraray Town House 25th May, 1765." Written in a different writing below is, "Charming Miss Tibby Dunstafnage."

Robert Burns the poet received a poor welcome when he visited Inveraray, and wrote on a window of the Argyll Hotel the lines:

> There's naething here but Hielan' pride,
> An' Hieland scab, an' hunger;
> If Providence has sent me here,
> 'Twere surely in His anger.

The Inveraray Cross, which stands beside the waters of Loch Fyne, is traditionally stated to have been carried thither from Iona. It appears to be of early fifteenth-century design and to commemorate Duncan MacGille Comghan, his son Patrick, and MacGille Muire, son of Patrick.

When the traveller Pennant visited Inveraray in 1771 some hundreds of fishing boats each evening set their herring nets on Loch Fyne. He records that on weekdays the cheerful noise of bagpipe and dance was heard by those on shore proceeding from the fishing fleet. "On the Sabbath, each boat approaches the land, and psalmody and devotion divide the day."

The vast shoals of herrings which roamed Loch Fyne in Pennant's day entered the loch from the Atlantic in July and remained in it until January. From September until Christmas between five and six hundred boats, each having a crew of four men, were employed in the fishing. The herring were salted for export, or were sold fresh to the people of the countryside, two or three hundred horses being brought to the shores of the loch each morning from all the neighbouring districts. Tunny used to frequent the loch, preying on the herrings. Pennant records a tunny of between four and five hundred pounds taken during his visit, and says these great fish were taken on a hook

The Pass of Brander, Loch Awe

baited with a herring, and when caught were cut in pieces and either sold fresh or salted in casks.

I remember my first visit to Inveraray Castle, in the spring of 1916, a night quiet and soft. The first world war was in progress, and I had been appointed Admiralty Patrol Officer for that part of the western seaboard and the Hebrides. I had occasion that evening to put in a trunk telephone call to England and was told that it would be impossible to get through, as a Zeppelin raid was in progress over Newcastle-on-Tyne.

MacCailein's sister, Lady Elspeth Campbell, a gracious and charming lady, had a deep interest in old legends, old traditions and old events. She was at one time a piper, in an age before ladies' pipe bands were thought of, and when women pipers were few and far between. She had an excellent gramophone, on which she loved to hear Gaelic songs sung by the best singers of the day.

The eagle who suns himself on the cairn of Beinn Bhuidhe and the wild geese which pass high overhead each autumn on their southward migration must have seen strange sights on the Loch Fyne hills during the years of the second world war—armed men fighting mock battles out on the high gloomy corries, often mist-filled. The sanctuaries of the red grouse and even the ptarmigan were disturbed by the rattle of machine guns, which must have made more noise than the Atholl men when they invaded MacCailein's country about the year 1680 and did much damage there.

From Inveraray, Glen Shira leads away into the hills. In that glen some five miles from Loch Fyne, is the small historic house, now roofless, in which the celebrated Highland riever Rob Roy MacGregor lived for ten years. A dirk, on which were Rob Roy's initials, was found near this house; his sporan is in Inveraray Castle.

The last time I was in Inveraray was on a clear May morning when the blue wood smoke from the chimneys of the castle rose, pungent and aromatic, into the still cold air. The old beeches were renewing their youth and the birds of the forest, chaffinch and robin, song-thrush and blackbird, were in song. I was crossing to Loch Awe, that sister loch of Loch Fyne, legend-haunted, and at the watershed between the two basins left the road to examine the prominent memorial to Neil Munro. Ahead of me I could see Loch Awe reflecting the deep blue of the sky, and beyond the loch Cruachan rising to the white clouds. This great hill, renowned from early times (is not

Hills of Mull and Firth of Lorne

its very name, Cruachan, the war and rallying cry of the Campbells?), is one of the few Highland hills in which the prefix "Ben" is placed after and not before the name. You may hear a stranger speak of Ben Cruachan, but to a native of the country the hill is always Cruachan Beann, the English translation of which is Haunch of Peaks—for there is more than one "Ben" in the massif. On this May day, as I looked upon Cruachan, clear and bright in the sunshine, a white snow cloud approached the hill and for a time I could see the snow falling gently on the higher reaches; when the cloud slowly moved away the mountain was snow-clad and the sun which once more shone upon it did not melt the snow.

Loch Awe is a loch of islands, each one with legends of the past. On Innisconnel (Innis Chonaill) is the ruined castle that has been called the Cradle of the Campbell Race. It is a small isle, and the castle, now a stately ruin, takes up almost the whole of it.

On another small island, Fraoch Eilean, was the ancestral castle of the MacNachtans, who also held Dundarave. Fraoch Eilean was held from the Crown on condition that the sovereign should be entertained if ever he should pass that way, and should be given a bed of clean straw to sleep on. On another island of the loch, Innishail, was an old Celtic convent: the nuns were renowned, according to an old account, both for the sanctity of their lives and the purity of their manners. Within and around the crumbling chapel situated on this island are many recumbent gravestones, some of them showing beautiful designs. One represents an angel offering the crucified Christ a drink from a cup while Roman soldiers stand smiling on either side.

At the head of Loch Awe is Kilchurn Castle, a picturesque ruin on a low island lying near the mainland. The castle is said to have been built by Sir Colin Campbell, Lord of Lochow, he who was known to the Gaels as Cailean Dubh na Roimh (Swarthy Colin of Rome) because of his frequent journeying to the sacred city. At the time of the Forty-five Kilchurn Castle was in the hands of the Breadalbane family, the great tower being garrisoned by Lord Breadalbane in order to prevent the Jacobites from crossing that way. The osprey at one time nested on the castle, which Pennant records as being a ruin in 1771.

Where the river Awe leaves Loch Awe is seen the wild and gloomy

34

Pass of Brander, the haunt, according to an old account, of eels of the thickness of a man's thigh, which broke the fishing lines of all who attempted to catch them, except those of an ancient man who had learned the method of capturing those monsters. We do not now hear much of the monster eels of Loch Awe, but the loch is the haunt of great brown trout, up to 14 lb. weight and more, which are caught by trolling.

The river Awe, a swift river of no great breadth, flows from the Pass of Brander to the sea waters of Loch Etive. The salmon of the Awe are probably larger than those of any other British river, and Major and Mrs. Huntingdon have the unique record of landing three salmon each exceeding 50 lb. The weights of the three salmon are, one of 57 lb. killed by Major A. W. Huntingdon on July 8, 1921; another of 51 lb. killed by the same angler on a fly on May 22, 1930; the third, a male fish of 55 lb. killed by Mrs. Huntingdon on September 19, 1927.

One February day an angler on the Awe had an interesting experience. He had fished unsuccessfully (February is early for this river) and was thinking of going home when he saw a seal chasing a salmon. So hot was the pursuit that the salmon in its efforts to escape came right out of the water, and was "caught" by the angler as it wriggled on the shingly banks of the river. This seal did not show such contempt of the angler as a seal did one October day on the Lochy. Here an angler had just caught a salmon of about 12 lb. when a seal came right out of the river and took the fish from the line on the shingly shore. The seals which enter Scottish rivers are usually *Phoca vitulina*, the common seal; the Atlantic seal, *Halichœrus grypus*, is a much larger animal and usually keeps to the open sea, although it takes the salmon out of the bag nets on the coast, often tearing the nets as well as destroying the fish.

The river Awe flows into Loch Etive, a sea-water loch, at Bonawe beside Taynuilt. Loch Etive takes its name from the goddess of the loch, a sprite or water nymph called Eiteag, who was capable of raising a tempest and of sending ships to their doom. This loch, which turns away to the north-east above the estuary of the Awe and penetrates into the heart of the hills, calls to mind a fjord of Norway. Its upper waters are so far from the sea, and receive so many hill streams, that the salinity here, especially after a dry spell, is low; that is why this loch freezes over in severe frost; sometimes indeed the ice is so thick that the motor-boat conveying the mails from Taynuilt is unable to complete its passage. This happened in December 1950.

Opposite Bonawe is the greatest granite quarry in the Highlands.

On the north side of Cruachan is Glen Noe, in Gaelic Gleann Nodha, "a verdant glen on the north-west skirts of Cruachan." The river Noe flows into Loch Etive some little distance up the loch from the estuary of the Awe. The chiefs of the Macintyres are traditionally believed to have held the lands of Glen Noe from the fourteenth century. A tombstone in Ardchattan Priory was made by the chief of the day for his grave and bears the date 1695. There is a tradition that the first chief of the Macintyres lived in Sleat in the Isle of Skye. He followed, it is said, a white fairy cow across the sea, and then inland until she halted at a spot in Glen Noe known as Làrach na Bá Baine—the Abode of the White Cow.

The chief of the Macintyres held his land of the Breadalbane Campbells on the conditions that he supplied a snowball each summer from the high corries of Cruachan and a white fatted calf reared on the land. The calf was delivered over a stone at the upper part of Glen Noe, the rock being named Clach an Laoigh Bhiata—Stone of the Fatted Calf.

Chapter III

OBAN AND ITS DISTRICT

THE main road to Oban winds north-westward beside the shore of Loch Etive. Here are grassy islands where colonies of common gulls and terns nest; here great northern divers spend the winter, and may be seen in their full breeding plumage diving for flounders as late as mid-May before leaving for their nesting haunts on the lakes of Iceland and Greenland. Many oystercatchers call shrilly from the low grassy shores or rocky skerries, and the resident mergansers are joined in winter by goosanders from the north. On the farther side of the loch stands Ardchattan Priory, founded in 1230 by Duncan MacCoul, ancestor of the MacDougalls of Lorne. It was annexed to the Bishoprick of Argyll by James VI in 1617. It is on record that Somerled MacDougall was abbot in 1500. An old account, written *circa* 1630, says that "friers, moncks, and Nunns" lived here "in ancient tyme." Robert the Bruce is said to have held a parliament at Ardchattan. The Priory, now the residence of the Campbell-Prestons of Ardchattan, is beautifully situated. I remember, when I stayed there long ago, hearing the piper play "Johnny Cope" early before breakfast outside the priory, to arouse its secular and Highland inmates from their sleep. At Connel Ferry, where Loch Etive enters the Firth of Lorne, are the Falls of Lora, where the Atlantic pours into the loch in a great river at flood tide and at the ebb pours over a rock, causing a fall which is said to be 20 feet high during certain spring tides. The Oban-Ballachulish railway crosses the loch here on a strong but inartistic viaduct which largely spoils the beauty of what (without its presence) would be one of the most inspiring scenes in the west Highlands.

At the estuary of Loch Etive stands the old castle of Dunstaffnage, where at one time was kept the Lia Fail, the celebrated Stone of Destiny on which the early Scottish kings were crowned, and which was said to have been brought from Ireland by the first king of Dalriada. Kenneth the second of Scotland had the stone removed from Dunstaffnage to Scone, whence Edward I brought it to Westminster Abbey. The king had the Coronation chair specially made to hold the oblong stone. Sitting above the block of reddish sandstone successive kings have been crowned. At each end of the stone is a very old rusty iron bar. In December, 1950, the stone was stolen from the Abbey.

Dunstaffnage Castle was in 1307 a seat and fortress of Alexander MacDougall, Lord of Lorne: a hundred and fifty years later it is said to have been a residence of the Lords of the Isles.

It commands a particularly wide and beautiful view, for it looks over the sea to Lismore—that long grassy isle well named by the Gaels the Great Garden—and, behind it, the high hills of Morvern. Westward rise the hills of the Isle of Mull.

One wonders what the Lord of the Isles would have thought of the daring raid on a convoy anchored off Lismore by a German bomber during the early years of the second world war. One of the bombed merchantmen succeeded in limping shoreward, and sank at the estuary of Loch Etive in water so shallow that her masts could be seen emerging from the sea for a number of years afterwards. She was carrying a cargo of valuable race-horses for export; some of them succeeded in swimming ashore in the darkness, but many were lost.

The descendants of the Lord of Lorne, who had his fortress in Dunstaffnage, which, according to the tradition of the district, was an ancient seat of the kings of Scotland, now live at Dunollie, a few miles westward along the coast.

We are now at the gateway of Oban, sometimes named the capital of the west Highlands, so let us return to Inveraray, whence we took the hill road to Loch Awe, and travel from Inveraray to Oban by the coast.

At Crarae, the seat of Sir George Campbell of Succoth, much afforestation has been done and the face of the country has been altered. Where the ground is wet, the fast-growing Sitka spruce, here as elsewhere in the Highlands, has been proved to be the best tree for profitable timber-growing. Despite the high rainfall, bird life is plentiful and varied on the land: on the waters of Loch Fyne there are fewer birds than might be expected, for the loch does not now support the fish population it formerly did and its shore waters are too deep for ducks to feed in with comfort. The buzzard is often seen here, and the raven flies over high above the loch, but does not alight on its shores.

In early times the Scrymgeours, hereditary standard-bearers to the

Scottish kings, were superiors of Minard and Crarae. Where Loch Fyne broadens Ardrishaig stands, the last port of call of the daily steamer from Glasgow. The road now for a time leaves the coast, passing Dunadd near Kilmartin and reaching the sea once more at Loch Melfort. Near Dunadd the Crinan Canal crosses the peninsula, from Loch Fyne to the Sound of Jura, enabling vessels of small size to pass from the Firth of Clyde to the western ocean without the long voyage round the Mull of Kintyre with its rough seas and strong tides. A road follows the canal, then turns south-west, soon reaching a narrow sea loch named Loch Sween and following its shore to Point of Knap. On the shore of the loch are the ruins of Castle Sween, known in early times as the Key of Knapdale. Red Sween (Suibhne Ruadh) was Thane of Knapdale in the thirteenth century. In the sixteenth century the castle passed into the hands of the MacMillans, and a part of the building, known as MacMillan's Tower, is said to have been erected by MacMillan Mór, in whose memory the MacMillan Cross was set up in the old burial-ground of Kilmory near the Point of Knap. MacMillan Mór was said to have had the charter of his lands in Knapdale engraved in Gaelic on a rock at the march of his property.

I remember calling on the last of the MacTaggarts, hereditary weavers of Knap, in the year 1914: the two handlooms in his house were said to be at least three hundred years old.

On the coast, not far from Dunadd, stands the old castle of Duntroon, built on a promontory of Loch Crinan. Duntroon is an ancient MacDonald stronghold, but the Earl of Argyll in 1616 collected a large force here, both of ships and men, preparatory to invading Islay. It may have been then that the event which I shall relate took place. Colla Ciotach, a kinsman of MacDonald of Islay, intended to attack his Campbell enemies, and sent forward his piper to reconnoitre. The piper gained admittance to the castle, but was later taken prisoner. When incarcerated in one of the turrets he saw his master's galleys approaching the place, and fearing that they might fall into a trap, played the pibroch which he composed on the spot, which is known as the "Piper's warning to his master." Colla Ciotach knew the language of the pipes, and hearing the warning urgently conveyed stood out to sea. Too late, the Campbells realised what the piper was doing. He was seized and bound, and as a punishment—the worst that could be inflicted on a piper—his fingers were cut off.

Perhaps happily for him he died of shock, and was buried beneath a large stone slab in the castle kitchen. His grave is still to be seen and his ghost is said to haunt the castle, in which, as in Dunvegan, the sound of ghostly piping is sometimes heard before moonrise when the night is dark and the sea wind sends in a multitude of waves to break upon the shore. There is another pibroch, "The sound of the waves against Duntroon Castle," of which the composer is, I think, unknown. It is a slow and sad refrain, and the original name, as in many of these old tunes, was perhaps a different one and is now lost.

At Barbreck, a few miles before Loch Melfort is reached, the road to Craignish branches away to the south-west. On a promontory overlooking rocky Scarba and the Gulf of Corryvreckan stands Craignish Castle. The country of Craignish, or as it was earlier named Craigness, is said to have been "fertill both of corne, butter and cheese and abundance of all kynd of fishes."

Craignish Castle was built about the year 1300 by a MacEachern. According to one tradition, he adopted a Campbell as his son. The lad fell in love with a daughter of MacDonald of Islay, and after much opposition succeeded in marrying her. In his *Highlanders of Scotland* the Celtic scholar Skene mentions the family of Craignish and states that, according to the tradition of their country, their real name (although they were usually referred to as the Campbells of Craignish) was MacEachern, and that they were of the same race as the MacDonalds. Skene mentions that the policy of the Argyll family was to compel those clans which had become dependent upon them to adopt the name of Campbell. In this instance the Mac-Eacherns are made to be the descendants of Dugall, an illegitimate son of one of the Campbells in the twelfth century, and because of this they were known as the Clan Dugall Craignish. They were for centuries a powerful family in these parts.

The fertile lands of Craignish must often have been looked upon with envy by other clans. Alasdair MacDonald (Alasdair mac Colla Ciotach), he who led 1,500 Irish to take part in the campaign of the Great Montrose in 1644, invaded the country of Craignish and besieged the castle. Campbell of Craignish, becoming aware of his enemies' approach, moved his cattle across to one of the islands, perhaps Scarba, and after a siege of six weeks the Irishmen withdrew.

Beyond Loch Melfort, and near the coast, stands Ardmaddy Castle. About a mile south of this castle near by an old road now grass-grown, a venerable hawthorn tree stands, and in it coins have been stuck in various places, so long ago that the bark has grown almost over them. There is probably a wishing well near. On Saint Maolruba's isle on Loch Maree is an old tree similarly marked; here the coins were placed as an offering to the saint, and it may be that a similar custom long ago was practised at Ardmaddy.

I know of no town in Britain with the charm of Oban. As one descends the hill into the town, either from the north or from the south, one looks over the grassy island of Kerrera across the Firth of Lorne to where the great hills of the Isle of Mull rise on the horizon. The view is at its best near sunset, when clouds of gold hang above, or descend lightly upon, those hills. In winter, when the hills are snow-covered, the snowy slopes for a few brief minutes before sunset are violet-tinted, and in contrast the amethystine waters of the sea deepen their colour until they are dark as the shades of night. After sunset the warm yellow rays from the lighthouse on Lismore shine through the gathering dusk, and the lights of shipping as vessels steer through the Sound of Mull shine like planets. There are autumn and winter nights when the northern sky above Morvern becomes luminous, and as the aurora or merry dancers spring to life the stars are dimmed and shafts of light, like searchlights, rise from a glowing arc. Sometimes the display is so powerful that pools of light rise, pulsating, to the zenith and beyond. The colour is almost always pale green. But there are rare occasions when deep red zones of light appear at the zenith. The Highland tradition is that an aurora of this colour is of bad omen; the two most remarkable displays of red aurora in recent years were seen early in the New Year of 1940 and again in 1949. On the first of these two occasions at least the old tradition was justified.

The Sound of Kerrera is half a mile in width. Here anchored King Haco's galleys on their southward voyage before the battle of Largs: here, probably in the now ruined Gylen Castle, died Alexander II of Scotland in the year 1249 of a fever.

Towards the end of the tourist season, in mid-September, is staged at Oban the Argyllshire Gathering. This is a two days' affair, and is considered to be one of the best-run Highland gatherings. The whole of the great county of Argyll supports it, from Ballachulish in the north to the Mull of Cantyre to the south. The march of the judges and stewards through the streets of Oban to the gathering ground followed—not preceded, be it noted—by the best pipers in Scotland is always impressive. The piping at this gathering is of a high standard, and I have in my time helped to judge some excellent performances. One day I recall when the cold was extreme and the hills of Mull topped with fresh snow, a rare thing in September. On that occasion the competition for the coveted gold medal went on the whole day, and I do not know who were the colder, competitors or judges. It was nearly six o'clock in the evening when the last man played, and we had been judging this competition since ten o'clock in the morning. The last piper was Pipe Major Chisholm, and I remember that he played the "Gathering of Clan Chattan" for his pibroch. He had very strong fingers, and seemed to be less affected by the cold than the other players. At all events he won the medal.

One of the best pibrochs which I heard played at the Oban Gathering was by Malcolm MacPherson, son of Angus MacPherson and grandson of the great Malcolm MacPherson, after whom he was named. His grandfather was an outstanding player fifty years ago. He again was the son of another Angus MacPherson who, according to his grandson and namesake Angus MacPherson of Invershin, received tuition from the celebrated John MacKay of Raasay, from John, last of the immortal MacCrimmons, and also from the Bruces of Skye, pupils of the MacCrimmons.

This Angus MacPherson was first prize winner at the Northern Meeting in Inverness in 1852, when Angus MacKay, John Ban MacKenzie and Donald Cameron were at their best. Angus gave tuition to his son Malcolm, who was also taught by Archibald Munro of Oban, the composer of "Glengarry's Lament." Angus Mac-Pherson (senior) was piper to Cluny MacPherson when John MacKay was piper at Drummond Castle and John Ban MacKenzie at Taymouth Castle, and after John MacKay retired to live at Kyleakin in the Isle of Skye, Angus MacPherson used to walk from Cluny Castle over the Pass of Corrieyaireag to stay with him, and to keep in touch with the playing of that great piper.

With a long line of outstanding pipers behind him it is only natural that "young Malcolm," as he is usually called, should have early come to the fore as a piper. The pibroch which I heard him play was a long and very beautiful one, "Lament for Donald Ban MacCrimmon," he who was killed at the Rout of Moy in 1746. It is a hard tune to play, and yet, if it is well played, it has a beauty and sadness that is perhaps unique among pibrochs. His performance on that occasion—it must have been in 1926 or 1927—was one of the best I have known at Oban over a long number of years.

I have not mentioned Pipe Major John MacDonald of Inverness, on whom the mantle of the MacCrimmons has descended. His pipe, alas! is silent. His performances were always marked by a delicacy and finish equalled by no other piper, and for that reason what would have been an outstanding performance in others was an ordinary performance in him.

At the north entrance to Oban bay stand the ivy-covered ruins of Dunollie Castle, the ancestral home of the MacDougalls, who trace their direct descent from Loarn, brother of Fergus, the founder of the kingdom of Dalriada and its first king. MacDougall of Mac-Dougall, chief of his clan, has his home in a pleasant house surrounded by stately trees through which swallows flit in summer after the white wave of snowdrops has spent itself, but while the wave of daffodils is still in full vigour. The chief of the clan was not "out" in the '45, for his lady, it is said in order to prevent his departure, poured a basin of boiling water over his feet. The present house was built in 1746, of stones taken from the old castle.

When Wordsworth visited Dunollie in 1831 he wrote thus of a captive eagle which he saw there:

> Dishonoured rock and ruin that, by law
> Tyrannic, keep the Bird of Jove embarred
> Like a lone criminal whose life is spared.
> Vexed is he, and screams aloud.

A priceless possession of the MacDougalls is the Brooch of Lorn. It was worn in his plaid by King Robert the Bruce at the battle of Dalrigh (Dalree), and in the heat of the fight a follower of Mac-Dougall attempted to drag the king from his horse. The Bruce dealt him a blow with his claymore, but with his dying grasp the Mac-Dougall clansman tore the king's plaid or cloak from its owner, and with it the brooch. It remained a cherished possession in the Mac-Dougall family until the year 1647, when it was discovered (although it had been carefully hidden) in Gylen Castle by a detachment of General Leslie's army who were searching the place. The brooch then came into the possession of MacDonnachaidh, or Campbell of

Inverawe, as he had been serving in the detachment. In the family of Inverawe it remained until the year 1826, when it was bought by General Duncan Campbell of Lochnell. He generously presented the brooch to the MacDougalls, who have had it since then. The centre-piece of the brooch is a large crystal of quartz; a warm glow seems to burn within it from whatever angle it is examined. Surrounding the crystal is a circle of pearls. The centre of the brooch unscrews; within the recess was formerly a small piece of bone, which may have been a saintly relic. Admiral MacDougall of MacDougall, the chief of that time, steered the royal barge in which Queen Victoria sailed up Loch Tay, and wore the brooch of Lorne in his plaid. The queen so greatly admired the brooch that she asked if she might wear it during her passage up the loch. It is not, I think, recorded whether this ancient brooch possessed some particular virtue, such as the Clach Dhearg of Ardvorlich, or the Lee Penny.

CHAPTER IV

APPIN AND GLENCOE

NORTH of Oban and Dunstaffnage, across the Falls of Lora. at the mouth of Loch Etive, is the district of Appin. The word "Appin" means Abbey-land, and the Celtic scholar MacBain has shown that it comes from the early Irish word "Apdaine." The abbey-lands here belonged to Lismore; they extended ten miles along the shore of Loch Linnhe and fifty miles inland, including Glencoe as far as King's House. The district is a sheltered and wooded one, and the sea waters of the Firth of Lorne and Loch Linnhe protect it from severe frosts. At Ledaig on the shore of Loch Nell are the remains of an old *dun* or fort, of which one of the old names is Dùn mhic Uisneach. It commemorates, no doubt, the great romance of Deirdre and Naoise, one of the sons of Uisneach, which came to its tragic end in the days when the Druids still possessed their magic powers. It may be recalled how Naoise and his brothers perished in the enchanted sea raised over the land at the behest of King Conchobar, Naoise's rival for the love of Deirdre. The more recent name of the fort is Beregonium. The old tradition is that there were seven forts on the summit of the small green hill and the ridge which extends from it. The main pass which leads to the hill is Bealach Banruinn Fhionnaghail—the Pass of Fingal's Queen. It has been said that Beregonium was a seat of the Pictish kings before they were driven from the district on the consolidating of the kingdom of Dalriada.

On the opposite side of the road stood Dùn Bhalaire, the name perhaps commemorating Balor of the Evil Eye, whose glance brought sudden death to him on whom it was directed.

As you travel north past Ledaig you leave the sea for awhile and pass through the richly wooded lands of Barcaldine, near which place is a factory for manufacturing various products from seaweed. The road winds round the head of Loch Creran, a sea loch in which mackerel and young coal fish play and seals disport themselves, and then enters the district of Appin, or "the Appin" as it was formerly named. On a small island, almost joined to the mainland, are the ruins of a small castle, Castle Stalker (in Gaelic, Caisteal an Stalcaire

—the Castle of the Stalker or Deer-hunter). Duncan Stewart of Appin is said to have built this castle in the reign of James IV and to have entertained the king in it. It was later lost to its owner because of a wager.

North of Appin is Ballachulish at the mouth of Loch Leven, which narrow sea loch forms the boundary between the counties of Argyll and Inverness and also, it is believed, the northern boundary of the old kingdom of Dalriada. On the old track, which was farther from the sea than the present road, is a small cairn, its stones moss-grown, which marks the spot where Colin Campbell of Glenure was shot and killed by a man in ambush, and for which crime James Stewart of the Glen, a natural brother of Stewart of Ardsheal, paid the extreme penalty. It was on a day of the year 1752 that Campbell of Glenure, accompanied by his servant and the sheriff officer, was travelling along that narrow road, now grass-grown, in order to evict certain Jacobite families. Because of his part in the rising of 1745 Stewart of Ardsheal had his estate forfeited, and Campbell of Glenure was appointed by the Government to be factor, at the modest salary of ten guineas a year. He himself seems to have been a decent, easy-going fellow. He was a brother of Campbell of Barcaldine, and his mother was a daughter of Sir Ewen Cameron of Lochiel. At the beginning of his tenure of office he had been on friendly enough terms with the people. This was reported to his superiors, and he was cautioned to be more strict in future to those who had, seven years earlier, risen against the Government, and, carrying out his un-welcome orders, now became a marked man. On this day, when he was travelling along the track beneath the hills, two shots rang out in quick succession, and as he fell, mortally wounded, his companions saw a furtive figure, whom they thought to be James Stewart, gliding through the trees. It is said that Glenure, thinking that they were attacked in force, called to his two companions to save themselves and leave him to his fate. It was known that James Stewart had recently been at enmity with Glenure, and he therefore was arrested and, as I have said, was tried and executed, being hung from a gibbet erected on a knoll, now wooded, within a stone's throw of the ferry slip at South Ballachulish. To the last he protested his innocence. His hanging took place on a day of storm, in the month of November. It was decided that the body of the unfortunate man should remain suspended as a grim example to the Jacobites in the district. It hung there, latterly as a skeleton, for more than two years, and when it fell to earth the skeleton was carefully replaced on the gibbet. This execution is still a topic of discussion in the west Highlands.

Not far from here, in the year 1880, a remarkable wooden image was dug from the peat. It was the figure of a female, fashioned, according to the evidence of experts, from the oak of the district. It aroused considerable interest at the time, but no certain date was assigned to it although, from the depth in the peat at which it was found, it must have been buried for many centuries, and it was conjectured to date from the Norse occupation.

The name "Ballachulish" means Township of the Straits. In the year 1522 the name is spelled "Ballecheles." The strait is narrow and the tides flow swiftly through it. In early summer there is much bird life to be seen here. Arctic terns fly daintily above the channels, and green cormorants fish in the strong stream. Beinn Bheitheir southward rises steeply to the clouds. At the foot of this hill lived a woman, a native of the Outer Hebrides, skilled in the dyeing of yarn with natural dyes. The secret of obtaining a bright red vegetable dye has now been almost lost, but she found that, by boiling the berries of the blaeberry or whortleberry, *Vaccinium myrtillus*, a good red dye for wool could be obtained. I have a pair of excellent red hose which she made and dyed for me.

This high hill above Ballachulish, Beinn Bheitheir, is supposed to have been named from a mythical hag who perhaps personified the spirit of winter and its rough storms. She may have had kinship with the Cailleach or Hag of Beinn Bhreac—she who forded the Sound of Mull without its waters reaching beyond her knees. There is a car ferry at Ballachulish and the branch line from Oban on the old L.M.S. Railway is near it.

Ballachulish has long been celebrated for its slate quarries. It stands at the entrance to Glen Coe, one of the most gloomy and impressive glens in western Scotland, even were its grimness not heightened by its associations with the massacre perpetrated here in 1692.

The Campbells were not at any time popular in the west, yet, allowing for exaggeration in the contemporary accounts of that event, it seems to be certain that a deed was done which indelibly stained those who were involved. Captain Campbell of Glenlyon, the officer who actually gave the order for the massacre, all his life felt the curse

47

of Glencoe upon him. That curse was so strong that it was believed it would influence future generations. It is said that Glenlyon's grandson, Colonel Campbell of Glenlyon, felt the curse in his actions. In 1771 he was ordered to superintend the execution of the sentence of a court-martial on a soldier of *marines*, condemned to be shot. It was arranged that at the last moment, when the man was on his knees ready to receive the sentence, he was to be pardoned, yet not a hint of that pardon was to be communicated to the firing party—their officer alone was in the secret. Glenlyon's orders were that, at the last moment, instead of dropping the white handkerchief which was the signal for the squad to fire, he was to take the reprieve from his pocket. When that moment arrived Glenlyon did indeed take from his pocket the paper on which the reprieve was written, but with it fell to the ground the white handkerchief, and the soldiers, seeing the signal, fired. Glenlyon is said to have exclaimed, "The curse of God and of Glencoe is upon me, I am an unfortunate man," and to have shortly afterwards resigned his commission, although no blame was imputed to him. Colonel Stewart relates this incident in his *Sketches*.

No fitter glen than Glen Coe for a dark deed could be imagined. The great hills which rise from it hide the summer sun. Highest of them all is Bidean nam Beann, 3,766 feet above the sea and the highest hill in Argyll. Near it stand Beinn Fhada (the Long Hill), 3,500 feet, and Stob Coire an Lochain, while at the head of the glen Buachaille Eite Mór, the Great Herdsman of Etive, rises in majesty to a height of 3,345 feet above the Atlantic.

The headwaters of the river Cona or Coe are in comparatively open country, and the stream enters the glen through a dark gorge, a place of gloomy waterfalls where the *uruisks* and other goblins may have sported in the old days, before the speedway which has been driven through the glen caused them to shun the place. The river hurries through the glen where, set high on the rocky slope of Aonach Dubh, is to be seen Ossian's Cave, inaccessible to all except skilled climbers. The Fèinne or Fingalians are elsewhere commemorated in the district, for the hill which rises to the east of the river near the foot of the glen is named Sgùrr na Fèinne—the Peak of the Fingalians. Ossian or Oisein was a leading member of the Fèinne.

There are many side glens throughout the length of Glencoe; they wind deep into the hills and are soon lost to view. The side glen

THE ANCIENT KINGDOM OF DALRIADA

that is chief in size, and also chief in interest, is Gleann Leac na Muidhe. This grassy glen, now almost unpopulated, had many living families in it during the early seventeenth century up to the night of the massacre. So intensively was the ground cultivated that on the steep slopes low walls of turf and stone were built in order to retain the soil, which would otherwise have been washed away by the rain storms of autumn and winter—for Glencoe is one of the wettest districts of the west Highlands, with a rainfall of over a hundred inches in the year.

The people of Glencoe are Episcopalians, and there is a Gaelic service in St. Mary's each Sunday. They are thus keeping alive the faith of the neighbouring glen, Glen Urchy or Glen Orchy, where a memorable scene was enacted on a Sunday many years ago. Stewart of Garth, relating the scene, says that it originated because Mr. David Lindsay, last Episcopal minister of Glenorchy, was ordered to surrender his charge to a Presbyterian minister appointed by the Duke of Argyll. On the first Sunday on which the new minister was to preach he found the whole population of the glen assembled outside the church. None of them, except Mr. Lindsay, would speak to him. There was silence and order until he attempted to enter the church, when he was surrounded by twelve men, fully armed, who ordered him to accompany them. "Disregarding all Mr. Lindsay's prayers and entreaties, they ordered the piper to play the march of death, and marched away with the minister to the confines of the parish. Here they made him swear on the Bible that he would never return, or attempt to disturb Mr. Lindsay. He kept his oath. The synod of Argyll were highly incensed at this violation of their authority, but seeing that the people were fully determined to resist, no further attempt was made, and Mr. Lindsay lived thirty years afterwards, and died Episcopal minister of Glenorchy, loved and revered by his flock."

The mind must go back long years to that winter day in February, 1692, when the snow which lay deep in the glen was reddened by the blood of those massacred. Trouble had been brewing for some time. MacDonald of Glencoe, he who in the Highlands was always known as MacIain, had incurred the enmity of the Campbells, and both Argyll and Breadalbane would have liked to have seen him and his small clan out of their way. The opportunity arose sooner than could have been expected. The Highland chiefs had been required

49   D

to swear allegiance to King William's Government before the first day of January, 1692. Glengarry, Lochiel and MacIain put off the swearing until the last possible moment. The two former chiefs had the support of powerful clans; besides, they may have just succeeded in making their submission before the close of the period of grace.

At the last minute MacIain of Glencoe rode through a storm of snow to Fort William, reaching the commandant's quarters at the Garrison (as Fort William was then called) at night. Colonel Hill received MacIain in a friendly manner, but told him that he had no power to swear him (which was true enough) and that he must ride at once to Inveraray to swear before Sir Colin Campbell of Ardkinglas, the sheriff. He had two days to cover the district—and he arrived too late. Too late by a single day.

His misfortunes did not end here, for Sir Colin was from home. Impatiently MacIain awaited his return, and when he did arrive three days afterwards he told the chieftain that he could do nothing for him, since the period of grace had expired. MacIain would not take this refusal, and represented to the sheriff that it was only because the heavy snow had made the journey hazardous that he was late. So in the end Sir Colin Campbell relented and agreed to swear him, although he was unable to say that the submission would be accepted by the Government. This was on January 6, 1692.

MacIain returned home and was at home when, at the end of January, a party of 120 men of the Earl of Argyll's regiment under the command of Captain Campbell of Glenlyon were seen marching through the glen. When he saw Glenlyon, MacIain no doubt recalled uneasily that his men had "lifted" the cattle from Glenlyon on their way home after the battle of Killiecrankie, and his welcome of the strangers cannot have been too enthusiastic. When it was seen who they were, his eldest son at the head of twenty men went forward to meet the Campbells and asked the reason of their visit. Glenlyon and his officers gave their "parole of honour" that they had come as friends, and asked that they might find quarters in the glen, giving as their reason the "thronged" state of the garrison quarters at Fort William. A younger son of MacIain was married to Glenlyon's niece, and this may have influenced the people of Glencoe in accepting the assurances of goodwill, plausibly given.

For a fortnight the military remained in Glencoe and during that time mistrust gradually gave place to goodwill. Captain Campbell

50

then received a fateful letter from Major Robert Duncanson. The letter is still in existence, and is in the Scottish National Library in Edinburgh. In it Captain Campbell is ordered to "fall upon the MacDonalds of Glenco, and to putt all to the sword under seventy." He is further ordered to "have a special care that the old fox and his sones doe not escape."

Captain Campbell of Glenlyon and his men were quartered up and down Glencoe. Canon MacInnes, who had lived in Glencoe for more than seventy years and was a man of much lore, told me that the firm tradition of the glen was that MacIain was not living at the time of the massacre at his house at Invercoe (as most accounts of the affair have stated), but at his sheep farm in Gleann Leac na Muidhe (incorrectly named by John Buchan in his *Massacre of Glencoe* as Gleann Leac-nam-Bhuidhe). Captain Campbell of Glenlyon, if we credit a letter written on April 20 of the year of the massacre, had the evening before played at cards with MacIain, who was entirely unsuspecting, until supper. The parting between the two had been friendly, and Glenlyon had accepted an invitation to dinner on the following day.

Although the orders for the massacre had been kept secret, some news of it leaked out. A soldier quartered on two brothers asked his hosts to take an evening walk with him. When they reached a large stone in a field the soldier thus addressed it, "Grey stone, if I were you, I would be moving from here, for great things will happen tonight." One of the brothers realised that he was being warned: he did not return home and escaped with his life, but his brother did return home, and was killed. On the night before the massacre MacIain's elder son, Alexander, having his suspicions, left the house. He saw a party of soldiers in the snow, was able to approach them unseen, and overheard a conversation. One soldier was saying there were things which even a common soldier could not be expected to do; that he was ready to fight the men of the glen, but not to murder them. His companion replied that duty was duty, however unpleasant it might be. Alexander at once returned to his father's house, told him what he had overheard, and urged him to leave. The old man could not bring himself to believe that things were as his son said, but agreed that he ought to continue his watch. It was some hours later that the suspicions of Alexander were confirmed. He then endeavoured to warn his father, but found the house closely surrounded by troops and was unable to pass through the cordon. At five o'clock in the morning, in the cold, grim hour before the winter dawn, he heard the report of a gun or small cannon. It was the signal for the massacre to begin.

Loud knocks on his door caused MacIain to start from his bed and to hurry to open it. As a welcome he received a mortal wound from a gun fired at point-blank range. "He fell," as we read in a contemporary account, "back into the arms of his lady, who uttered a dreadful shriek. She was stripped naked, ruffians pulled the rings from her fingers with their teeth, and she received such treatment that she died the following day." Meanwhile men and boys were being slain without mercy. There is a story that a woman escaped with her child and hid in the bed of a precipitous burn. An officer saw them, and sent a soldier to kill the pair. This man disliked his orders so much that he killed a dog and, returning, showed his officer the animal's blood on his sword as proof that he had carried out his orders. Thirty-eight men, women and children were murdered that February morning; many more perished in the flight across the hill passes, "wrestling with a storm" as a contemporary account has it. At the head of the glen was Colonel Hamilton with 400 men. His orders had been to march down the glen before daylight and cut off those endeavouring to escape to the south. He arrived late, being impeded, as he said, by the extreme severity of the weather, and his tardy arrival undoubtedly saved many lives. He is indeed credited with having slain an old man of over 80 years, the sole survivor of the people of the glen. It is said that MacIain's grandson, with his nurse, was for some years after the massacre sheltered in secret by the Campbells of Dunstaffnage, who were related by marriage to the MacDonalds. The houses of the unfortunate people were fired, and a letter of the time records that 900 cows, 200 horses, and many sheep and goats were driven from the glen.

The men of Glencoe, taken thus by surprise, what chance had they of defending themselves? Very little, yet it is known that they accounted for at least three members of Argyll's regiment. The grave of one soldier is beneath a very old hawthorn bush which, it is said in the glen, was an old tree even at the time of the massacre. The two other soldiers were buried at a place named Cladh nan Guibhneach, near the old road. The word "Guibhneach" is dialectal for Duibhneach, and means a member of the Clan Campbell, so that eminent Celtic scholar Professor W. J. Watson told me. Glencoe is still a desolate glen; it has never recovered from that night's work of long ago. The side glen where MacIain was living—Gleann Leac na Muidhe—still shows the ruins of small dwellings, but there is now only one house in that glen. Scarcely visible are the ruins of MacIain's house, for water from the hills has brought down much debris during the centuries and a part of the ruined walls is now buried. A bagpipe chanter was not so long ago unearthed here; it may have been silent since the evening before the massacre, when a sacred Highland tradition was violated and the honour of those in high places deeply involved.

The croak of the raven and, more rarely, the shrill yelp of the eagle break the great silence in Glencoe. Sometimes, in spring, the roar of an avalanche from the high ridges of Bidean nam Beann sounds like prolonged thunder, so that the deer seek safety in flight and the ptarmigan rise, white-winged, into the heavens. The winds often rush through the glen, and lift the water from the swaying cascades so that, defying the law of gravity, it disappears into the clouds that are tempest-torn as they race over the jagged peaks. But when you have emerged from the glen, and have reached King's House, you find here an open country, still wet and stormy it is true, but giving wide views and receiving the benefit of any sunshine there may be.

CHAPTER V

BLACK MOUNT TO LOCH LOMOND

THE inn at King's House stands near the Mother Loch of Etive, in Gaelic Lochan Mathair Eite. From this tarn flows the stream that later becomes the river Etive and empties itself into the head of Loch Etive. No one who has interest in the events of olden times should fail to make the journey from King's House to Loch Etive. At the head of the glen northward stands that noble hill Buachaille Eite Mór, the Great Herdsman of Etive, and to the south Clach Leathad, an even higher hill. The road winds down Glen Etive on the north bank of the river. At a turn of the river about halfway down the glen is Dalness. Here was the home of Deirdre of the fatal beauty, on the grassy slope that rises from the south bank of the river; here too was her *grianan* or sun bower. At a much later date Duncan Bàn Macintyre, the renowned Gaelic poet, had his home at Dalness. Until recent years the ruins of his house could be seen between two streams and shaded by old ash trees. Duncan Bàn Macintyre, he who is always known to the Gael as Donnchadh Bàn nan Oran (Fair-haired Duncan of the Songs), is to the Highlander what Robert Burns is to the Lowlander. His greatest poem is that in which he praises Ben Doran: the rhythm is in the form of a classical piece of music for the Highland bagpipe. His poems are the more remarkable in that he could neither read nor write. There is a story that, while serving in the army, he was one day seen holding a newspaper the wrong way up. An acquaintance walked over to him and said, "Duncan, it is the wrong end of the paper you have up." At once Duncan retorted, "It matters not to a good scholar which end of it is up."

Let us return to King's House and travel south, over the wild country of the Monadh Dubh, the Black Mount Forest. The main road passes near Loch Baa, with its birch-clad island where herons make their nests. On this isle, perhaps even in the same birches, the sea eagle had her eyrie 100 years ago. Great hills form the horizon. To the east are Schiehallion and Ben Lawers. South are the steep slopes of Ben Dorain. To the west are the lofty hills of the Black Mount Forest, Clachlet and Stob Gabhar. Here, too, is that wild

54

corrie, Corrichi-ba, the home of the white hind of the Black Mount, an animal that is said to have lived to a very great age.

There is in the Black Book of Taymouth a record that in February, 1622, "the king's majesty send John Skandebar, Englishman, with other two Englishmen in his company, to see ane quhyt hynd that was in Corrishiba." Scrope in his *Days of Deer Stalking* mentions more than one white hind. That of Loch Treig in Lochaber was particularly renowned. Captain MacDonald of Tulloch, who died at the age of 86 in 1776, knew the white hind of Loch Treig for the last fifty years of his life, his father knew her for an equal length of time before him, and his grandfather knew her for sixty years of his own time—and she preceded his days.

That the Highlanders firmly believed in the longevity of the red deer is seen from the following adage, of which the original is in Gaelic:

> Thrice the age of a dog the age of a horse,
> Thrice the age of a horse the age of a man,
> Thrice the age of a man the age of a stag,
> Thrice the age of a stag the age of an eagle,
> Thrice the age of an eagle the age of an oak.

Loch Tulla of the Black Mount, old pines sheltering its western shore, is the home of many water fowl in spring, and golden-eyes are there long after the local mallard are nesting. The black-throated diver has nested on some of the lochs in the forest, although the red-throated diver is unknown here.

Near the hotel at Inveroran beside Loch Tulla are to be seen the ruins of the house in which Duncan Bàn Macintyre was born. His wife, Mairi Nighean Neacail (Mary Daughter of Nicol) was the daughter of the keeper of the old inn at Inveroran. She was the poet's loved companion throughout his life, and when an acquaintance once said to him that his wife was scarcely as beautiful as he had led him to believe, Duncan replied, "Cha n'fhaca tusa i leis na suilean agamsa" ("You have not seen her with my eyes").

Inveroran is near Bridge of Orchy. Here the traveller may either continue by way of Glen Orchy, along a pleasant salmon river, and find himself at Dalmally on the main road to Oban near Loch Awe, or he may follow the main south road over the watershed and drop down to Tyndrum, which is on the county march between Perth and Argyll. Close to the march is a small loch named Lochan na Bi

—Tarn of Pitch Pine. This name may be a very old one, for there are no pines now in sight of the loch. I recall, one day of early summer, watching goosanders fishing on this loch, the home of many trout. The birds, swimming in line, were driving the trout before them during their frequent and prolonged dives. It was a day of sunshine, and there were no ripples on the loch except those caused by the fishing duck. Here, at the watershed between Perth and Argyll and between the rivers Awe and Tay, spring comes late. The white grasslands (there is little heather in this district) around the loch and on the hillsides above it were still without a tinge of green. There was snow upon Ben Lui (which does not usually free itself of its last snow-bed until late in the summer), and a great snowdrift lay across the face of Ben More beyond Crianlarich. But the curlew had arrived, and their rippling songs echoed from the sunlit corries.

I dropped down to Tyndrum, and saw the small loch, Lochan nan Arm (Tarn of the Arms), which, according to tradition, received its name from an event at the battle of Dail Righ (Dalree) when King Robert the Bruce, being hard pressed when mounted on his steed, threw his sword into the tarn. This was the historic fight in which the MacDougall clansman tore the king's cloak, together with the Brooch of Lorne, from the king's person, and in which the Bruce killed three of these clansmen with his battle-axe.

Glen Dochart, which has its beginnings here, in those days must have been a lonely glen, without road or track. At the present day it has for a short distance a main road and two railways running through it. From Tyndrum to Crianlarich the Oban-Stirling railway is on the west side of the glen and the Glasgow-Fort William is on the east side.

There are few families now in Glen Dochart, a glen with a heavy rainfall and with grass rather than heather on its hills. In olden times the glen was more populous, and there must have been many strangers visiting it, if only because of the sacred pool in the young river not far from Tyndrum. The pool is named Linne Fhaolain— St. Fillan's Pool. It is a deep pool, and was believed to have miraculous properties, especially in mental illness. Mentally afflicted persons were thrown in with a rope tied to their middle. He or she was then instructed to take three stones from the bottom of the pool and to walk three times sunwise round three cairns which then stood on the bank

56

Sunset over Lismore, from Oban
Castle Stalker in Appin

of the stream. They left on the cairns a portion of their clothing covering the afflicted parts.

The ruins of the old priory, which stand below the railway from Crianlarich to Fort William, commemorate another rite in the healing of a person in St. Fillan's Pool. After the immersion he or she was bound securely and left all night to lie within the priory. Robert the Bruce decreed that goats should have free grazing in Strath Fillan. After the battle of Dalrigh the king spent the night in a goatherd's home, and was delighted with the cleanliness of the goat's milk he was given to drink.

The head waters of the Dochart are in what is usually named Strath Fillan and not Glen Dochart, and the river here is called the water of Fillan and does not receive the name Dochart until it reaches Crianlarich.

Looking west from the old priory and healing pool of St. Fillan the traveller sees the noble cone of Ben Lui, in winter deeply snow-clad like some Alpine peak, in summer blue and clear, the snow beds in its east-facing corrie a brilliant white beneath the June sun. He sees, too, the old pines dark on the face of Beinn Dubh-chraige, another mighty hill of 3,374 feet against the 3,708 feet of Ben Lui, from which it is divided by a deep and narrow glen. The watershed on the Ben Lui massif is a narrow one. On its north-west face the hill burns find their way into the river Orchy, thence into Loch Awe and through Loch Awe into the river Awe, which reaches the Atlantic at Loch Etive. South, the streams flow into Loch Lomond, thence into the Firth of Clyde; south-west, they travel into Glen Fyne and thence to salt water in Loch Fyne. East, a greater volume of water leaves the hill, and here may be said to be the headwaters of the river Tay, which enters the east sea below Perth. The confluence of these waters is, at first, named Amhuinn Choininish, then Fillan Water, later the river Dochart which flows into Loch Tay, and reappears as the river Tay.   At Crianlarich let us take the road southward to Loch Lomond. This road passes along Glen Falloch, where are ancient, storm-beaten pines on the high ground and, nearer Loch Lomond, many birch trees, green and feathery in the summer sun, still graceful when leafless at mid-winter, plum-coloured in early spring before the green buds have opened.

The view down Loch Lomond, from the head of the loch, is of singular beauty and charm, with the cone of Ben Lomond standing

In Glencoe
Kingshouse Hotel and the Black Mount Forest

sentinel on the horizon. At Inveruglas the water of Sloy enters the loch, and here are to be seen evidences of the mighty hydro-electric scheme which has harnessed the waters of Loch Sloy and the rivers and streams which enter and flow from that hill loch, once among the wildest and most beautiful in the Highlands.

On the opposite shore of Loch Lomond from Inveruglas is Inversnaid, where there was at one time a ferry across Loch Lomond. Inveruglas is old MacFarlane territory. "Loch Sloy" was the rallying cry of that wild clan, who often raided the lowlands to lift the cattle and return to their fastness with their *creach*. By the lowlanders the moon was named MacFarlane's Lantern, and at the times of full moon they guarded their flocks and herds with particular care. The chief of the MacFarlanes was living in 1729 at Inerioch, near the head of Loch Long. On the upper waters of Loch Lomond are two islands which were MacFarlane strongholds. The castle on Eilean Uglas was burnt by Cromwell's orders, and the chief then built himself another castle on Eilean a' Bhuth. There are very old yew trees on this island, which was a former nesting haunt of the osprey until the hen bird was shot. The yew trees of the Loch Lomond district are celebrated. In olden days they were of considerable importance because the bows used by the Highlander both in war and in the chase were fashioned of yew wood. Near the north shore of Loch Lomond, at Firkin, is a yew which is obviously of great age. The tradition of the district is that Robert the Bruce and his followers sheltered beneath that tree before the battle of Bannockburn, as the king's army was being ferried over the loch in a small and leaking boat. There is nothing improbable in this tradition, for the yew is our longest-lived tree—witness the celebrated yew at Fortingall, which is said to be more than 3,000 years old. On the day when we crossed to Eilean a' Bhuth and saw the venerable yew at Firkin my friend Sir George Campbell of Succoth, who is keenly interested in afforestation and has noteworthy plantations and woods on his land at Crarae on Loch Fyne, brought away a cutting from the tree and it soon took root, strong and healthy, in his garden. He later gave it to me. Some trees grow easily from cuttings, but the yew is not one of them. The parent yew of this cutting may have stood, strong and sturdy, when the kingdom of Dalriada was formed; it may have been a grown tree when Angus Mór of Islay before the battle of Largs caused his galleys to be dragged overland from Loch Long, and ravaged the country of Loch Lomond and its fertile islands with fire and sword.

It was from a yew growing in a rock that MacFarlane hung the "savage" commemorated in the clan's crest. The story is that the chief's wife had had a baby in the castle on Eilean a' Bhuth. She died in, or soon after, childbirth, and when MacFarlane heard that the wife of one of the ancient inhabitants of the country, then living on the hill on the mainland opposite the castle, had an infant of the same age, he had her seized and brought to his castle to suckle his baby. The "savage" avenged himself by seizing MacFarlane's dairymaid when she crossed to the mainland shore to milk the cows and cutting off her breasts. MacFarlane then caught and hanged the savage on the yew tree growing from the rock, and took his likeness, naked and carrying a sheaf-ful of arms, as his crest. Graham of Duchray states that the MacFarlanes were still living on Eilean a' Bhuth in 1724.

At Tarbet, Loch Lomond bends rather toward the west. It was to Tarbet that Angus Mór of Islay before the battle of Largs crossed in his war galleys from Loch Long to harry the lands of Lennox. Four miles down Loch Lomond is Rowardennan, on the east shore. Professor Watson believed the name means Point of Adamnan's Cape, named after Adamnan, abbot of Iona and chronicler of the life of St. Columba. Here "Row" stands for Rudha, a Point or Promontory. At Rowardennan Loch Lomond is less than a mile wide and a ferry at one time plied here. Graham of Duchray, writing in 1724, mentions an old tradition that Rowardennan at one period was the end of Loch Lomond, and that south of it was an agricultural country, fertile and inhabited. Then, for some unknown reason, the loch overflowed across this level land, inundating it. He mentions that fishermen on Loch Lomond, in times of drought when the loch had greatly shrunk, have seen the ruins of houses, on which their boats have sometimes stranded, and have stood on the old walls to push off their boats. Two miles from the mouth of the river Leven they sometimes saw the ruins of a particularly large building. He also mentions the ruins of a church called by tradition Kildavie that is seen rising from the loch near the shore of the island of Inchcaillioch.

In the same old account it is stated that in Loch Lomond near the mouth of the river Enrick (now Endrick) "the Water Horse or Hippotam" is sometimes seen.

Graham of Duchray writes of Ben Lomond, "reckon'd the highest hill in Scotland," and states, "off the top of this mountain in a clear day a person will discover not only the Cape of Kintyre tho eightie miles distant to the west, but also some of the mountains of the County of Donegall in Ireland, and some hills in Cumberland and Northumberland in England." The record of this wide view, written as it was more than 200 years ago, is of unusual interest. When a friend and I climbed Ben Lomond on a November day the air was very clear and the islands of Jura, Islay and Mull were plain. The Arran steamer could be seen crossing to that island from the mainland.

We were fortunate that day to have a near view of a covey of ptarmigan sun-bathing on the south face of the hill. Ben Lomond is the most southerly hill in Britain where ptarmigan have their home. In calm weather the birds are often reluctant to move and may be closely approached. In November they have partly assumed their white winter dress and are beginning to be conspicuous on the hills if the snow should delay its coming.

A considerable number of islands, of varying sizes, rise from Loch Lomond in the southern part of the loch. The parish of Buchanan was at one time named Inchcaillioch, after the island of that name, and the ruins of an old church on that island were pointed out in Graham of Duchray's time as the old parish church. On Inchmurren, the most southerly of the islands, where fallow deer roamed, are the ruins of a castle which was an ancient seat of the Earls of Lennox, and near it "an old ruinous chappell called the Chappell of St. Mirren." On another island, Inchlonaig by name, a wood of yew trees flourish. Graham of Duchray in his account of the district names the isle Inchconnachan, but the local opinion is that he was mistaken; at all events no yews now grow on this isle. Mention is made in this old account of the "Gyants Castle built all of prodigious big quhinstone without lyme or cement. The founder therof said to be one Keith Mac Indoill or Keith the son of Doillus who is reported to be contemporary with the famous Finmacoell and consequently to have lived in the fifth century of the Christian Epocha."

As the high-road winds down Loch Lomond from Tarbet to Balloch at the foot of the loch it passes the village of Luss and, two miles farther down the loch, Rossdhu, the home of the Colquhouns of Luss. The house stands close to the loch, and Sir Iain Culquhoun of Luss told me that on one occasion he and his terrier had watched three otters playing in the loch quite near them. He watched them for three-quarters of an hour and the terrier stood on the shore only a few feet from the otters. They gazed at one another, he said, with the greatest interest but with no sign of fear or antagonism. Eventually the otters started a sort of game with the terrier, two of them actually coming ashore. Bird life is varied on and around Loch Lomond. Capercaillies still roost on the old Scots firs of Inch Caillioch and everywhere, both on island and mainland, willow warblers sing softly in May and June. The gannet might be expected to visit Loch Lomond, to fish for the powan or fresh-water herring which have their home in the loch. A gamekeeper who lived beside the loch for more than thirty years told me that he had only on one occasion seen a gannet fishing here. The reluctance of the species to fly over land is well known, and although many doubtless fish in Loch Long the strip of land which separates the two lochs at Arrochar is no doubt sufficient to deter them from crossing to Loch Lomond.

Major Leckie-Ewing, whose reputation as an angler adds weight to his testimony, has kindly given me some notes on the fishing on Loch Lomond. He writes:

The deeper knowledge an angler (or his boatman) has of the position of the various under-water banks and rocks around the shore and various islands of Loch Lomond, the better his chances are when angling for salmon or sea trout. As the loch is twenty-two miles long and covers some 21,000 acres, it is obvious that this knowledge cannot be picked up in a day. Local anglers have the advantage that on windless days they can work their boats round the islands and the shore, and take note of the position of the various banks. Speaking generally, on the north and west sides of the islands there are extensive banks (said to have been formed during the Ice Age) where fish lie.

On the east shore of the loch, six or seven miles from where the river Leven flows from the loch, the river Endrick enters Loch Lomond: on either side of the Endrick mouth the ground is level. The loch bottom here is of sand, which runs out for 100 yards or more into the loch, with the water gradually deepening to 4 or 5 feet, when the depth suddenly increases to 10-12 feet. This is known as the Endrick Bank, and I believe that more salmon have been taken by rod and line here than in any other part of the loch. If the boatman knows the water, he can manipulate the angler's boat so that the angler's flies work the edge of the shallow and deep water. A good stiff breeze is required here, preferably on shore or off-shore.

In fishing Loch Lomond, as opposed to a river, one is so dependent on the wind. There may be no fishable breeze for many days, and so the total bag of salmon or sea trout for a season may appear small in comparison perhaps to only a month's sport on rivers such as the Dee or Spey. According to the records in the late Henry Lamond's book *Loch Lomond*, between 1903 and 1930 the three best seasons were 1925 with 465 salmon, 1926 with 328, and 1927 with 460. The average weight of these fish worked out to 12·5 lb. The record rod-caught salmon was one of 44 lb., got by Mr. E. Cochran trolling with a blue-and-silver phantom in 1930. The previous record, a fish of 42 lb., was caught near Balloch in 1912 by Mr. W. Millar, also on a blue-and-silver. In the year 1886, Mr. Hamilton Maxwell caught on a fly a fish of $31\frac{1}{2}$ lb.; this stood as the record fly-caught salmon until June 30, 1927, when Mrs. Leckie-Ewing, fishing off the east end of Inchfad, caught a salmon of $36\frac{1}{2}$ lb. The day was dull, with a stiff east wind blowing. The fish took a No. 7 mallard and yellow, was 46 inches long, and had a girth of 24 inches.

As regards numbers of salmon caught in one day to one boat, the best bag was five, weighing 60 lb., all taken on the fly, in 1919. In 1920 Mr. J. S. Sellar had five salmon, also on fly. Several anglers have taken three or four salmon in a day, not necessarily all on a fly. In my own boat the best result, as regards weight, was 71 lb., in three salmon taken on fly, on two successive afternoons' fishing.

The Loch Lomond sea trout lie in deeper water than the salmon. The salmon lie in water 6 to 8 feet deep; the sea trout in water 12 to 16 feet deep. In May or June the larger class of sea trout, fish around 4 lb. to 5 lb., arrive in the loch. In July the main run arrives, and from then until October shoals of whitling or finnock, known locally as black-nebs, run up the river Leven. The Loch Lomond whitling are larger than the normal, and weigh usually from $\frac{3}{4}$ lb. to $1\frac{1}{2}$ lb. On the various banks on which they lie, given reasonable conditions, the sea trout rise freely. In 1925 a Luss angler caught a sea trout $11\frac{1}{2}$ lb., a record for the fly, and in August, 1938, I had one of 12 lb. on a No. 8 Irishman. This was a well-shaped cock fish, a little dark in colour, and was $30\frac{1}{2}$ inches in length. The scale reading, by the Scottish Fishery Department, showed that the fish was seven years old, and had spawned only once (in 1937).

As a foot-note to this interesting account by Major Leckie-Ewing, Mrs. Leckie-Ewing, whose almost uncanny skill in taming wild birds is well known, narrates the affairs of a pair of coots which nested in the bay where they kept their boat. When the seven or eight chicks hatched, she used to throw pieces of biscuit to them, and eventually when they saw the boat coming they would "scutter" along the surface of the water to the boat. By the time they were almost full-grown they had become so tame that they would come to Mrs. Leckie-Ewing as she sat beside the loch, and would climb on to her lap to take bits of biscuit from her hands, and even her mouth. The parents had meanwhile nested again, and when Mrs. Leckie-Ewing waded out to the nest both parent birds would take scraps from her hands. The bird which was brooding at the time would stand up on the nest and, as Mrs. Leckie-Ewing bent down, would take food from her mouth. The taming of the adult coots was more remarkable than the taming of the young.

South of Luss and Rossdhu the water of Fruin enters Loch Lomond. Glen Fruin leads far into the hills, and the headwaters of the stream are less than two miles from Loch Long. The old clan fight between the MacGregors and the Colquhouns is known as the Rout of Glen Fruin, and is commemorated in a wild Pibroch, no doubt a Mac-Gregor composition from its triumphant song.

The MacGregors, a wild, turbulent clan from Glen Strae and Glen Orchy in Argyll, in the year 1602 attacked the Colquhouns of Luss, and after a bitter conflict defeated and pursued them to the gates of the castle, driving away as booty 600 head of cattle, 300 horses and 800 sheep and goats. The MacGregors had never been popular with the "powers that be," and this brought matters to a head. By an Act of the Privy Council, dated April 3, 1603, the name of MacGregor was expressly abolished, and those who had hitherto borne it were commanded to change it for other surnames, under pain of death. It was also decreed that all those who had been at the Rout of Glen Fruin should be prohibited from carrying weapons, except a pointless knife with which to cut their victuals. Should any of the tribe formerly called MacGregor assemble to the number exceeding four, the penalty would be death if they were apprehended. The chief was Alasdair MacGregor of Glen Strae. The Earl of Argyll promised to convey him to England and to plead his cause at Court. When they had reached Berwick-on-Tweed, Argyll, saying that he had fulfilled the first part of his promise, conveyed his victim back to Edinburgh, where he was hanged. In the declaration MacGregor made before

63

his death he accused Argyll of inciting him to war against the Colquhouns for his own ends, and also against the Laird of Buchanan and others.

There is a track across the shoulder of the hills from Glen Fruin to Gareloch-head, from which place Loch Long is less than two miles distant. Loch Long, a sea loch, might be expected to have received its name from its length, for it is a long and narrow loch, with hills rising steeply from it. The meaning of the name, however is Loch of Ships, and its Norse name was Skipafjord. Its chief branch is Loch Goil, a lonely loch, on the shore of which is the site of the ruins of ancient Carrick Castle, no more than twelve miles up the coast from Dunoon. There is a tradition that the last wild boar slain in Scotland was killed not far from Carrick Castle.

Although this country is at no great distance from Glasgow the golden eagle still breeds here, and the peregrine and the raven remain in their ancestral haunts. I was told that during the severe spring of 1947, when the ground was frost-bound for six weeks and the frost continued until after the laying season of the raven, the clutches of eggs in this district were very small, averaging no more than two. In the Loch Lomond and Loch Long districts the severe weather which affected the raven clutches had also a disastrous effect on many other species of birds, and the following spring curlews and lapwings were rare where formerly they had been numerous. They are still scarce in the spring of 1949.

PART II

THE KINGDOM OF THE PICTS

CHAPTER I

LOCH LOMOND TO HARLAW

FROM Helensburgh in the west to Aberdeen in the east is a wide country, differing in its geology, in its climate, in its people. The distance as the eagle flies is no more than 120 miles, although by road it is very much farther. The clans are different, the customs are different, the outlook of the inhabitants is different, for their traditions, anchored deep in the past, have a different origin.

If Helensburgh had existed in the time of the kingdom of Dalriada it would have found itself on the borders of, or just within, that kingdom, and would have endured a life of constant anxiety, never knowing when a descent by the Picts might not bring strife and bloodshed. No doubt the galleys of the kings and nobles of Dalriada from time to time sailed into its Gareloch: at a later time the Norse galleys must have aroused mistrust on the occasions when they visited the coast, for this district, unlike the Hebrides, was outside the rule of the vikings.

The eagle on his flight from Helensburgh to Aberdeen would pass directly over the southern isles of Loch Lomond. He would see the noble cone of Ben Lomond rise a few miles to the north, would pass immediately over Aberfoyle (where the fairy minister, the Reverend Robert Kirk, laboured some centuries ago) and above Callander, then, after flying over some high and lonely country, would reach the river Earn between Comrie and Crieff. As he passed over the Sma' Glen he would see the houses and churches of the city of Perth, with the sun shining silver on the Tay beside them, a little way toward the south-east. Perhaps when over Dunkeld, which would be directly on his course, the eagle would pause, and would sail awhile high in contemplation, for when Iona was sacked by the Danes the relics of St. Columba were transferred for greater safety partly to Kells in Eire and partly to Dunkeld. The church of Dunkeld was treated with high honour by the Picts and the abbot of Dunkeld was placed at the head of the Pictish church.

From Dunkeld the eagle would fly over Angus, previously called Forfar, seeing from his aerial way the historic castles of Cortachy and

Glamis, then would cross remote Glen Clova, where winter blizzards often seal the glen, so that food supplies have to be dropped by air. Crossing the high pass of Cairn o' Mount, the eagle would reach the Dee valley at Crathes, and would continue east to Aberdeen. He would be less at his ease over the last twelve or fifteen miles of lowland country, with its rich cultivation, and would, I am sure, gain altitude before seeing far beneath him the city of Aberdeen—the Silver City by the Sea as it has sometimes been called—with its strong white granite buildings flashing in the sun, its narrow river estuary, and the green waters of the North Sea beyond.

Aberdeen and the agricultural district north of the city are lowland country and do not strictly come within the province of this book. But the battle of Harlaw, being fought by Highlanders on both sides, merits some mention.

The battle of Harlaw was fought near Inverurie, some fifteen miles north of Aberdeen, on July 24, 1411, the opposing leaders being Donald, Lord of the Isles, and Alexander, Earl of Mar. Donald of the Isles was at variance with his uncle, Duke of Albany and Regent of Scotland, over the Earldom of Ross. The Lord of the Isles, with justice as most historians think, considered that he, or rather his wife, had the right to this title, but Albany had it conferred on his own son, the Earl of Buchan, and with it the fertile lands of Buchan which went with the old title. Hence the battle of Harlaw.

The Earl of Mar, who opposed Donald of the Isles, was his first cousin. Mar was the natural son of the Wolf of Badenoch by a Highland girl whose name, Mairead or Margaret, is Latinised as Mariota by the writers of that day. He was thus an illegitimate grandson of a Scottish king.

Most historians have taken the view that the battle was between a Highland force on the one hand and a smaller but better-disciplined Lowland army on the other, but, as the late William MacKay, LL.D., of Inverness, the Highland scholar and historian, has pointed out, the Earl of Mar was purely Highland, for he was brought up in Badenoch, spoke Gaelic, and appears to have been a good Gaelic bard. His opponent Donald, Lord of the Isles, the reputed Highland barbarian, was an undergraduate at Oxford. Lord Lindsay, Master of Balliol College, Oxford, has been good enough to make some enquiries for me and tells me that the Principal of St. Edmund Hall has record of "Donald, son of John de Out Isles, or De Insulis, clerk, who was granted a safe conduct on August 1, 1378, to enable him to proceed to Oxford for study for six years." It is Mar who acted as the wild cateran—did he not besiege the widowed Countess of Mar in her castle of Kildrummy and compel her to marry him after he had captured her castle?

Aberdeen, as I have said, is not strictly in the Highland area, which the eagle would enter once more as he flew north over Monymusk, the Cabrach, Dufftown and Craigellachie. At Craigellachie the eagle would feel more at home, for here he would find himself above a Highland river, the renowned Spey, the haunt of many a salmon and sea trout. From Craigellachie he would fly over the hills to Forres, and would continue near the shores of the Moray Firth to Nairn and Inverness. From Inverness he would fly above the Caledonian Canal to Fort William, cross the hills to Bridge of Orchy and Crianlarich, and, flying down Loch Lomond, would reach his starting-point above Helensburgh.

He would have passed, on his flight (which would have taken him perhaps five hours) the territories of many clans. At his starting- and finishing-point he would have been over Colquhoun territory, and, had the flight been on a dark November day of the year 1948, he would perhaps have seen a small craft sailing up Loch Lomond with the mortal remains of one of the best-loved chiefs of the Highlands, Sir Iain Colquhoun of Luss, and would have heard the lament the piper played on the boat. The family of Colquhoun have been on Loch Lomond-side for more than five centuries, and during that time have played a leading part in the affairs of that district. The passing of that brave, upright and humble man Sir Iain is a loss not to the Highlands alone, but to all Scotland.

Across Loch Lomond are the ancestral lands of the Buchanans, which for some centuries have been owned by the Dukes of Montrose, chiefs of the clan Graham. The present holder of the title is one of the great public figures in Scotland. Across the hills from Buchanan to Aberfoyle in the Trossachs is a distance of nine miles, over rough country where sheep feed and in spring the curlew sings his wild, melancholy song. Aberfoyle has close associations with Sir Walter Scott's historical novel *Rob Roy*, and that strange personage the Rev. Robert Kirk was minister here. He was a seventh son, and his book dealing with *The Secret Commonwealth of Elves, Fauns and Fairies*, written in the year 1691, has on several occasions been reprinted.

Sir Walter Scott in his own *Demonology and Witchcraft* notes that "it was printed with the author's name in 1691," but there is now no record of that first edition. The edition of 1815 consisted of one hundred copies. In the book are remarkable instances of second sight, telepathy, and other occult phenomena. In the Trossachs, in the neighbourhood of Aberfoyle, is Loch Ard, set in a scene of great beauty, woods of birch and oak intermingling. On this loch are two small islands, the larger named of old St. Mallo, having the ruins of a chapel on it. On the lesser isle, or rather rock, Dundochill by name, according to Alexander Graham of Duchray's account of 1724, "is the ruines of an old litle Castell called the Duke's Castell said to be built by Murdo Stewart Duke of Albany Earl of Fife and Montreath Regent of Scotland. And ther's a tradition that it was out of this Castle, he was taken when he was execut at Stirling, after the ransom of King James the first from his captivity in England."

There are many trout in Loch Ard, and the angler, if the fish are not on the take, can watch the sandpipers courting on sunny days of early May on the shores of the loch, from time to time flitting delicately over it on wings driven so fast that they seem to tremble, the while their twittering song carries on the breeze. From the oaks and birches, the oaks bronze, the birches a soft green, come the husky calls of invisible cuckoos, while from the topmost branches of some venerable oak a missel-thrush hurls his loud imperious song, a song that sounds like a challenge to all within earshot—as perhaps it is. Soft cadences from the throats of invisible willow warblers are heard from these birches. At times the golden eagle flies high over Loch Ard, perhaps to visit his ancestral eyrie on Ben Venue, and the peregrine with strong flight moves toward his eyrie on the high rocks on the north face of that hill. At sunset the cone of Ben Lomond glows as though afire, and a wandering cloud that rests awhile here is suffused by rosy rays. Then comes the moment of sunset, and one can visualise that view from the hill-top as the sun dips behind the Paps of Jura, far westward, or, if the season is early spring, behind the high hills of Donegal in Ireland.

Rob Roy, the Robin Hood of Scotland, a kinsman of the chief of the MacGregors, is the legendary hero of the Aberfoyle district—as indeed he is of other districts of the south-west Highlands. The following story is typical of the man. One day of the year 1716 when on his way from Inversnaid on the east shore of Loch Lomond to

Aberfoyle he was told of the plight of a widow on the Duke of Montrose's estate. She was in arrears with the rent of her small farm. Rob
was informed that the estate factor was that very day about to sell her
belongings to the value of the overdue rent. He at once decided to
help her. He called at the house and advanced her the sum of money
she was due the estate. His one stipulation was that she should obtain
a written receipt from the factor or land agent for the money. Then
Rob Roy with some of his men proceeded to an inn near, where he
knew that the factor was likely to call for refreshment on his way
home. Sure enough, later in the day the factor arrived, and after he
had had his dram was departing in a happy frame of mind when Rob
Roy and his men, who had carefully concealed themselves, sprang
out, seized him, and relieved him of the £20 which the widow had
paid him. Rob Roy thus got his money back, and for interest had the
excitement on which he throve. Since the widow was able to show a
written receipt, the estate could not call upon her for further rent
that year. Of the innumerable tales of the remarkable Rob Roy I
take one more. The scene is this time at Tyndrum, near the Healing
Pool of St. Fillan, of which I have already written. Rob Roy was
"wanted" by the government for more than one misdemeanour in
the eyes of the law, and when word was brought to the troops in
the district that the wanted man was at Tyndrum a party at once
set off hopefully to that place with the object of arresting him. They
began a careful search of the district from their quarters at the inn.
News of their plans being brought to Rob Roy, that worthy disguised
himself as a beggar and came boldly to the inn, walking into the
kitchen and sitting down among the soldiers. After a time the soldiers,
warmed by drink, started to poke fun at the beggar, and to play tricks
on him because of his transparent simplicity. At last the beggar,
apparently losing his temper, said, "If you do not stop your games I
will tell Rob Roy." At the mention of their quarry's name the soldiers
were all attention. They plied the beggar with eager questions and
he, apparently greatly pleased by the interest he had aroused, said he
knew the great man well, "and what is more, I know where he is
in hiding at the present time." The soldiers at once informed their
officer, who, taking the beggar aside, engaged him in earnest conversation, and asked him for his help in tracking down Rob Roy, promising
him great riches if he did this. The beggar appeared to hesitate, but
in the end said that Rob Roy was at Crianlarich with his men, and

71

that their arms were in one house and they themselves in another, so there should be little difficulty in capturing them all. The party in great spirits started on their journey of three miles down the glen. It was necessary for them to ford the river, then in spate. The ford was near St. Fillan's Pool, and the stream was running so swiftly that the soldiers were unwilling to cross. They prevailed upon the beggar, who was a tall, powerful man, to carry them over. This he did for the payment of a penny for each man. His strength was such that he was able to carry the lighter soldiers across two at a time.

As the party approached Crianlarich the beggar said that he would go on ahead, in order not to arouse suspicions, and engage Rob Roy in conversation in order that he should not be on his guard. He gave them minute directions as to the whereabouts and appearance of the house, and as a final injunction added these words: "Order your men to the back of the house, while you, with the sergeant and your two best men, walk in at the front door. When you enter the door, call out loudly that all within are your prisoners." His final words to the officer were that he must not be surprised if he saw the beggar at the head of the company, as he was high in Rob Roy's favour.

The officer did as he was told, and leaving the rest of his company at the back of the house rushed in through the front door, accompanied by two of his best men and the sergeant, shouting that all were his prisoners and that it was useless to defend themselves. In a room within they saw the beggar standing at the head of the table, but at once the door was closed and they were seized and bound. The beggar then went out and shouted loudly that two more men were wanted inside. When the two had hurried in, they also were swiftly seized. The beggar continued to call at intervals for two more men, until the whole company were inside the house and securely bound. In the morning Rob Roy, the beggar in disguise, gave each man an excellent breakfast before taking their parole to return to their garrison, saying he was sorry that he would have to keep their arms.

When the Duke of Montrose succeeded in having Rob Roy outlawed, the Duke of Argyll allowed him to use a cave in Glen Shira, and subsequently built him a house there. Upon Montrose remonstrating with Argyll on his harbouring this outlaw, Argyll replied, "You feed him, but all he gets from me is a cave and water."

Chapter II

TROSSACHS AND LOCH EARN

The great bulk of Ben Venue dominates Aberfoyle. At the southern
base of the hill is the farm of Ledard, where it is said that Sir Walter
Scott on one occasion stayed, perhaps when gathering material for his
historical novel *Rob Roy*. Beneath the oak trees wild hyacinths flower
in early summer, among them the wood sorrel and the wood anemone.
Higher up the Ledard burn birches replace the oaks, and on the May
day when I climbed the hill these trees were at the most beautiful
stage of their foliage. When I reached the high ground of Ben Venue
I could see the hills of Arran rising clearly on the south-west horizon.
I was here sheltered from the cold north-east wind, and on the sun-
warmed slopes the aromatic leaves of the crowberry were scenting
the air. I had now reached the home of the ptarmigan, whose white
feathers, moulted from the winter plumage, rested here and there on
the crowberry leaves: of the birds themselves there was no sign.
When I had reached the hill-top the view that lay spread out before
me was of great extent and clearness. Far to the north-west rose,
beyond lesser intervening hills, Cruachan Beann. On the county
march between Perth and Argyll Ben Lui was still sleeping beneath
its winter snow-cap. The air was of that extreme clearness associated
with a north-easterly type of weather in early summer. The sky was
deep blue; here and there white fair-weather clouds, stately and
dignified, drifted idly. The hills of Arran rose beyond the Firth of
Clyde. Beneath me was a land of glens and lochs, of birches and oaks
in the radiance of their young foliage. Each loch reflected the blue of
the sky, and showed colours so vivid that an artist who had faithfully
portrayed them would have been accused of exaggeration. I do not
think enough has been written of this remarkable colour which both
fresh-water and sea-water lochs in the Highlands sometimes assume
in early summer, and perhaps at no other season. To me that colour
is the most beautiful and the most remarkable to be seen in the British
Islands at any season of the year. It is not often seen, for the weather
and the season of the year must be just right for it to be apparent.
It may result from an unusual quality in the atmosphere; or an un-

usual quality in the blueness of the sky: I do not remember having seen it except in May or early June.

The lochs of the Trossachs—Loch Ard and Loch Con, Loch Arklet, Loch Vennachar, and Loch Katrine—what visions their names evoke in the minds of those who have seen and known them in all their beauty. Chief among these lochs is perhaps Loch Katrine. It has now been tamed by steamships and by innumerable tourists, but in olden times it was remote and wild, respected and even feared. Does not Coire nan Uruisgean, the Demons' Corrie, rise from its shore? Is not the water bull still seen plunging at dusk in its dark waters? Is not the loch's original name, in old Gaelic, Loch Ceiteirein, Loch of the Furies or Fiends? It is not so long ago since all the demons in Scotland were accustomed to gather in the corrie which bears their name, on days of mist and rain, when the grey wind from the west hurried over the dark loch, sweeping the surface waters before it in columns and clouds of spindrift; when the mists eddied in the corrie and the red grouse sought what shelter they could on heathery banks. The weeping birches, their branches naked, then swayed in the wind which scattered the raindrops which attempted to form on them. Perhaps the peregrine, he who has his home on the high rock above the loch, watched from his perch the gathering of the demons, and the eagle—he who had his eyrie high on Ben Venue but who has been banished by the hand of man from the district— looked down on the scene.

There are in the Highlands two species of birch. One of them is the pendulous variety, *Betula pendula*, which is found in the Trossachs: in the valleys of the Spey and Dee and elsewhere. It is more beautiful by far than the birch of the western seaboard and the Hebrides, which botanists have recently named *Betula glutinosa*, and which is sturdy and upright in character. In some districts the two species may be seen growing almost side by side.

At the head of Loch Katrine is Glen Gyle, the birthplace of Rob Roy. Behind the house of Glen Gyle is an old MacGregor burialplace, the recumbent gravestones showing on them the fir tree, emblem of the clan, and the crown which proclaims their descent from very early Scottish kings. There are ancient summer shielings in Glen Gyle, which may have been in use when those old copper beeches that grow so nobly beside Glen Gyle house were planted. Perhaps the trees were planted by Grigor Glun Dubh, Gregor Black Knee—

he who passed through Aberfoyle with two hundred strong men on a Sunday to join Prince Charlie. They halted on the green at Aberfoyle, where the girls of the district presented them with white cockades (the white cockade was the emblem of the house of Stuart, the black rose was the emblem of the House of Hanover). At the lower end of Loch Katrine rises Ellen's Isle, immortalised by Sir Walter Scott: it was he who gave the island the name it now bears. To see that isle at its best it must be viewed on a day of early summer sunshine, when the fresh young foliage of the island trees, swaying gently in the breeze, contrasts in colour with the blue waters of the loch from which the trees draw their moisture.

Below Loch Katrine is Loch Vennachar, and below Loch Vennachar is Callander. Let us take the road northward from Callander by way of Strathyre to Loch Earn, that long loch from which the river Earn flows. The road goes by the Pass of Leny, then along the shore of Loch Lubnaig (Loch Lubanach, the Winding Loch), with Ben Ledi, 2,875 feet, rising steeply from the foot of the loch. There is a very old tradition that in pre-Christian times the people from districts far and near assembled at the summer solstice on the summit of Ben Ledi. The great assembly, which was presided over by Druids, remained on the hill-top for three days. The old Statistical Account mentions that the summit of the hill is smoothed and free of stones, "which seems to be the work of art, but no stones with inscriptions on them have been found in the vicinity." Loch Lubnaig, according to an old account "produces of fishes rid weams [char], trouts and some salmond." The stream which flows from Loch Lubnaig was formerly called Garbh Uisge or Rough Water, a name no doubt given it because of its impetuous rapids and falls; it is now known as the river Leny. Two miles beyond Loch Lubnaig is a road which branches west to Balquhidder and carries on beyond it to Loch Voil and Loch Daoine. Rob Roy was buried at Balquhidder churchyard. On the recumbent stone which marks his grave is incised a sword, but no inscription of any kind. Inside the church is a stone, standing upright, of which the name is Clach Aonghuis or Leac Aonghuis, the Stone of Angus. On the stone is a figure of an ecclesiastic who may be Angus, patron saint of Balquhidder. This stone was formerly in the old church. The place where Angus preached is still pointed out, but little is known of him. Balquhidder, being off the main road, retains much of its simplicity and charm. The Braes of Balquhidder rise steeply from the shore of Loch Voil, and only a few miles to the north-west are the high tops of Stob Inneoin (3,821 feet) and Ben More (3,843 feet). I remember once sitting on a calm summer day on the summit of Stob Inneoin and watching a raven fly overhead when of a sudden a whirlwind arose, lifting the dry grass and moss and even small stones high into the air. As suddenly as it had arisen the wind dropped: the effect was curious and almost uncanny.

If, instead of striking west, the traveller continues north by the main road, he soon reaches Lochearnhead, and sees beneath him Loch Earn, a pleasant loch with wooded shores. South of this loch rise two noble hills, Ben Vorlich and its neighbour Stuic a' Chròin, of which the English translation is Rock of the Murmuring. I have seen both these hills at a great distance from the east when airborne. It is probable that Stuic a' Chròin has received its name from the hill loch which lies half a mile from its summit, and which is named Loch a' Chròin, perhaps from the outcry made by the gusts of wind as they rush down upon it, or from the music of the gale on the hill above it. The head-waters of the stream which flows through Glen Artney have their birth between Stuic a' Chròin and Ben Vorlich, and join the Earn at Comrie.

Ben Vorlich is the ancestral hill of the Stewarts of Ardvorlich, who have lived for centuries at their house of Ardvorlich beneath it. At Ardvorlich is to be seen the renowned Clach Dhearg, or Red Stone, which, like the Lee Penny and other charms, was believed to have miraculous healing properties. It imparted its healing powers to the water in which it was dipped. It was important to move the stone sunwise (deiseil) thrice round the pail, and it is likely also that certain runes were recited while this was being done; if so they have been lost. The water in which the stone had been dipped was often carried long distances to be given to sick cattle. There is a tradition in the family of the Stewarts of Ardvorlich that the crystal was brought back from the Holy Land by an ancestor after a crusade in the fourteenth century. The Lee Penny, described by Sir Walter Scott in *The Talisman*, a small dark red stone whose miraculous properties are more widely known, is also said to have had its origin in the Holy Land, from which it was brought back by Sir Simon de Lockhart, who had carried the heart of the Bruce there for burial. The house of Ardvorlich stands beside Loch Earn, where old natural woods of oak and birch grow. The Gaelic name of the loch is Loch Eireann, and Celtic scholars are inclined to believe that here we have the same name as Erin, and that settlers from Eire, who very early, perhaps when the kingdom of Dalriada was broken up, came to the district, gave it the name of their motherland. The word is also found in the place-name Drummond Eireannach in the same district; Drummond of Drummond Eireannach was the king's forester in the royal forest of Glen Artney.

There is a tragic connection between Drummond Eireannach and Ardvorlich. Stewart of Ardvorlich married, near the close of the sixteenth century, the daughter of Drummond of Drummond Eireannach. Being the king's forester, he dealt drastically with a party of MacGregors whom he found killing deer without authority in the royal forest, for he ordered their ears to be cut off. One's sympathies go out to the unfortunate MacGregors, even if they had been doing a bit of poaching on their own. Drummond must have realised that these men would be revenged sooner or later; perhaps the injured men bided their time and did not make their plans for revenge until they hoped their victim would have put the incident from his mind. One day Drummond was hunting alone in the forest. He had little chance against the body of men who surrounded and slew him in a lonely corrie and then cut off his head and carried it, wrapped in a plaid, to the house of Ardvorlich to complete their revenge. They had heard that Stewart of Ardvorlich was from home and that his wife, daughter of their enemy, was alone. They therefore demanded hospitality; nor could it be refused them, for the law on this matter was strict in the Highlands. The lady of the house asked the men to enter, placed bread and cheese before them, then left the room. She was later called back by the strangers, and when she opened the door saw on the table the blood-stained head of her father, a piece of bread and cheese in its mouth. Uttering a piercing shriek she fled from the house, her reason gone. When Stewart of Ardvorlich returned home he learnt of the affair, and although search was made near and far no trace of his wife could be found. It was summer, and the people who lived beside Loch Earn had gone to the summer shielings high in Glen Vorlich according to the old Highland custom. A few days later it was found that the cows belonging to some of the shielings were giving surprisingly little milk. Fairies were suspected, but a watch was kept and one night a woman was seen milking a cow on the hillside. She was carefully followed and was discovered sheltering by the shore of a small hill loch which ever since has borne the name Lochan na Mnà, the Woman's Loch. This was the poor wife, who never recovered from the shock. The MacGregors carried the head to Balquhidder, then sought their chief, MacGregor of Glenstrae, in Argyll, and told him what had happened, although they did not surely describe the grim scene at the house of Ardvorlich. Glenstrae summoned the clan and before the high altar in the church of Balquhidder each MacGregor clansman, placing his hand on the head there displayed, swore that he would defend with his life those who had done the deed.

At the eastern end of Loch Earn, not far from the shore, is a small island with trees growing thick upon it. Its name is Eilean nan Naoiseach, in English the Neishes' Island. Here a tragedy yet more grim than that enacted at Ardvorlich took place in the reign of King James V of Scotland. The Neishes and the MacNabs who lived across the hills at the head of Loch Tay were at variance—as most Highland clans were in those days—and when the Neishes saw the MacNabs returning home laden with wine and delicacies for Christmas (they had perhaps brought them from Crieff or Perth) they set upon them and relieved the travellers of their goods. When word of this outrage was brought across the moors to MacNab, the chief of the clan at his home at Bovain (Both Mheadhon), he became, it is said, "of an unsocial humour." He called his twelve sons to him, told them what had happened, and ended with the words: "The night is the night if the lads were the lads." The sons were quick to act. How were they to reach the island of their enemies? Their own boat was on Loch Tay. The distance from the nearest point of Loch Tay to Loch Earn is, as the eagle flies, a full seven miles; as a man walks considerably farther, because of the rough, uneven ground, often boggy. Thoughts of revenge made the MacNabs tireless. They rowed down Loch Tay to Ardeonaig, then shouldered the heavy boat and carried it over the hills, launching it upon the dark waters of Loch Earn before the dawn flushed the eastern sky. Quietly they rowed down the loch, still more quietly approached the isle of their enemies. The eldest MacNab, he who was known as Iain Min, Smooth John, leaped ashore and knocked at the door of the Neishes' stronghold. There was at first no reply, for the stolen wine was strong and all within the castle had indulged freely and now slept dreamlessly. At last old Neish, the tumult without increasing, called out, no doubt with misgivings in his heart, "Co tha sinn?"—Who is there? The reply came, "Who would you least like to be here?" "Iain Min," replied old Neish haltingly. The voice without then said, "If he has hitherto been smooth, you will find him rough enough for this one night." The MacNabs forced the door and rushed in, killing all they found. The head of old Neish they wrapped in a plaid and carried over the hill to their father. Their boat they carried halfway and then left it at the watershed between Earn and Tay. There, deeply embedded in the peat, its remains were still to be seen in 1854.

Old MacNab impatiently awaited the coming of his twelve sons. At last they entered the house, weary but triumphant, and silently unwrapped the plaid, displaying the head of their enemy. MacNab looked long upon it, then said these words: "The night *was* the night, and the lads *were* lads." The MacNab thereafter took as his crest the head of Neish.

CHAPTER III

LOCH TAY AND BEN LAWERS

I HAVE mentioned that the MacNabs, who claim descent from the lay abbots of Glen Dochart, had their home at the head of Loch Tay, into which the river Dochart flows. The loch is a large one and in length is fifteen miles. From its shore rises that great hill Ben Lawers, which wants only fourteen feet to make it one of the small and select band of Scottish hills of 4,000 feet and over, but of this more anon. Francis, twelfth chief of the MacNabs, is immortalised in that magnificent portrait by Raeburn showing him, a grand figure of a man, in full Highland dress. The last of the residences of the MacNabs was the House of Kinnell, now one of the seats of the Earl of Breadalbane. It has in it old MacNab furniture, showing the head of the unfortunate Neish as the MacNabs' crest. The Kinnell vine, planted in 1832, is believed to be the finest vine in all Europe. In 1940 it covered an area of 171 by 25 feet, and the glasshouse in which it grows has had to be frequently enlarged. At a height of 6 feet above the ground the vine in 1940 was 54 feet in circumference. The number of grapes it bears is remarkable. In the year 1936 it bore 5,429 bunches, of which 4,673 were removed as thinnings, leaving a crop of 756 bunches to mature. In growth and bearing capacity it has remained approximately the same since 1940.

The Dochart roars through the village of Killin at the head of Loch Tay before entering the loch. A short distance east of Killin is the historic castle of Finlarig, ancestral home of the Campbells of Glen Orchy and Breadalbane. It was built by Sir Duncan Campbell, seventh of Glenurchy, he who was known as Donnchadh Dubh a' Churraic, Black Duncan of the Cowl. Black Duncan was a pioneer in afforestation; he even insisted that each of his numerous tenants and cottars should yearly plant a certain number of trees on their land. His gardeners supplied the trees for the small sum of twopence each. Like Loch Earn, Loch Tay has an island near its eastern end. It is Eilean nam Bannaomh, Island of the Blessed Women or Female Saints. The old name is in danger of being lost and it is now usually known as the Isle of Loch Tay—a name without charm, and one which gives no description of the island's history. This island has

Loch Long, Dumbartonshire, looking North

religious associations from a very early period. Its name appears in the year 1122, when the Scottish king granted it in a charter to the monks of Scone Abbey, in memory of his queen Sybilla, who had died on the island and had been buried there. The priory, which in very early times was on the island, was replaced by a nunnery. The Glenurchy Campbells used the convent as a castle, enlarging and fortifying it. It was besieged by Montrose and was later held by one of Cromwell's generals.

I have mentioned that Ben Lawers, which overlooks Loch Tay and its saintly isle, is only 14 feet short of an elevation of 4,000 feet. A native of the district, Malcolm Fergusson by name, determined to add stature to the hill. He built, between fifty and sixty years ago, a cairn on the summit of sufficient height to reach an altitude of 4,000 feet above the sea. That cairn, although strongly built, could not withstand the tempests and the rains of this elevation and has crumbled until there is now little left of it. I am giving away no secret when I say that Ben Lawers is the home of rare alpine plants, one of which, *Saxifraga cernua*, is found nowhere else in Britain. Although rare birds are protected by Act of Parliament, rare plants have no protection afforded them, perhaps because such protection would be impossible to enforce. As there are collectors of rare birds and their eggs, so there are collectors of rare plants, and I would appeal to all who may find rare alpine flowers on the Scottish hills to leave them in position, in order that those who come afterwards may have the pleasure of seeing them also. A correspondent who was anxious to find one of the rarest British alpines wrote to me to ask where it (*Arabis alpina*) was to be found. I gave him the information, but added that I hoped he was not a plant collector. He replied that all he wished to do was to paint the plant in the high rocky country where it grew, and I have thought since that a valuable and delightful book might be written and illustrated by some plant-loving artist of the rare alpines of Britain in their natural habitat, for so far as I know this has never been done.

I was on Ben Lawers with a friend one windy day of September when, a short distance from the summit, we came upon a considerable gathering of meadow pipits. The altitude was 3,900 feet above sea level, unusually high for this species to be seen even during the nesting season, and it is probable that the birds were on migration. That day we saw no ptarmigan, although this species lives throughout

Edinample on Loch Earn

the year on Ben Lawers. On the lower slopes of the hill curlews nest, but they do not approach the summit, nor do they ascend the hillsides so high as the swift-flying golden plover, whose mournful whistle travels far on the hill wind. On one occasion I saw a sparrow-hawk almost at the summit of the hill; the bird was, I think, on migration. There is little heather on Ben Lawers; the hills in this district and further west are mostly under grass. Yet I wonder whether there may not have been considerably more heather before sheep pastured on these hills. There are, of course, large acres of boggy land where heather would not flourish, but a stock of sheep on the ground and the heavy burning of sheep pasture in early spring favour grass and are adverse to heather. As an example of heather being dormant or suppressed on grass land the following occurrence may be related. On a certain hill slope, facing south, where the ground was under grass and no heather was visible, an area was fenced in as protection against sheep before being planted with young trees. A remarkable transformation in the character of the ground resulted. Heather appeared and flourished, and the grass soon became a secondary growth. Again, I crossed a moor in the west Highlands recently. Two years before my visit a heather fire had burnt a considerable area of the moor. That area, and the strip where the fire had been extinguished were still plain. The whole of the burnt area was now under grass and few young heather plants were showing in it; the whole of the moor on either side of it was almost pure heather. That shows the effect of burning a moor which is pastured by cattle and sheep.

From Loch Tay at Fearnan across the hill road to Fortingall in Glen Lyon is a distance of only two miles. At Fortingall is a venerable yew which some experts believe to be at least 3,000 years old. It is a magnificent tree and as long ago as 1772 measured 56 feet in circumference. There are those who say that the tree was probably associated with Druidic worship: this is possible, as the tree may have been more than 1,000 years old even at the birth of Christ. Fortingall will be always associated by Celtic scholars with the Book of the Dean of Lismore. This is the earliest known collection of Gaelic poems in Scotland, having been written over 400 years ago. It was edited by Sir James MacGregor, Dean of Lismore and vicar of Fortingall, and it is said that Finlay MacNab, chief of the clan in and around the year 1500, by his advice and inspiration had much to do with the undertaking of this invaluable work.

CHAPTER IV

THE LYON AND CASTLE MENZIES

THE river Lyon is celebrated among anglers because of its early run of spring, or rather winter, salmon—strong silvery fish which are caught in January, at a time when most of the Highland rivers are still closed to anglers. The temperature of the water in a river has a good deal to do with the season at which the salmon begin to run. The Tay, flowing as it does from Loch Tay with its deep and relatively warm waters, is naturally an early river, but it is perhaps to be wondered at that the early fish should run up the Lyon, which enters the Tay four miles above Aberfeldy and, since it is an upland river with only a small loch at its source, has waters which in winter are presumably considerably colder than those of the Tay.

Where the Tay leaves Loch Tay is situated Taymouth Castle, formerly named Balloch, the ancestral home of the Breadalbane Campbells. It is said that when Sir Colin Campbell, who built the castle, was asked why he chose a site at the eastern end of his great property, he replied that he would extend his lands in time equally far to the east as they already existed westward. This ambition would have been difficult to gratify, for the Breadalbane property extended, at the close of the nineteenth century, from Aberfeldy to Oban, a distance of nearly 100 miles. A valuable possession of the Breadalbane family is the Black Book of Taymouth, which goes back for many centuries and records contemporary events as well as the family history of the Breadalbanes. The Black Book records that Sir Colin Campbell, sixth knight of Lochow, who was the builder of the original Balloch Castle, died in the year 1583, and that he

> was ane great justiciar all his tyme throchtht quhille he sustenit that dadlie feid of the Clangregour ane lang space. And besydis that the caused execust to the death many notable lymmeris. He behaddit the Laird M'Gregr himselff at Candmoir (Kenmore) in presence of the Erle of Atholl, the justice clerk, and sundrie other noblemen.

The chief who was executed was apparently Donnchadh Laidir, Duncan the Strong, and before his execution he composed a poem on his life and on the scenes of his forays. This poem in manuscript long remained at Taymouth Castle.

Below Taymouth Castle the valley of the Tay broadens and is subjected to floods. So much so that Castle Menzies, ancestral seat of the chiefs of Clan Menzies, is now uninhabited, since there is insufficient fall between the castle and the river to give proper drainage. The chief of the Menzies still holds the 'Red Book of Menzies,' in which the affairs of the family are from an early date recorded. The clan rose for Prince Charlie in 1745, and suffered accordingly.

At Castle Menzies were preserved the claymore wielded by the chief at the battle of Bannockburn and the bagpipe played at the same fight by the chief's piper. This old pipe, which I have seen, has only one drone. The hereditary pipers to the Menzies were the Macintyres, one of whom, John Macintyre, is believed to have composed that wild Pibroch named the "Prince's Salute," which was composed in 1715, not at the rising of 1745 as is sometimes stated. The Pibroch associated with the "Forty-five" is another Macintyre composition named "Thainig mo Righ air tir am Muideart," or, in English, "My King has landed in Moidart." This is a strikingly beautiful tune and was played by Norman MacRae, Lochiel's piper, at the celebrations held at Glenfinnan in 1945 to mark the bicentenary of the raising of the Prince's standard in 1745. On the death of Sir Neil Menzies the chiefship of the clan devolved on Major Steuart Menzies of Culdares, and after his death his son, Colonel Ronald Menzies, succeeded his father as chief. East of Castle Menzies the Tay is crossed by a particularly striking bridge. Consisting of five graceful arches, it was built, according to the contemporary description on the bridge, within a single year, in 1733. If we except the bridge of Perth, it was the first bridge to span the river Tay, and Marshal Wade regarded it as the climax of his ten years' work in the construction of roads and bridges in the Highlands in order to open up the country after the Jacobite rising in 1715. Twelve years after the bridge was finished it was tested by the passage of Sir John Cope's army with its artillery. In order that the retreating Jacobites in 1746 after Culloden should not have the opportunity of using the bridge, Cumberland sent a detachment of troops to guard it. Near the bridge is a lofty cairn raised to commemorate the first mustering of the Black Watch in October, 1739. This monument should serve as a guide to those persons contemplating memorials at the present day, for its execution is masterly, and it would delight the eye of the most critical artist. On the top of the cairn stands a Highlander of striking and distinguished appearance, wearing the old uniform of the 42nd. In his Highland broad bonnet he wears a single flight feather of a golden eagle; his right hand is in the act of drawing his sword. The expression of the Highlander and the attitude in which he is shown are admirable, and the figure itself seems to live.

On the bank of a small burn above Aberfeldy tradition has it that the renowned Andrea Ferara had his smithy in the sixteenth century. His celebrated claymores he fashioned from iron dug from the surrounding hills, and smelted them in fires kindled of birch. The blades he tempered in the stream beside which his smithy stood, a stream which had qualities in its water specially suited for the purpose. There was a broadsword or claymore of his preserved in Castle Menzies 5 feet 8 inches in length, including the handle. The swords made by Andrea Ferara had stamped on them the smith's name and a St. Andrew's Cross. The hilt of the sword was sometimes composed entirely of St. Andrew's Crosses. I have given the local tradition as it is recorded in MacMillan's *Highland Tay*, but think it is unlikely that the great Italian smith ever lived in the Aberfeldy district, although it has been said that he came from Ferara in Italy to Banff, where he set up his workshop.

There are, it is believed, many Ferara blades which are in reality not the work of the master but were made in Germany, in Spain, and even possibly in the Scottish Highlands. It has been said that nearly every Highlander of distinction who fought at Culloden carried a Ferara sword, which could be identified by its great breadth, suppleness, and fine temper. The Ferara sword of MacDonald of Keppoch, who was killed at Culloden, bears a gold cross and ball on both sides, which the authority Noel Paton, according to Lord Archibald Campbell, regarded as the hall-mark of the genuine Andrea Ferara.

Who the true Andrea Ferara was, and where he worked, is a mystery. One authority believes that he was Andrea dei Ferari, and that he fashioned his famous swords at Belluno in Venetia in the second half of the sixteenth century.

The broadsword was a formidable weapon. With his trusty claymore Gillies MacBean of Kinchyle killed fourteen Campbells at Culloden before he himself fell.

The falls of Moness near Aberfeldy were made celebrated by the poet Burns, who describes them in his well-known poem "The Birks of Aberfeldy." It was in the shelter of these falls that the demon Peallaidh, after whom Aberfeldy was named, is said to have had his home.

At Ballinluig the Tay joins the Tummel, and the two continue eastward through Dunkeld to Perth.

CHAPTER V

THE TAY AND ITS SALMON

AT Inver, on the river Braan, near Dunkeld, lived Neil Gow, perhaps the most celebrated Highland fiddler. He was renowned not only in the Scottish Highlands but in London, where the Duke of Atholl often took him to play at entertainments and society functions. Neil Gow died in his eightieth year, in 1807. He was painted by Raeburn, wearing not the kilt but tartan knee-breeches, his chin resting on his fiddle, his inseparable companion. In the grounds of Dunkeld House still stands one of the first two larch trees ever planted in Britain. They were brought by Menzies of Culdares from the Tyrol in the year 1738, and have a curious history. They were considered so precious that they were planted in a greenhouse, but since they sickened, they were thrown out on to a heap of garden refuse. Here they took root, and grew into splendid trees. There are so many larch woods in Britain at the present day that some people believe the tree is a native of this country, but this is not so. It has been claimed that the larch was planted at Dawyck in the County of Peebles ten years before those at Dunkeld, but the Dunkeld trees are at least the first Highland larches planted. Dunkeld Cathedral, of which King David I laid the foundation in the year 1127, was added to at different periods, and combines the Norman and the Pointed styles. It occupies the site of the still older monastery, and in the middle of the gable may be seen reddish dressed stones which formed part of that monastery. The choir was built in the First Pointed style in 1318, and the nave, now in ruins, was built about 1406 in the Second Pointed style. In 1466 the great Tower, 96 feet high, and Chapter House were begun by Bishop Lauder and were completed in seven years. At the Reformation the cathedral was unroofed. In 1689 the Tower was fortified and mounted with small cannon to guard the town of Dunkeld from the adherents of James VII.

Near Dunkeld is the King's Seat, which in olden days was used as a look-out place for red deer in the royal forest. Here William the Lion hunted, and later the tragic Queen Mary during a great deer drive in her honour narrowly escaped being trampled by the stampeding deer. In the vicinity is Birnam Hill, from which eminence may be seen, at a distance of some twelve miles to the north-west, the celebrated hill of Dunsinnane. On the top of Dunsinnane is a hill fort known as MacBeth's Castle. Shakespeare's immortal lines may be recalled:

> MacBeth shall never vanquished be, until
> Great Birnam Wood to high Dunsinnane Hill
> Shall come against him.

And again:

> I will not be afraid of
> death and bane
> Till Birnam Forest come
> to Dunsinnane

These lines refer to the large branches of trees which were in olden times carried by a besieging force for the double purpose of shielding and defending the attackers. Rather less than a mile below Dunkeld Bridge, on the south bank of the Tay, stand what are believed to be the only two surviving trees of the old Birnam wood. One is an oak, the other a sycamore. The height of the two trees is not remarkable, but when you stand beneath them you realise their great size and venerable appearance. Both trees are locally believed to exceed the age of a thousand years.

No account of the Tay would be complete without mentioning the salmon which each year ascend the river. The heaviest salmon landed on the Tay was one of 64 lb. It was caught by Miss G. W. Ballantine, daughter of the fisherman on the Glendelvine beat of the river, on October 7, 1922. This great salmon was in length 54 inches, and in girth 28½ inches: its head was 12 inches long and its tail 11 inches. Miss Ballantine's father was rowing home in the evening, and had a rod out with a large spinning bait. The bait was seized and Ballantine told his daughter to take hold of the rod. I never heard a description of the great fight that must have followed. The huge fish ran down stream and passed below Caputh bridge. In the end it was landed on shingle on the right bank of the river about a quarter of a mile below the bridge. The best day's fishing I ever had on the Tay was on April 4, 1927. I was staying with the Duke of Portland at Dunkeld House. He rented the Lower Stanley and the Dunkeld beats from the Atholl estate. It was a grey day with cold south-east wind blowing up the river and the Dunkeld beat had done nothing for weeks. When I went up to fish it the boatmen were pessimistic and I had little hopes of any success. For some reason the salmon that day were everywhere on the take. I had to catch the afternoon train to Aviemore, so had only a short day on the river, but I landed three salmon of 20, 20, and 17 lb. I later heard that fifteen salmon in all had been killed that day on the two beats of Dunkeld and Lower Stanley, and thirteen of the fifteen averaged 20 lb. The late Duke of Portland had the Dunkeld beat for a number of years, and also Lower Stanley and Benchill. In 1930 he had an unusually successful season, killing in five weeks six salmon each of over 30 lb. weight. The actual weights were 37, 35, 33, 30, 30 and 30 lb. His best day on Lower Stanley was March 11, 1930, when he landed thirteen fish in three and a half hours' fishing. On March 9, 1922, an old friend of the Duke of Portland, Major Baker Carr, landed no fewer than seventeen salmon on the Lower Stanley beat. The total weight of the fish was 276 lb. and the heaviest was 30 lb. The Duke was devoted to "B. Carr" as he called him, and I do not think he was ever the same man after his friend died.

On January 18, 1944, Commander Edmund Fergusson of Baledmund and I fished the Islamouth beat of the Tay. The second world war was raging at the time, and as a result Summer Time had been kept on throughout the winter. I was surprised that the boatmen on the beat—the fishing was all harling from a boat—took no account of the change in the time, which at this season of mid-winter is an important factor. We began fishing at 9.30 a.m. when it was scarcely daylight, and the two men had rowed for an hour and a half before the first fish—a kelt—moved. From then onward fish were showing almost continuously. Most of them were kelts, of which the river is always full at that season of the year, but we saw some beautiful early spring salmon. I hooked and landed a heavy male fish which weighed 32 lb., and Commander Fergusson had a beautiful hen fish of 18 lb., with sides like burnished silver. We landed, and of course returned, ten kelts or spawned fish, and also one late unspawned autumn fish. Mr. Gilbert Malloch of Perth from his examination of scales of the 32 lb. fish came to the conclusion that it was a little over five years old. Going down to the sea as a smolt, growth during its first summer in the sea was very good. Less weight was put on in its second summer in the sea and rather more in its third summer,

89

its last in the sea before returning as a late winter fish to the Tay. Apart from the exciting fishing the day was noteworthy because of the abundance and variety of bird life upon and above the river.

Many gaggles of grey-lag geese passed over making for the fields of winter wheat which are a favourite feeding-ground of theirs. They sometimes crop the young wheat almost to the ground, but do little harm to it; indeed, it is sometimes said that the plants thus grazed are stronger in spring. There were large numbers of duck of various species swimming on the pools or flying swiftly up and down the river. On land the day was mild, with a strong south-west wind; whenever the boat was rowed out from the shore an appreciable drop in the temperature was felt, for the river temperature was 10 degrees lower than that of the air. On the lower Tay the river is too broad to permit of fishing from the bank, and harling from a boat is the only form of angling possible. In harling three rods usually are fished over the stern of the boat, which is rowed diagonally over the pool by two men. The centre rod has a spinning bait attached to it, and the rod on either side a fly. If one angler is in charge of all three rods he cannot hold them all, but the two which are fishing of themselves have each a stone placed on the line, between the reel and the first ring of the rod. This stone "strikes" a fish automatically when it is hooked. When this happens the lines of the other two rods must be reeled in as quickly as possible so that the playing fish does not foul them.

The river Tay after leaving Dunkeld makes a wide detour before reaching Perth and its tidal reaches. At Meiklour is to be seen a remarkable beech hedge planted in the year 1746. It now reaches a height of 85 feet. The length of this unique hedge is 580 yards. It is believed to have been trimmed each year for the first forty to sixty years of its life. There was then a period when it grew untrained. From the early nineteenth century until the present time the great hedge has been regularly trimmed and pruned every five or seven years. Lord Lansdowne, who has kindly supplied this information, tells me that his great-grandmother, who rebuilt Meiklour house in 1870, had a 30-foot double ladder, supported on four wheels, constructed; this greatly facilitated the trimming, but, even so, there remained a considerable height which could not be reached in this way. The higher parts were reached by climbing, and the branches trimmed with a bill-hook. Fire-escape ladders were used on several occasions. The last hedge-cutting, in 1947, was formidable as, because of the intervening war years, it was overdue. The labour was carried out successfully by the estate foresters, assisted by certain athletic German P.O.W.s, without any mechanical aids. The road passes beneath this great hedge, and when it is seen in May, in its first delicate green foliage, it is beautiful and most impressive in its stately height.

Perth was at one time the chief city of Scotland. Its church of St. John the Baptist is a building of grace and beauty. It is of great age and was rebuilt in the year 1328 by command of Robert the Bruce. At the Salutation Hotel in Perth Prince Charlie had his headquarters during the campaign of 1745; the room in which he slept is still in use. The church of St. John was already used as a place of worship in the time when the old kings of Scotland were crowned in the Abbey of Scone, of which no trace remains. The Stone of Destiny or Stone of Scone, of which the old Celtic name is Lia Fail, came from Eire to Scotland when the kingdom of Dalriada was established, and for a time, as I have elsewhere in this book mentioned, was at Dunstaffnage Castle near Oban. It was later taken to the abbey of Scone, and on it the Scottish kings were crowned. It was carried off by Edward I of England and made part of the coronation chair at Westminster Abbey. The stone is an oblong block of red sandstone 26 inches long, 16 inches broad, and $10\frac{1}{2}$ inches deep. It is reputed to be the stone which Jacob used as a pillow at Bethel and then set up as a pillar and anointed with oil. It became the pedestal of the ark in the Temple. It was brought to Egypt from Syria by Gathelus, who sailed from the Nile with it and landed in Spain. Gathelus after he had invaded Eire caused the stone to be brought to that country, from which it was later brought to Scotland.

Chapter VI

THE SMA' GLEN AND THE ATHOLL HIGHLANDERS

I HAVE described the country of Loch Earn, and the association of the district with Eire in very early times. The river Earn is, for a Highland river, slow-flowing. It travels, by way of St. Fillan's, Comrie and Crieff, to join the Tay below Perth. Its fame as a salmon river does not approach that of the Tay, but heavy salmon are caught in it, especially in the autumn. The lower valley of the Earn is the feeding-ground of great numbers of wild geese.

From Crieff a road crosses the hill country northward through one of the beauty spots of the Highlands—the Sma' Glen. The old name of the glen was, in Gaelic, An Caol Ghleann, which means the Narrow Glen; the present name is modern. It is truly Highland in character, and it is hard to realise that the comparatively Lowland country of Strath Earn is only a few miles away. It is a short glen, and near its head, between the road and the water of Almond, is a huge, ice-marked boulder of which the old name is Clach Oisein— the Stone of Ossian. He whom the boulder commemorates was the bard of the Fingalians fifteen hundred years ago, and he, Ossian, is traditionally said to have been buried here. When General Wade was driving his road through the Sma' Glen he ordered his soldiers to move the boulder, which they did with difficulty. Beneath it they found a small cavity, 2 feet square, built in on all sides by square flat stones. In the hollow were ashes, scraps of bones, and half-burnt stalks of heather. The officer in charge of the work intended to preserve these remains for the commander-in-chief's inspection, but when the Highlanders heard of the discovery they assembled in strength, gathered up the relics and marched with them in solemn procession to a new place of burial which they had chosen, the whereabouts of which is now unknown. Having deposited the remains in a new grave, they discharged their fire-arms in salute before they separated.

Aberfeldy is twenty miles north of the Sma' Glen; Dunkeld, by way of Strath Braan, is much nearer.

Let us return to Ballinluig, where Tay and Tummel meet, and

explore the valleys of the Tummel and, later, the Garry which joins it. About five miles up the Tummel is the town of Pitlochry, much frequented by visitors, especially during the summer months. The ambitious hydro-electric scheme which has transformed the waters of the Tummel into a large loch has quite altered the appearance of the valley here. It is unfortunate that one of the most beautiful reaches of the Tummel, Faskally, has been inundated, for the dam extends as far as the Falls of Tummel. At Faskally the river still flows in a series of deep pools and high rocky banks, and despite the activities of hundreds of labourers in the neighbourhood the bird life of the district and the river is (I write this in 1948) as yet unaffected. Oystercatchers, including a bird of unusual plumage, have their spring and summer homes near the river, and sandpipers arrive in mid-April from the south. Dippers or water ousels nest on the rocky banks of the river, where pied and grey wagtails also have their homes. The sandpipers may adapt themselves to the changed surroundings and may nest on the shores of the dam, but the shingle beds and fields where the oystercatchers have nested will be flooded and the birds will have to move elsewhere. The dippers, too, will be evicted, for their nesting sites will disappear. The salmon pools—among the finest in Scotland—will be submerged deeply in the dam, or loch. It is a pity, but who heeds, in the present progressive days, whether a beauty spot peopled with birds disappears? Who heeds whether some of the best salmon fishing in the Highlands is lost? A salmon fisherman has in these days what is vulgarly called a "poor press." Perhaps by now the ravens which often pass high over the Tummel valley have become accustomed to the strange scene. They see the valley gradually changing its appearance; they see the trees on the Tummel banks being felled, many of them when in the beauty of their summer foliage. They watch bulldozers and excavators at work, and from time to time they hear heavy explosions as charges are fired to break up and dislodge the solid rock. They see the foundations for a great dam being prepared by their old enemy man. Perhaps they wonder idly what these things may mean, for the raven is traditionally said in the Highlands to be the bird of wisdom, but their thoughts soon turn again to more practical matters—to the repair of their nest high on Ben Vrackie, or where to find the carcase of a deer or a sheep on the hills to provide nourishment for themselves and their family. The golden-eye duck which haunt the Tummel, as they do other Highland rivers, will find, perhaps, that great dam to their liking, and may be seen swimming and diving here in years to come. This attractive duck, small, compact and fast-flying, and resembling the tufted duck, from which it may be distinguished by the white patch behind either eye, remains late in the spring at its winter haunts on Highland rivers. It is still there in May when the local nesting ducks have eggs, and when the mallard have hatched out their broods, and I am assured by fishermen on the Spey that it has bred on that river. I do not, however, think that the nesting of the golden-eye in Scotland has been authenticated, and the explanation of the birds' late stay in spring is that their nesting haunts are in Lapland and the north of Russia, where in May the snow still lies deep, and where the rivers are still under ice, so that the birds would find a poor welcome awaiting them if they crossed the sea and arrived in Lapland in May.

Below Faskally the Tummel valley widens; the pools are long, rather swift, and less deep. There is here the ever-present danger that the river may in times of heavy spate flood the neighbouring lands. At East Haugh the arable land which adjoins the river has on more than one occasion in recent years been flooded and considerable damage done. The East Haugh beat of the Tummel (the property is owned by a keen fisherman and his wife) nearly always does well on the opening day of the salmon fishing. These hardy anglers are unfailingly on the river bank soon after daylight each year on January 15. The ground is usually deeply snow-covered, and the frost so keen that the line freezes to the rings of the rod, yet the fresh-run fish are in the pools, and several beautiful clean-run salmon, with silvery sides, may lie on the snowy bank before the blood-red sun sinks on the frosty horizon and the hardy water ousel takes his last cold bath before flying home to roost. Winter fishing is a sport only for those who have a circulation impervious to wind and snow. A friend of mine believed in doing himself well on the river. He lived in the days before austerity was a household word and spent most of the winter day fishing the pool close to his house on the river bank. At one o'clock he went home to lunch, in a centrally heated house with large fires to add to the warmth, and after an excellent lunch washed down with port and Madeira, emerged into the cold air fortified for his afternoon by the river. He used to have large fires in the bothies which stood beside each pool—in some of them it would have been possible to have lodged for the night in comfort—and these fires were grateful to stand or sit by after one had changed from waders. These fishing bothies, which are to be found on most of the Highland rivers, lessen the austerities of winter salmon fishing. On a certain beat of the river Spey a well-known peeress insisted on cooking a full-course lunch for her fishing guests: I still remember the stewed steaks at which she excelled—a juicy steak fried in butter softened the disappointment of a blank morning by the river.

Above Faskally the river divides. The Tummel turns towards the west and its large tributary the Garry goes north.

The birch woods of the Tummel are among the finest in Scotland. The district is a sheltered one and, being inland, experiences much frost and a good deal of snow during the winter months, but not many gales. There is, I think, an advantage in a cold winter from the point of view of a hardy tree such as the birch, in that it does not come into growth at too early a date and thus have its young leaves and shoots destroyed by subsequent frost. I have known the ice on a small loch on the Fincastle estate strong enough for skating from December until April. That was, it is true, in an exceptional season, but I do not think the mildest winter passes without a spell of frost and snow in this district, which is of no unusual height above the sea.

Five miles west of the junction of Tummel and Garry is birch-fringed Loch Tummel, a loch three miles long. Ten miles west of Loch Tummel is Kinloch Rannoch, a village standing at the mouth of Loch Rannoch, a large loch ten miles in length. I have often wondered whether the name Kinloch Rannoch has been transferred from the district at the head of the loch, because "Kinloch" means the "Head or Upper Part." I find no record of the name Kinloch Rannoch in the three volumes of MacFarlane's *Geographical Collections*, which are valuable in giving the old forms of Gaelic place-names. Above the southern shore of Loch Rannoch is the celebrated Black Wood of Rannoch, a wood of old Scots pines which are a link with the old Caledonian Forest. The wood was partly felled during the years of the second world war.

On the high ground to the south of Loch Rannoch two collie dogs one winter's day a good many years ago showed sublime devotion towards their master. The shepherd left home with his dogs one morning. The weather was stormy, and the ground was snow-covered. Perhaps he was anxious about the safety of some of his sheep in the outlying corries. He was five miles from home when a blizzard arose,

95

and even with his knowledge of the hills he at last lost his way. What happened then shows the love the collie is capable of bearing his master, and also the wisdom of the dog. One of the collies made his way home through the drift, and when he had reached the shepherd's home by his actions showed that he wished a search party to set out: when the party started the collie guided them unerringly through the drift to where his master lay. The second dog was then found lifeless, lying on his master's chest to give him all the warmth and shelter possible. The man, thanks to the dog, still lived, and recovered from his grim experience. It is obvious that the two collies must have conferred before deciding on their course of conduct, but to a dog lover there is nothing remarkable in this.

The headwaters of the Tummel are in Loch Laidon, the anglicised form of Loch nan Lodan (Loch of the Pools), and, still higher, in Loch Ba and the river Ba. There is indeed less than a mile between the headwaters of the Tummel and those of the Etive, out on the high ground of the Moor of Rannoch, one of the wildest districts in the Highlands. Many a night has the train from Fort William to Glasgow fought its way through drift across this moor. Sometimes the drifts have been too heavy and passengers have found themselves stranded for the night until their train was dug out.

In every Highland glen there are signs that the population has gone, but here on the uplands of Rannoch there was never a population of human beings and the red deer and the eagle, the raven and the peregrine, have since time immemorial had the place to themselves.

The main road to the north after passing Pitlochry leaves the Tummel and winds beside the Garry, through the Pass of Killiecrankie where, in the year 1680, the last wolf in Perthshire was killed by Sir Ewen Cameron of Lochiel.

Nine years after that date the battle of Killiecrankie was fought, in which the Highlanders, under the command of John Graham of Claverhouse, Viscount Dundee, utterly defeated the army of MacKay of Scourie, William of Orange's general. Although the Highlanders were outnumbered by two to one they killed 2,000 of MacKay's men and took prisoner another 500, but their commander was mortally wounded through his breastplate. The stone beside which he fell may be seen near the north entrance to the Pass of Killiecrankie, and his grave beside the church of St. Bride above Blair Castle. It is said that

96

Yew tree at Fortingall, Glen Lyon

General MacKay, finding his retreat unhindered, said, "Had Dundee been alive I should not have been suffered to retreat unmolested."

Four miles north of Killiecrankie, where the strath broadens somewhat, stands Blair Castle, the ancestral seat of the Earls and Dukes of Atholl, where Prince Charlie stayed for several days. Comyn's Tower, the central part of the castle, is said to have been built by the Red Comyn in the year 1280. Here many house martins make their nests, and very early in the morning in June their twittering awakens the light sleeper. Blair, like many another Highland castle, is no longer the home of its old owner. There are indeed few chiefs at the present day who live, or can afford to live, in their castles. Many of the castles have been sold, some of them stand deserted. The country has lost in this, for no government, and no government department, can do so much good locally as a landowner of the right sort. One has only to meet the people of Blair Atholl to realise what a fine type has been evolved through the centuries by the ducal family of Murray. One of the privileges of the head of the Atholl family was to present a white rose to the Sovereign when he or she should arrive at, or pass through, Blair Atholl. Queen Victoria in her Memoirs records that a white rose was given her by the Duke of Atholl. The late duke and his duchess kept up the old traditions. The duke had a great love for the Gaelic; it was indeed said that in earlier times no one was employed on the staff of Blair Castle who was not a native of the estate, or who could not speak Gaelic. The Atholl Highlanders, or 77th Regiment, were raised by the young Duke of Atholl in the year 1778, the Government of the day having given him authority to raise 1,000 men for the service of the State; this regiment served until 1783, when it was disbanded

The Atholl Highlanders, which succeeded the earlier regiment of the same name to which I have briefly referred, were organised in 1822. It was intended that they should act as the retinue or body-guard of the fourth Duke of Atholl when he attended on George IV in Edinburgh. In the end they did not go to Edinburgh. In or around 1837 they appeared as a bodyguard to the duke when he attended the Eglinton Tournament. There the distinguished bearing and appearance of the Highlanders created a deep impression. The same men, many of them the grandsons of those who had been out in the Forty-five—acted as a guard of honour to Queen Victoria when she passed through Dunkeld in 1842 on her first visit to the Highlands.

General Wade's Bridge and
Black Watch Memorial, Aberfeldy

In the year 1843, when Blair Castle was lent her, she presented the Atholl Highlanders with colours—a gift which is usually conferred by the reigning Sovereign only on a national regiment. Because of this honour the Atholl Highlanders can wear their uniform at Court. This distinguishes them from the Duff Highlanders and the Invercauld Highlanders, whose uniform is not court dress. From 1843 until 1913 the Atholl Highlanders paraded annually at the Atholl Gathering. This was unique among Highland gatherings, for it was confined to Atholl men: there was always excellent piping to be heard there, for the pipers of the district have long been renowned.

The last occasion on which the Atholl Highlanders paraded was shortly before the second world war, when the Appin flag was handed over to the museum at Edinburgh Castle.

The great hill, Beinn a' Ghlo, stands sentinel to the north of Blair Castle, and on the far side of the Tilt, which flows down from beyond that hill, is a small moorland loch of singular charm—Loch Moraig by name. It is a good trout loch, but its chief attraction to my mind lies in its spring and summer bird population. I think that almost everywhere in the Highlands there are now fewer birds than there were fifty years ago; Loch Moraig is the exception. Around the loch, on the windy acres between it and the foot of Beinn a' Ghlo, many curlews, lapwings and red grouse nest. The grouse have their home here throughout the year; the lapwings and curlews arrive in early spring and stay until the end of July. The air is vibrant with their song on days of April, May and early June. It is a curious loch to find in high, inland country, and seems to have affinity rather with the Outer Hebrides. One can imagine the machair lands, scented with bedstraw and other aromatic herbs, lying near it, and beyond the machair the white sands, tern-haunted, and lonely skerries where the surf breaks white in summer sun and where Atlantic seals sun themselves and fall into deep sleep at ebb tide. The country of Loch Moraig is not a tern country, but one day when two companions and I visited the loch at the end of June a tern—I think a common tern—was there, and was hawking insects with great energy and persistence. There was a strong north wind blowing across from the Beinn a' Ghlo hills, and the air was cold, almost wintry, although not so cold as at Braemar, which we had left that morning. The wind was sufficiently strong to raise white waves on the loch, but notwithstanding the apparently adverse conditions there was a large hatch of flies and the tern was dipping swallow-like to the surface to pick the insects delicately from the water. Large numbers of sand martins and swallows were also flycatching, and at least half a dozen swifts were dashing here and there across the loch with their mad, impetuous flight. The scene was thus a most animated and pleasant one, beneath a grey sky, which now and again showed areas of blue as the wind drove the mist from Beinn a' Ghlo high over us. Loch Moraig is actually across the Atholl march, on the Lude property. The old family of Robertson of Lude were the owners of a famous harp, given to Miss Robertson of Lude by Queen Mary about the year 1564. The harp was a very ancient musical instrument in the Highlands. Skene in his *Highlanders of Scotland* (vol. I., p. 216) mentions that in the lord high treasurer's accounts of May 10, 1503, a certain sum is given to "Makberty, the clairsha, to pass to the Isles," and on September 3, 1506, nine shillings is given to "Maklain's clairsha" and on the following day payment is made to "Earl of Argyle's clairsha and to Duncan Campbell's bard." The word "clairsha" is for *clarsair*, the Gaelic word for harper, from *clarsach*, a harp.

When was the *clarsach* first played? Skene mentions a sculptured pillar, of which the date is believed to be ninth century, on which an armed figure, playing on the harp, is seated; on another sculptured stone, believed to date from a still earlier period, is a harp of exactly similar construction. The harp rapidly declined in popularity in the Highlands during the seventeenth century, the cause being the civil wars which began during that period, and made the bagpipe with its shrill martial music more popular. The style of the Highland airs suited the *clasarch*, for Highland music is remarkable for its simplicity, wildness and pathos. The scale is different from the ordinary or diatonic scale, and is defective, wanting the fourth and the seventh, but, in the words of Skene, "this very defect gives rise to the pleasing simplicity and plaintiveness of the Highland melody, and imparts to their music a character peculiarly adapted to the nature of their poetry."

At Blair the main road continues north-west to cross the march between the counties of Perth and Inverness three miles beyond Dalnaspidal; at Blair, too, there is a right-of-way north-eastward through Glen Tilt to Mar and Upper Deeside. This is a walk through the glens rather than, like Lairig Ghru, through the hills, but it gives some outstanding views, looking back, as you gradually rise from

Blair Atholl, on to the hills westward. Notable among those hills is Schiehallion, a stately cone rising from the shore of Loch Rannoch.

The main road on leaving Blair first follows the birch-filled valley of the Garry (which, by the way, must not be confused with the Garry of the Great Glen), then ascends, over wild upland country, to a height of 1,422 feet above sea level at Dalnaspidal station. From the carriage window of the Perth-Inverness train travelling at speed across the pass I have watched a golden eagle driving grouse, and the country retains its wildness despite the fact that both road and railway cross the Pass of Drumochter. The districts of Atholl and Badenoch are here commemorated in the two hills, Sow of Atholl to the south, and Boar of Badenoch to the north. Trains are sometimes snowed up on the pass, and the road is often impassable to cars. During a blizzard I have seen from the train abandoned vehicles on the road, drifting snow sweeping over them; the drivers and passengers must have found shelter, although for many miles there is no house on this lonely road. During a snowstorm, railway locomotives with snow-ploughs attached maintain a ceaseless patrol here night and day; I have known snow-ploughs used in May.

CHAPTER VII

BADENOCH AND CLUNY

AT Drumochter (Druim Uachdar—Ridge of the Upper Ground)
the wayfarer stands with his face towards the wild, upland confines
of Badenoch, named of old Bàideanach, the Submerged or Drowned
Lands, because of the habit of the Spey of overflowing the haughs or
low grounds which lie between Kingussie and Loch Insh.

Badenoch since very early times has been the territory of the
MacPhersons, that proud Highland family who have for their crest
a wild cat, and who have for long disputed the chiefship of Clan
Chattan with the Macintoshes. But as yet, at Drumochter, with An
Torc, the Boar of Badenoch, standing guard above us, and perhaps
the May snows curling airily around the high brow of Marcaonach,
we are far from the Drowned Lands, nor can we even see from here
the great river Spey of which Timothy Pont, minister of Dunnet,
writing in the middle of the sixteenth century, states that it is among
Scottish rivers, "swyft above them all," yet he does not fail to note
that "it is most myld and calme in the courss as it runneth through
Badenoch, afterward lower down a great deal more furious."

On wind-swept Drumochter, almost 1,500 feet above the level of
the distant ocean, the country is not such as might be expected to
attract the oystercatcher, bird of the tides, as a nesting site, yet I have
seen these birds here, already paired, in mid-March, when the ground
had been only a few days free of snow. The birds on Drumochter
are as far from the sea, in any direction, as it is possible to be in
Scotland; they must often endure hunger when frost and snow, as
is common in March, April, and even early May, seal off food
supplies, yet their love for the high strath where they were born and
bred brings them back from the coast year after year to their native
land. Here they must see the eagle flying high overhead; must hear
the grouse becking at dawn, and at times even hear the croak of the
ptarmigan from the high hills on either side of the pass.

In winter there is no lesser bird on Drumochter except the snow
bunting and the dipper. The dipper, or water ousel as he is called in
Scotland, haunts the headwaters of the Truim, which rises on Drum-

ochter and flows north-west and then north to join the Spey at New-tonmore. The soft subdued song of the dipper in a snow-clad strath in winter brings to the mind thoughts of spring. Do not believe it when you are told that the singer is here to feast on the ova of trout and salmon. His food is the larvæ of various species of insects; I have watched the dipper feeding equally eagerly on the bed of the Dee on the Braeriach plateau 4,000 feet above the sea, and in the Garbh Uisge on Ben MacDhui at an almost equal height. Both these clear streams are more than 1,000 feet higher than the highest trout, yet the food supply is sufficiently attractive to tempt the water ousels up from the glens far beneath. I do not say that the water ousel *never* feeds on ova, but I do assert confidently that the damage it does in this way is negligible, and any harm it does is far outweighed by the beauty and charm it adds to the Highland rivers, streams and lochs.

At Dalwhinnie, north-west some eight miles from the Pass of Drumochter, the road passes near, though scarcely in view of, Loch Ericht (in Gaelic Loch Eireachd—Loch of Meetings). This loch, with the magnificent outline of Ben Alder rising behind it, is seen from the railway. A strange tale is told of Loch Ericht. It is said that the west end of the loch was once a fertile strath and that after a subterranean upheaval this was inundated by the loch, submerging the houses. During recent work in connection with a hydro-electric scheme an old gravestone was dredged from the loch 20 feet below the present level of its waters. There is always snow to be seen on Ben Alder in July, and on occasion it remains throughout the year. At Dalwhinnie is one of the weather reporting stations of the Central Highlands, telegrams being sent off to the Air Ministry four times daily.

I have written of the snowstorms of Drumochter. They are severe in the pass; what must they be on the high tops above it! One of the most severe blizzards in living memory was experienced here in early March, 1947. The wind was from the south-east, and the three high hills, Chaoruinn (3,004 feet), AmBuidhe Aonach and Carn na Caim (3,087 feet), which here form the Inverness-Perth county march, had a remarkable depth of snow drifted into their north-western corries. I was travelling along the main road—it passes only a couple of miles from these corries—in mid-July, and estimated that there were two snowfields at least 50 feet in depth remaining at that time. In August they were still there, and I heard that the last of them did not disappear until October. That storm was unusual, and I saw a winter snowfield lying on Cheviot in Northumberland on July 8.

I remember being at Dalwhinnie a great many years ago—I think it was in 1908—and experiencing, in early July, nights when there was no darkness. It was said, if I remember rightly, that the volcanic dust of Hekla in Iceland, then in eruption, was reflecting from a vast height the sun's rays. During those two or three nights it was almost as light at Dalwhinnie—and presumably in other parts of the Highlands—as it would have been in Iceland.

The hills of the Dalwhinnie district are rounded and are a nesting-place for the dotterel—that confiding bird whose eggs are a prize among collectors. One of the gamekeepers in the district told me that he had sometimes seen car after car parked on the roadside on the high pass, and that there were so many egg collectors on these hills that he wondered that any dotterel were able to hatch their eggs. The number of egg collectors is probably less now than before the second world war.

Below Dalwhinnie is the house of Glentruim, the home for many years of a good Highlander, skilled angler, and friend whose kindness and hospitality I often experienced. Redwings have been heard in song in May and June around Glentruin House, and it may be that they have nested here, in some of the pines and silver firs which the laird planted during his long life and which have here a climate greatly to their liking. There is an Ordnance Survey mark in a dry-stone wall near Glentruim House which is said to show the precise centre of Scotland, between the east coast and the west coast. The Spey and the Truim meet at some little distance below the house. A clan fight was fought on the level haughs here between the Camerons and the MacPhersons in, or about, the year 1370. The Camerons from Lochaber were on their way to harry the country of Mackintosh of Mackintosh, and found their way opposed by a force of Mackintoshes, MacPhersons and Davidsons. The tradition is that the MacPhersons claimed their traditional honour of the right wing of the battle, and when the Davidsons for some reason took the right wing the MacPhersons withdrew from the fight and, as they ate their lunch on a knoll near the river, watched with apparent indifference the course of the battle. The Mackintoshes and the Davidsons got the worst of the encounter. The chief of the Davidsons was slain, and seven of his sons shared the same fate, yet, seeing this, the Mac-

Phersons still refused to help. It was curious conduct, for which they atoned when they a little later pursued the victorious Camerons and at a place called Coire Thearlaich in the Loch Ericht district engaged and defeated them. Here was fought the epic duel with bow and arrow between MacGill'an Fhaidh (patronymic of Cameron of Strone and Invermallie) and one of the chief men of the MacPhersons, MacIain Ceann Dubh. The two were close friends, and were by arrangement firing their arrows so that these should fall short, or over them, when the chief of the MacPhersons, seeing his own dead who had succumbed to the arrows of the Cameron chief, angrily taunted his kinsman on his bad aim, saying, "Surely you had a Cameron for your mother!" Stung by this taunt, MacIain Ceann Dubh (MacIain Black Head) called then to his adversary, "Umam—is umad—a Thearlaich!" ("For me—and for you—Charles!"). Both then took careful aim at each other, and both fell mortally wounded. The cairn where the two friends rested in death can be seen on the hillside east of Loch Patag. It must have been a large cairn, but now, after the storms and frosts of nearly 600 years, little of it remains, although it is still visible from the forest road leading from Loch Laggan to Loch Ericht.

It was on an early day of April that my friend and I climbed by way of the glen of the swiftly flowing Patag river to visit that old cairn. The birches, as yet leafless, showed that deep blue colour which beautifies them in early spring before the buds begin to open. On the high hills, cloud-capped and gloomy, great snowfields lay. Not a green plover was to be seen—the species in this, and in other parts of the Highlands, was almost wiped out by the great frost of 1947.

A herd of deer were grazing on the grassy flats beside the river and, being alarmed, forded a pool in so crowded a company that the water was churned into foam. One of the deer on reaching the farther grassy bank began to romp and dart from side to side as a dog might have done in similar circumstances. The sight of these retreating stags reminded Finlay Mackintosh, the head stalker, a man who has spent half a century studying deer and probably knows as much about them as any person now living, of the hardships of the deer of his forest during the intense and prolonged frost of January, February and the first half of March in 1947. One day he noticed a stag licking a lump of ice. He fetched a pick-axe, and opened a small hole in the ice of the loch—the ice was 13 inches thick. He believes that the deer must have scented the water, for in fifteen minutes stags were literally queueing up at the hole, to drink in turn. He told us that they drank delicately, as though the water felt cold to their teeth. He subsequently enlarged the hole and kept it open, and each day stags were seen drinking at it. This episode has an added interest, because some authorities on the red deer believe that this animal does not drink. Four hundred stags and hinds were lost in this forest during the exceptionally severe spell. A fourteen-pointer and two royals died so near one another that the three were buried in a common grave.

We heard, too, the story of the white, or cream-coloured, hind which has haunted the forest for the past fifteen years. But the main impression I hold is of standing beside the historic cairn on that wind-swept hill-face 1,800 feet above the sea. Perhaps on that day of 1370 the weather was as wild, when the two friends by the grim irony of war were obliged to slay one another. I have seen other reputedly old cairns—as, for example, that on Iona, said to have been built by Columba—but none have conveyed the same sense of age. Eight-tenths of its stones have fallen and are partly overgrown by moss and grass; were they gathered and re-erected the majesty of the memorial would be irrevocably destroyed. The rain, driven by the rising gale, struck one's face like hail. Everywhere the gloom was unrelieved; a break in the cloud for a moment seemed to point to better things, but from the invisible basin of Loch Ericht came the rain, yet more relentless and persistent. In one version of the duel, one of those who fought it is said to have been MacDhomhnall Duibh, chief of all the Camerons—he who would now be termed Lochiel. But the chief of that time was named Allan, and this man was, as we have seen, Charles.

We must go forward in time from 1370 to 1746 to describe how the defeat of Prince Charles Edward on Culloden Moor affected the fortunes of those in Badenoch. Rising steeply from the Spey is a rocky hill of which the name is Creag Dhubh (Black Rock), 2,350 feet above the sea. The lower slopes of the hill are birch-clad; rather more than halfway up is a high rock-face, haunt of raven, peregrine falcon, and wild cat. High up on this rocky face is Uaimh Cluanaidh— in English, Cluny's Cave.

Cluny MacPherson, or Cluny as he was always named in his own country, had been "out" for the prince, and after Culloden he, like so many other leading Highlanders, found himself homeless and a hunted man. His clansmen were in no better plight, yet they hid and fed their chief for nine long years until, in 1755, Cluny escaped to France and died there, a broken-hearted man, a year later.

During most of his time in hiding his place of concealment was a small recess, which later became known as Cluny's Cave (it must not be confused with another of his hiding-places, Cluny's Cage, high on Ben Alder). He may have seen his castle fired by government troops, and the *saighdeiran dearg*—the red soldiers—marching through the strath below. The cave is almost impossible to discover unless one has knowledge of its precise location, and must have afforded an ideal hiding-place for a hunted chief. Yet the men of his clan, in order that their chief's safety should be still better guarded, made for him a second hiding-place at the foot of Creag Dhubh, near the slow-flowing Spey, which here meanders eastward through peaty pools and swamps—a curious youth for the swift and mighty river of its middle reaches. This second hiding-place was a subterranean dwelling, and those who worked at it toiled always at night and before daylight threw the sand and gravel excavated into the river. Cluny sometimes used this alternative hiding-place, but when it was discovered, by a man falling through the roof, he moved to another place of concealment in the old house of Dalchully. Although the government offered a reward of £1,000 to anyone who should reveal Cluny's hiding-place, there was no person during those nine years who could be persuaded to betray him. It was indeed remarkable that the fugitive was not taken, for parties of soldiers were continually searching the district, and there was in addition a force of eighty soldiers stationed in the district to intimidate the inhabitants.

To the west of Cluny's Cave a magnificent waterfall drops from the high ground in a single fall of perhaps 500 feet. It is only after heavy and prolonged rain that the fall springs to life. I passed that way in mid-October under these conditions, and, although I know the district well, had no idea until that day of the grandeur of this high fall.

A sequel to the days when Cluny hid in the underground dwelling was the discovery, in the nineteenth century, of six claymores near the place. The find was made by a piper of renown, Sandy Mac-Donald, father of that supreme piper John MacDonald of Inverness, he who has sometimes been named King of Pipers. Sandy was piper to the MacPhersons of Glentruim, and one day when he was ferreting rabbits moved some large stones and found six old swords concealed beneath them.

Cluny Castle, which stands beside the Spey near Laggan, was the repository of the Green Banner of Clan Chattan—the Bratach Uaine, as it is named in Gaelic. It was held to have miraculous properties when carried into battle. The banner was sold in 1943, but was purchased by a committee of representative clansmen, to be kept henceforward in the possession of the Clan Chattan. Another relic which in old days was even more highly prized than the Green Banner was a pipe chanter named the Feadan Dubh, or Black Chanter of Clan Chattan. This chanter is said to have fallen from heaven during the battle of the North Inch of Perth in 1396, playing, as it fell, a pibroch so sublime that those who heard it were bespelled. As it reached the ground it struck a stone or hard ground; at all events the slight crack in it was said to have been received on that historic occasion. Another version is that the Fairy Chanter was fashioned from a crystal and that the present one is a replica. It was at Cluny Castle that one of the most celebrated pipers of recent times was accustomed to play. He was Calum MacPherson, a man of imposing presence, with flowing beard and locks and the proud eye of the MacPhersons. He was piper to Cluny, and many a prize he won at the various Highland gatherings. John MacDonald, he to whom I have referred above as king of pipers, was a pupil of Malcolm or Calum MacPherson, and has told me of the skill of his veteran teacher. He told me a thing that, as a piper, greatly impressed me—that he had never heard Calum MacPherson miss a grace note, or fail to give justice to each grace note, in the intricate *Crunluadh* variation of a pibroch. Calum MacPherson's son, Angus, is still with us, and on occasion will impart the lore of piping which he learned from his gifted father beside the peat fire at Catt Lodge in Badenoch. When the news was received that a prince had been born to Princess Elizabeth and the Duke of Edinburgh, Angus celebrated the auspicious occasion by playing, beside the river Shin, the pibroch known as "The Prince's Salute," a tune that was composed in the year 1715. There must have been many pipers throughout the world who celebrated that event on their martial pipes, but I doubt whether any of them played that difficult and stirring composition, which was composed to celebrate the arrival of another prince in Scotland more than 200 years ago.

If you travel along the road westward past Cluny Castle you will see, shortly after crossing the river Spey, a small piece of land fenced in against stock and having a plantation of trees on it. This is known as Johnny Cope's About-Turn, because at this point the government General Cope retreated towards Inverness when he heard that the army of Prince Charles Edward was crossing the pass of Corrieyaireag towards him. Farther west is Loch Laggan, the home of great trout, sometimes known as *salmo ferox*.

CHAPTER VIII

LOCH LAGGAN

On the shore of Loch Laggan I had a curious encounter with a cock capercaillie on a morning of mid-October. My wife and I were driving along the road, which follows the birch-clad north shore of Loch Laggan. On the road ahead of us we saw a cock capercaillie. We drove on, expecting the bird to take wing, but it did not fly, and stood at the roadside. We had ample opportunity of admiring its glossy black plumage at close quarters after the car had been stopped. The capercaillie now began to feed on the green fronds of the bracken, which had been protected by the sheltering birches from the frost, seeming to take only those fronds which were spore-bearing. It paid no heed to the motor-car standing a few yards away. Sometimes a bird does not mind a car, but will at once fly off when the occupant of that car opens the door and shows himself or herself. When I opened the door of the car and stepped out on to the road I expected the capercaillie to take precipitate flight. Nothing of the sort happened. The bird continued to feed calmly, and I was able to take a number of photographs of it. I then made sure that its wing must be broken and that it was therefore incapable of flight. After feeding for a time the caper climbed up (by leaping, with no help from its wings) to the lichen-covered boughs of an old birch and from this perch placidly surveyed me. At last with no warning it took wing and, skimming low above the bracken, disappeared from sight. Had there been a house in the neighbourhood I should have thought the bird hand-reared, but here the loch-side is for some miles without any house. This encounter made me remember the tame cock capercaillie which at one time lived in Rothiemurchus Forest and made itself feared by attacking children on their way to and from school, and ladies walking in the forest. It was said that the sight of a lady wearing silk stockings (these were pre-war days!) used to cause that old caper special annoyance, and it would run up and peck, from behind, the legs of the offending female. During the years of the second world war great disturbance must have been caused to the capercaillie population in the Highlands, for much of the old woodlands was then felled, and this felling is not yet ended. I was fishing the Balmoral water of the Dee one day when I saw a curious bird flying down the river towards me. The bird when first seen was a considerable distance away, and during the time it was approaching I was wondering to myself what on earth it could be. The only bird it resembled was a cormorant, yet I had never seen, nor heard of, a cormorant on these upper waters of the Dee. As it passed me, the bird solved my difficulty by showing itself to be a very fine and large male capercaillie. The riverside country where I saw it was comparatively treeless, and the bird was evidently on passage from the forests of Scots pine to the west, where extensive felling operations were then in progress. Although it is normally a stay-at-home bird, the capercaillie has a powerful flight and is capable of flying long distances should occasion demand it. A capercaillie which was shot by my father-in-law, Howard Pease of Otterburn, on Strathmashie ground in Upper Strathspey was taken by him to the Outer Hebrides. When he arrived at the lodge in North Uist where he was staying, the cook asked his hostess with agitation how she was to cook "the eagle." A friend of mine on one occasion saw a thrilling pursuit of a cock capercaillie by a golden eagle: the eagle stooped at tremendous speed, but the caper by a split second succeeded in gaining the cover of some pines. The same result on another occasion followed the pursuit of a caper by a peregrine falcon. The friend who witnessed this occurrence said he had never seen anything move so fast as that falcon, yet the caper eluded its fierce enemy in this instance also and dived into a thick wood, where it was safe.

The castle of Ardverikie stands on the south shore of Loch Laggan. When Queen Victoria and the Prince Consort were house-hunting in the Highlands they stayed at Ardverikie, and inspected Cluny Castle, which tradition says they intended to buy. But the weather was so wet that they decided on a district with a smaller rainfall, and later acquired Balmoral.

It was in the Loch Laggan district that the wild cat had one of its last strongholds before the war years brought about a great increase in the numbers of this species—the only animal in the British Isles which has never been tamed. Since the wild cat is the crest of the MacPhersons, it is fitting that it should survive on the ancestral lands of this proud clan. An epic combat was observed one day in the Loch Laggan country between a golden eagle and a wild cat. The eagle was seen to stoop between thirty and forty times at the cat; on two occasions the cat at the last moment sprang into the air, striking at the eagle with its claws; these springs were so high that the observer watching through a stalking glass was able to see the cat momentarily suspended in the air. It was later found that the cat had kittens in a cairn near by. Fights between golden eagle and wild cat are not common. A deer stalker in a well-known forest of western Ross-shire one day found a wild cat's track in deep snow near his house. He and his terrier followed the cat's tracks along a steep slope and came on signs of a struggle in the snow. There were feathers from the head and neck of a golden eagle, and marks in the virgin snow where the eagle alighted, the impress of the bird's wings in the snow being plain. From the marks of the struggle it seemed that the eagle had attempted to lift the cat but she had been too quick for him, and had caught him by the head. The eagle and the cat had rolled down the steep slope to where, thirty yards below, the ground became more level. There was to be seen here further marks of the struggle—a few drops of blood and more feathers lying on the snow. The eagle apparently had then flown away, and in the snow were tracks showing that the cat had run in circles as though dazed, before travelling to rocky ground some little distance away. What happened to the eagle? About the same time a dead golden eagle was found on Blaven, a high hill near the Cuillin range in the Isle of Skye. The bird had severe wounds on the neck, and had apparently succumbed to those injuries. As the eagle flies, the distance from the scene of the fight to the slopes of Blaven is perhaps thirty miles, and thus it seems likely that the bird found in Skye was the same as that which attacked the wild cat, with disastrous results for itself.

There is grandeur in the Loch Laggan country, especially in summer before the snows have disappeared from the high hills. One July day, as I made my way along the shore of the loch, I saw great snowfields high on Creag Meaghaidh (3,700 feet) show white below the dun clouds; the vivid green of the grass below and, quite near, those snow-beds heightened the Alpine character of the scene. The country is wild and lonely north of Loch Laggan. Beneath Creag Meaghaidh, but still 2,046 feet above sea level, is the mountain tarn Lochan a' Choire, which lies in the well-known corrie of Corarder (Coire Ardobhair—Corrie of High Water). Here, too, is that well-known landmark as seen from the east—Uinneag Choire Ardair (the Window of Corarder). The "Window" is an opening or pass on the hillside: I have often seen it from the high tops of the Cairn-gorms and from the high ground of Gaick Forest, where it was first pointed out to me by Ormiston, the head stalker, a great hillman, a good companion, and one steeped in the lore of red deer and deer stalking.

In recent years Loch Laggan has been made approximately four miles longer towards the west by a great dam, which sends the waters of the river Spean through an underground passage into Loch Treig, whence they are taken in a tunnel beneath the heart of Ben Nevis to supply power for the aluminium works at Fort William. This great engineering feat took a number of years to complete. It has had the effect of drying the river Spean completely in rainless weather, and of doing the same thing to the river Treig. When drought persists, Loch Laggan becomes so low that great areas of sand and mud are exposed along its shores. An ancient canoe was found in the mud. It may have been in use in the time of King Fergus, who is said to have had a hunting lodge on the small island that still bears the name Eilean an Righ (the King's Isle), not far from Eilean nan Con (the Island of the Hounds), where the royal deer-hounds were kept. There is good brown trout fishing on the loch from the hotel at Kinloch Laggan and *ferox* trout up to 14 lb. have been caught. It is, I suppose, impossible to construct a great dam, capable of withstanding immense pressure of imprisoned waters, which can look anything but inartistic and utilitarian. The Loch Laggan dam is no exception, but the scene here, after heavy and prolonged rains spread over a number of weeks or even months, can be most impressive and even awe-inspiring. Picture a huge pipe opening halfway down the granite face of the dam. The flood waters, forced through it under high pressure, shoot out horizontally, for a time defying the law of gravity. They then fall with the noise of continuous thunder into the deep pool which they have formed, and which must ever be growing more deep. The spray from that great fall eddies above the pool and is often blown back, rainbow-tinted when the sun shines. Besides this great jet of solid water, there is a smaller jet below it, and at the same time there are cascades of considerable power falling over the top of the dam. There is a road crossing the dam; if you stand, in times of flood, on the bridge which carries the road, you feel a constant trembling of the solid granite structure, as though the earth itself were shaken by the torrent of water which seeks to free itself from its prison—from the bonds set upon it by the hand of man.

112

Schiehallion from Loch Rannoch

At Tulloch station Spean and Treig meet, and continue to flow west as the Spean, through woods of birch and oak, where in spring primroses are bright beneath the trees before the grass has changed its winter hue of brown to the young green of May. At Roy Bridge the Spean is joined by the Roy. It is already, if the season be a rainy one, an impetuous torrent which has rushed with irresistible might through its rocky gorge in view of both the road and railway which traverse its glen. The Roy rises within half a mile of the source of the Spey, and flows west, while the Spey flows east.

When the great Montrose was making his epic forced march from the Great Glen near Fort Augustus to surprise the Campbells at Inverlochy, he passed through Glen Roy and perhaps found the Parallel Roads of service to him. These curious "roads" or terraces are supposed by geologists to mark successive levels of a loch which at one time filled Glen Roy. A great glacier flowing down Glen Treig and Glen Spean blocked the passage through the foot of the glen and held the waters imprisoned. The early kings of Scotland made use of these "roads" when hunting, and at one time they were known to the people of the district as the King's Hunting Roads. They are a remarkable feature of the glen, the terraces rising one above the other, and each one exactly parallel. It is believed that at the time the highest of the "roads" was formed by the waves of the loch the water from this great glacier-hemmed loch in Glen Roy emptied itself eastward into Loch Spey and thereafter into the river Spey, which must therefore have been at that time a larger river in its upper reaches than it is now. It is curious that a glacier should be the means of changing a watershed; to have done so it must have been of vast height and extent. The loch which then filled Glen Roy must have been at least as deep as Loch Ness, although not perhaps as deep as Loch Morar (1,080 feet in depth), the deepest of all the Highland lochs. When the lowest of the Parallel Roads was formed the loch in Glen Roy joined Loch Laggan, the two forming a long, winding loch with its outflow eastward, to join the Spey at Laggan Bridge or beyond it. It is strange to think that this great loch in Glen Roy was in all probability nameless throughout its history, for the land was then under ice and snow, and no human beings lived here.

Soldier's Leap, Pass of Killiecrankie

LOCH TREIG

As you walk down Glen Roy, a fine view of the Ben Nevis massif unfolds itself. The great snowfield which extends along the upper slope of Aonach Mór (I always think this hill is unfortunate in being made 3,999 feet in height, and therefore by a foot missing the small and select band of 4,000-feet Scottish peaks) is a prominent feature of the landscape until late in summer. Aonach Mór is often mistaken, especially when seen from a distance (as from the Cairngorms), for Ben Nevis itself. Not more than two miles separate the two hills, and when seen from the east they seem to merge. Aonach Beag (4,060 feet), Aonach Mór, Carn Mór Dearg, and Carn Dearg (3,961 feet) all rise close to their chief, Ben Nevis. Beneath the foot-hills of Ben Nevis lies Lianachan, ancestral home of the Kennedys. A Glaistig, or Fairy Woman, is said to have put a curse on the Kennedys, so that they grow old before their time and meet other misfortunes through life.

There is an old drove road through the hills from Roy Bridge to Corrour at the head of Loch Treig. It is better to do the walk from the Corrour end, for thus the walker has the advantage of beginning the expedition at a height of 1,334 feet above sea level—this is the height of Corrour station—whereas the station at Roy Bridge is only 300 feet above the sea. The old track, by name Lairig Leacach— Pass of Flagstones—is picked up at the head of dark Loch Treig, a loch which in Gaelic lore has associations with the golden eagle. There is a saying, "As old as the eagle of Loch Treig." It was also said that an eagle's feather from Loch Treig made the most excellent wings for an arrow shaft.

There is an old tale of Loch Treig which may bear the re-telling. One spring of long ago the first day of May, or Beltane, came in with a frost so intense that the old eagle who had her eyrie on the rocks of Stob Choire an Easain Mhóir thought that she had never experienced such cold in May month. She had a great friend in the old water-ousel who lived beside the loch. She sailed down to the loch, found her friend, and asked him, "Have you in all your long years of living ever felt so cold a Beltane dawn?" "Indeed I have not," replied the dipper, but go you to the blackbird who lives in yonder wood; he is even older than I am, and he may well remember a May dawn of equal cold." The eagle found the blackbird, and put the same question to him. "No indeed," replied the blackbird, "but there is a stag in Coire an Easain Mhóir who is older than I; go you and ask him." The eagle sailed up, easily and lightly as is her wont, to the high corrie, and she found there the old stag, scraping away at the snow with his forefeet to search for the brown, withered grass beneath it. The eagle put the same question to him. "Indeed I never saw the like," said the stag, "but surely the water-ousel told you of the old trout in Loch Treig? He is older than all of us, and it would be well for you to put the same question to him." So back the eagle went to Loch Treig, and with her strong yelping cries called to the trout that she wanted to have speech with him. But the old trout was doing his best to keep warm, and was deep, deep down in Loch Treig, and it was long before he heard, and the eagle was growing weary, and was thinking of going away to search for a hare or a rabbit for her breakfast, when at last he came to the surface. The eagle put the same question to him. "Yes indeed," he replied, "I have known a Beltane dawn with greater cold in it. It was many, many years ago, perhaps before the mother who reared yourself from the egg was born. On that Beltane I leaped (for I was young and foolish then) out of the loch and, would you believe it, my body, arched with my leap, was frozen stiff before it touched the water again." "Indeed," said the eagle, at last satisfied, "that must have been the great cold."

When a friend and I did that walk through Lairig Leacach the season was May, but the frosts had gone even from this high country. The grey clouds of morning were slowly rising from the high tops, and light, wandering airs played upon the waters of Loch Treig as we rounded the head of the loch (depositing magazines with the shepherd who lives his lonely life here) from which rises the steep, rocky face of Creag Ghuanach, immortalised in a well-known Gaelic song. As we looked across Loch Treig we saw three goosanders—a drake and two ducks—fly up the loch on rapidly driven wings that showed white against the dark waters. At the head of the loch one of the ducks turned; the other two continued in swift flight above the burn which entered the loch quietly, almost stealthily, beside the shepherd's house. The sun broke through the clouds and a raven, flying so high that he seemed no larger than a jackdaw, crossed the pass ahead of us as he made his way to his nest and brood high on Creag Ghuanach. Wheatears darted cheerily over the moor, and meadow pipits, rising lark-like a little way, sailed delicately to earth, the while singing their simple song. We soon left behind us the few birch trees and, walking above the stream named Uisge na Lairig, saw ahead of us the sharp cone of Stob Bàn (3,217 feet) rise against the sky, now blue and studded with white, fleecy clouds. Sunlight flooded the Lairig where long ago drovers, wearing the old-fashioned knitted blue bonnet, drove the cattle, which had perhaps come from Skye, or even from the Outer Hebrides, southward to the Falkirk tryst or market. The old track is stony and winds sometimes beside the burn, sometimes across the hill-face considerably above it. When we had arrived at a point near the watershed of the Lairig we left the track and climbed eastward beside a stream that dropped from the high slopes of Stob Coire an Easain Mhóir—Peak of the Corrie of the Great Waterfall—an imposing hill which rises to a height of 3,658 feet, its upper slopes on this day the home of snowfields which gleamed in the strong May sunshine. It is curious that there should be two great hills, not farther than four miles from one another as the eagle flies, both bearing a name that is rare among Highland hills. The hill which we were climbing is Stob Coire an Easain Mhóir; that four miles to the west is named on the map as Stob Coire an Easain— Peak of the Corrie of the Waterfall—and is 3,548 feet in height. As we climbed (disturbing a pair of ptarmigan) we often looked back across the Lairig to admire the noble peak Stob Bàn—the Light-coloured Peak—which, 3,217 feet high but appearing higher because of its imposing outline, rose as an outpost of even higher hills west-ward. A hind sprang from long heather beside the burn. She was weak from the privations of winter; when she attempted to leap the burn, she fell to her knees on its farther bank, which was rocky and steep, but at once rose, scrambled up that bank, and made off at her best speed across the hill-face. On dry, heather-grown ridges *Azalea procumbens* showed its small dark-red flower buds, which would not open for several weeks. May is early spring on the high hills, and as we climbed we saw that the leaves of *Alchemilla alpina*, the Alpine lady's mantle, were only now beginning to uncurl.

The sky westward became rapidly overcast. For a time the sun continued to shine on the snowy summit of Ben Nevis—the snow-cap here appeared still to be unbroken—but the clouds, dropping, soon rested on that high hill-top and hid it from our gaze. The sun, too, had gone from our hill before we gained the summit and rested awhile behind its well-built cairn. The western slopes of Stob Coire an Easain Mhóir had been only moderately steep, but we now saw that the hill northward dropped almost sheer to a green corrie far beneath; east, the drop to Loch Treig, in Gaelic tradition the haunt of ferocious water horses, was almost as steep. A deer stalker, sound of wind and limb, once pursued a wounded stag over Stob Coire an Easain Mhóir, thence down the steep slope to Loch Treig. At the end of that stern chase he still had the energy to swim far into the loch, following his wounded quarry, which had taken to the water, and there he administered the *coup de grace* to the wounded animal, swimming back with it afterwards to the shore.

On the far eastern horizon rose the Cairngorm hill range, the Monadh Ruadh of the Gael. We could see the high, stony corries of Braeriach and, beyond and rather to the right of them, the broad, rounded summit of Ben MacDhui, on which the snow still lay, deep and unbroken. South-east rose the sharp, unmistakable cone of Schiehallion above Loch Rannoch, one of the most distinctive hills of the Highlands. South was Ben Dorain, praised by that great natural poet Duncan Bàn Macintyre; south-west were the Black Mount tops and, north of them, Bidean nam Beann, highest hill in Argyll, and Beinn Bheitheir above Ballachulish. North-west rain clouds advancing from the Atlantic hid the far view; it is likely the Cuillin of Skye are visible from here in clear weather. The sun had gone for the day from Stob Coire an Easain Mhóir, and in the backing wind was a cold dampness which is usually the forerunner of rain, but far east the sun still shone on the snowy slopes of the Cairngorms and at times also upon the great hill Ben Alder, much nearer at hand. It was high on a southern spur of Ben Alder that Prince Charles Edward and Cluny Mac-Pherson were in hiding for a time after Culloden. The place was known as Cluny's Cage. The Cage or shelter was in a thicket of hollies. The shanty which was constructed here had two floors or stories, was built largely of holly wood, and was covered with moss as a thatch. The upper room served as dining-room and bedroom, the lower to store the food and drink. As a contemporary MS. puts it, "At the back part was a proper hearth for cook and baiker and the face of the mountain had so much the colour and resemblance of smoke, no person could ever discover that there was either fire or habitation in the place. Round this lodge were placed their sentinels at proper stations, some nearer and some at greater distances."

On the Ordnance Survey maps is marked, near the course of the Alder Burn, a rude shelter named Prince Charles's Cave. This may be the site of Cluny's Cage; if so, the thicket of holly has entirely disappeared, yet it might well have been burnt by government troops if they had found within it the suspicious shelter after its inmates had left it. Prince Charlie was hiding in Cluny's Cage for six days—from September 6 to September 12, 1746.

We left the hill-top and with reluctance descended once more toward Lairig Leacach, but for long Bidean nam Beann and the high tops of the Black Mount kept us company, and gave us their strong and silent fellowship. The blueness of evening had already enfolded these great hills, where much snow still lay. Here and there we could see that an avalanche had recently fallen from some narrow summit ridge; its track was marked by blocks of snow, discoloured by grit and earth, lying on the boulders and grass below the steep slope. As a contrast to this scene of winter, we could discern northwards the smoke of a moorland fire, the fire itself hidden by intervening hills, rising lazily into the air against a darkening sky. We reached the Lairig—after having a brief view eastwards of Loch Laggan—crossed to its north side, and at once saw below us the broad valley of the Spean. Birches grow almost to the head of Lairig Leacach on its north side. These birches were in their first foliage of diaphanous green, trees of grace and beauty; their young leaves scented the quiet air with an exquisite perfume, and I could not but be sorry that the maidens of the Highlands no longer know the art of preparing perfume from the birch; surely no scent could be more sweet.

At length we came in sight of that moorland fire, the smoke of which we had seen for long. Although a shower of rain fell, the line of red flames, apparently impervious to that gentle rain, ran along the ground, beyond and above which towered, aloof, the long snowy ridge of Aonach Mór. No song of curlew or lapwing drifted to us on the light breeze, now shifting toward the north and sending back the smoke of the fire to its starting-place. A pair of golden plover, black-breasted and handsome, fed on a field of rough pasture near the Spean, and sandpipers courted above the river where the young foliage of the oaks was bronze and the scent of birches was still with us.

CHAPTER X

KINGUSSIE AND GAICK

In the last chapter we travelled as far east as Glen Truim, Creag Dhubh, and the old battle-field at Invernahaven. The main road to Inverness continues north-east, past Newtonmore and, three miles beyond it, Kingussie, sometimes known as the capital of Badenoch. The name Newtonmore is a singular one, the "more" here standing not for *mór*, "big," but for the English word "moor." The Gaelic is Baile Ùr an t-Sléibh—the New Town of the Moor. Here the river Calder, rising in the Monadh Liath hill range, joins the Spey. Midway between Newtonmore and Kingussie is the House of Balachroan, and above it the site of Coulinlinn, the ancestral home of an old branch of the MacPhersons. It was Captain MacPherson of Balachroan who, with four other deer hunters, was killed by an avalanche while asleep in a bothy on a Christmas night in the year 1799, in the Forest of Gaick, a place which a Gaelic poet describes as "Gàig nan creagan gruamach—Gaick of the grim rocks." Call Ghaig—the Loss of Gaick—made so great an impression on the district of Badenoch that old people used to count their years by it and say that they were of such and such an age at the time of the Loss of Gaick. Kingussie is an old name; it is found written Kinguscy as early as the beginning of the twelfth century. This place-name is a memorial of the time when the district stood at the head of the great pine forest of Strathspey, of which a remnant is still found at Rothiemurchus, Glenmore, and Abernethy. The Celtic scholar MacBain gives the original form as Cinn Ghiùthsaich—Head of the Pine Forest. Across the Spey from Kingussie is Ruthven Castle; near it is the site of Gordon Hall, the residence of the Gordon lords of Badenoch when Ruthven Castle, their former seat, became a barracks. In 1390 Alexander, son of King Robert II, he who was so greatly feared that he received the title of Wolf of Badenoch, lived in Ruthven Castle, and from that place made the expedition in which he burnt Elgin Cathedral. His eldest son became Earl of Mar, and this title, one of the oldest in Scotland, still survives. In the year 1451 the lordship of Badenoch passed to the Earl of Huntly, ancestor of the last Duke of Gordon who died in

119

1836, and Ruthven Castle became a seat of the Huntly family, although the original building had been largely demolished and had to be re-built. In 1546 Huntly imprisoned Lochiel and MacDonald of Keppoch in Ruthven Castle; these two chiefs were later convicted at Elgin of high treason and were executed. The castle was burnt by a force under Viscount Dundee in 1689 and remained a ruin until Ruthven Barracks were built on the same site in the year 1718. One of the most outstanding pictures by the late Sir D. Y. Cameron shows Ruthven Castle standing out in bright sunshine against a dark background; with his touch of genius he has made the castle live.

Near Ruthven Castle the Tromie river enters the Spey. Glen Tromie leads south into the hills. In the neighbourhood of Glentromie Lodge the glen is almost covered with birches, where redstarts, tree pipits and spotted flycatchers nest. The trees are soon left behind and at Loch an t-Seilich—Loch of the Willow—the hillside rises steeply from the loch. It was at the head of this loch that the avalanche swept down on the party of hunters in 1799; avalanches still periodically occur at this spot, and in or around the year 1922 I remember that a great fall of snow from a cornice on the hill high above swept into the birch wood above the east shore of the loch, killing a number of hinds which were sheltering here. There are heavy trout in Loch an t-Seilich, and near where the river leaves the loch is a pool where salmon are taken in early summer. Late in the year there are many salmon in the river, but they are then on the way to the spawning beds and few of the fish are worth catching.

At Gaick Lodge, situated above Loch an t-Seilich, Robert and Guy Hargreaves had the stalking for many years. Both were keen sportsmen and tireless on the hill. Breakfast in September and up to the end of the stalking season in mid-October was at seven o'clock; by eight the stalkers had left the lodge for distant beats. I remember that there was a powerful telescope at the lodge. On a Sunday much time was spent spying the hills and corries for stags. The glass was so powerful that it brought the deer, which often fed on the slopes of Sron Bhui-rich, two miles to the south, quite close.

There is a right-of-way through the hills from Gaick to Dalna-cardach in Atholl, past Loch Vrodin and Loch an Duin. According to Gaelic tradition, Loch Vrodin, or Loch Bhrodainn, received its name from a jet-black dog, Bhrodainn by name, owned by a deer hunter. The pup was left with the hunter by a demon, who first broke its leg. The hunter decided to try the dog out on the fairy deer of Ben Alder. This deer was white without blemish, and, as was natural, led a charmed life. The deer was found, and was chased by the fairy dog all the way from Ben Alder to Loch Vrodin. When they reached the loch the hound was gaining on the deer: the two plunged into the loch, and halfway across Brodainn seized the deer. They both disappeared instantly and were never seen again: the incident is commemorated in the name of the loch. MacBain, who describes the hunt in his *Place Names of the Highlands and Islands of Scotland*, a valuable and scholarly work, believes that the word "Bhrodainn" is from the early Irish Brot-chú, meaning a Mastiff.

I had a curious experience many years ago on the plateau of a high hill south of Loch Vrodin. I was photographing a bird, and had been sitting quietly beside my camera for some time when I felt slight pressure against my side. My thoughts were not of the fairy hound, and being intent on my photography I dismissed the occurrence from my mind. When I had finished with my bird "sitter" I made a movement to rise to my feet, but found that I was unable to move. I looked quickly round, and there, sound asleep, I saw a very small red deer calf, lying close to my side for warmth. I then recalled that some time before I had seen a hind running over the hill-top, but had thought no more of that incident. I now realised that the hind and her small calf must have been together. It may have been the little one's first expedition, and he had insufficient strength to quicken his pace and follow his mother. Seeing me, he had done the next best thing—he had walked up quietly to me and laid himself down in my shelter. When I rose to my feet, the small calf attempted to follow me, and did so for about half a mile, when, becoming weary, he lay down in the heather, and there I left him, hoping that his mother would find him. It was strange that she had not returned to look for him on the hill plateau, especially as I had made no movement over a long period.

Loch an Duin, on the county march between Inverness-shire and Perthshire, is a loch with high rocks overshadowing it, and in these rocks a peregrine falcon for many years had her eyrie. It is a wild loch in storms, the wind sweeping through the narrow pass and lifting the waters high into the air in clouds of grey spindrift. Perhaps under those tempestuous conditions the Witch of Badenoch is abroad—she who could at will assume the form of wild cat or raven—or the Leannan Sith, the Fairy Sweetheart, who was wont to appear to hunters in Gaick Forest. She, unlike the witch, was young and beautiful, but, like most fairies, capricious and jealous.

By returning to Ruthven Castle and following the road along the south side of the river Spey the river Feshie is reached at Feshie Bridge after a distance of five miles. Glen Feshie has often been in the news during the last quarter of a century and more because of the suggestion —which has so far come to nothing—that a road should be made through the glen from Braemar to Kingussie to link the valleys of the Dee and the Spey. The road would begin at the Linn of Dee and would follow the Dee westward, and thereafter the Geldie to Geldie Lodge. It would then cross the watershed at a height of 1,834 feet (Geldie Lodge stands 1,700 feet above the sea) and would continue down Glen Feshie. The country all the way is well suited for the making of a road, but the cost is prohibitive unless the undertaking should be financed by the Government. At one time I felt that the road would largely spoil the beauty of Glen Feshie, but the breath of the second world war seared this lonely glen. Many of the old pines which had stood in their beauty for centuries were felled, lumber camps were established, roads were driven up the hillsides, and the salmon were dynamited in the river.

Glen Feshie has associations with the great animal artist Landseer, and the remains of a frescoe of his on the wall of the small ruined chapel in Glen Feshie, in the pine forest beyond the lodge, were to be seen certainly until a few years ago. On the high rocky face above the chapel my friend Mr. J. C. Harrison, the well-known bird artist, had the rare good fortune to see three snowy owls migrating north on the first day of May. The ground that morning was snow-covered, and it must have been almost as cold as the Beltane day when the Loch Treig eagle asked his oldest neighbours whether they had ever seen the like. The raven which nested in the rocks flew out over the glen, croaking nervously, and my friend had just time to observe the three great white birds fly over in a stately manner and disappear over the sky-line. He made a sketch of the birds, which I have as a record of that unusual scene. The same artist one day when near the top of the Feshie found a clean-run salmon lying on the bank of the river. There was a bite out of the shoulder of the fish, and the otters which had their den near the pool, being fastidious feeders, had left the salmon after eating the most tasty portion. My friend, being less particular than the otter or otters, took the salmon home and ate it for several days: he told me afterwards that it was one of the best fish he had tasted.

The river Feshie flows into the Spey near Loch Insh, in Gaelic Loch Innis—Loch of the Island. Its island is, at the present time at all events, an island only when the loch is in flood: its site is near where the Spey leaves the loch. In an old account of the district it is termed a "half Yland." The island, or peninsula, is high and wooded. A church is built on it, and in the church is an ancient bronze bell, which is said to be St. Adamnan's bell. The mound on which the church stands is called sometimes Tom Eunan or Eónan, and Eónan is the name by which Adamnan is usually known in the Highlands— as, for example, in the place-name Ard Eonaig by the shore of Loch Tay. Adamnan, celebrated for his *Life of St. Columba*, was the ninth abbot of Hy (Iona). There is a legend that the bell was stolen and carried over the pass of Drumochter by the thieves. The theft was of no avail, for the bell of itself returned over the hills, and as it sped through the air is said to have intoned its name "Tom Eonan" for all to hear.

It is between Loch Insh and Kingussie that the river Spey habitually floods the low-lying, almost level, land through which it flows, and it thus gave the district its name "Drowned Lands." It was said of old that the water sprite of the Spey was not satisfied unless she claimed one human victim a year. Did she claim that victim by pursuing him over the fertile lands of Badenoch, which she floods with her cold dark waters, or was he swept to his doom where she surges seaward in fierce flood at Knockando? Of the Spey at Badenoch it was written as early as 1630 that:

Oftimes this river in tyme of speat or stormie weather will be alse bigg as if it were a Logh, and also as broad, and overflowes all the low corne lands of the Countrey next to itself.

Even when the river keeps to its proper course there are pools and lochans in this low land between Kingussie and Loch Insh, and during the winter and early spring months whooper swans make their home here before they fly north-west to their nesting grounds in Iceland. Sometimes the swans assemble at the west end of Loch Insh: in frosty weather the loch quickly freezes and the swans then fly farther down the Spey valley. One winter's day I had the rare experience of seeing

123

the three species of British swans, Bewick's swan, whooper swan and mute swan, swimming together on Loch Insh at sunset. There was only one Bewick's swan, and it was noticeably smaller than either of the other two species. Bewick's swan is becoming much scarcer. On the Hebridean island of Tiree, where formerly I could count on seeing a herd of over one hundred any day of winter, not a single bird is now recorded. It may be they were killed and their eggs were taken during the war years in their summer home in Siberia.

The call of the whooper swan has been likened to a whooping or hooping cry, hence the bird's name. The swans are regal in flight, progressing with a stately, measured gliding that is apparently slow, yet in reality is faster than it appears to be. On one occasion I saw whoopers heading north-west into the Atlantic on a warm and sunny day in late March. The migrants had then finished their land travel and had more than seven hundred miles of ocean ahead of them. It is not often that the swans alight on the open sea, although on occasion I have seen them do this when held up on migration by adverse winds. The whooper's food is fresh-water weed, and also short grass, which I have seen a pair cropping beyond sight of any loch. Bewick's swan, on the other hand, seems to be equally at home on a fresh-water loch or in a tidal estuary. I often used to see them haunting Loch Cuan, a sea loch in the north of the Isle of Mull.

There are pike and char in Loch Insh and good trout, both brown trout, sea trout and finnock. For a few weeks in spring the loch gives excellent salmon fishing. Three or four estates and the parish minister have the right of a boat on it. I have not heard of a salmon taking a fly on Loch Insh; the fishing here is trolling, and the lure a Devon minnow. March, April and May are the best salmon months; I have not heard of a salmon being caught after the end of May.

During the war Indian troops were encamped beside Loch Insh; one met them, galloping furiously on horseback, on sequestered forest paths, crouching on their horses and balancing skilfully on the sharp bends, their black beards streaming in the wind. In appearance some of these Indian hillmen were not unlike the old type of Highland deer stalker; their bearing on foot was erect; they were tireless in walking, their keen eyes flashed. On one occasion, when a troop of Indian horsemen, rounding a sharp bend in a forest path, almost swept me from it, I wondered to myself what the old people of the district would have said had they been suddenly confronted by what they would have imagined to be apparitions. The Indians went through a long period of training on upper Strathspey and were liked by the natives, for their manners were exemplary, and no doubt they felt at home in a hill country.

PART III

THE CAIRNGORM AREA

The Pass of Revoan and the Cairngorms

CHAPTER I

CAIRNGORM

THREE miles north-east of Loch Insh with its oystercatchers, tufted duck, sandpipers and redshanks the main road passes Loch Alvie, a loch with birches growing thickly near it. Near the loch is Lynwilg, its hotel much sought after by summer visitors. The name Lynwilg is a curious and rare one; indeed I recall no other similar Highland place-name. The meaning, as given me by that distinguished Celtic scholar, the late Professor W. J. Watson, is Lainn Bhuilg, Field of the Bag or Bulge. There is a Loch Builg below Ben A'an in the eastern Cairngorms.

We are now approaching Aviemore (Agaidh Mhór, Big Gap), and the birches which clothe the hillsides are a feature of this upland district. They are of especial beauty in September and October, when they become trees of gold for a short period before the high winds and the keen night frosts send the leaves in showers to the ground; even the river Spey is then golden with birch leaves after wind or a night's frost. From Aviemore the view southward over the Cairngorm range is attractive, and if the visitor climbs the comparatively small hill of Craigellachie the panorama of that high range is yet more striking. The high Cairngorms are perhaps seen at their best in early summer, when there is still much snow in their corries but when the snow has gone from their tops which, before rain, appear dark-blue—does not the name Cairngorm, now given to the whole range but originally to the hill of Cairngorm (4084 feet), mean Blue Hill? From Aviemore, even from the main road or the railway station, the course of the Lairig Ghru, that high pass traversing the range from Strathspey to Glen Dee, is plain on a day free of mist. Changed days have come to the Cairngorms. Their land was at one time a great deer forest, or rather a number of deer forests. Then came the second world war, and many of the deer were shot for food, and Highland cattle were pastured on the foothills and in the pine forest. Canadian lumber men made great inroads into all the old Highland pine forests, and many of the lesser hills, which were formerly wooded, are now bare and desolate, and are strewn with the dead branches and limbs of the forest

Cairngorm (4,084 ft.) from Loch Morlich

giants which formerly flourished here. The second world war has ended; the tree felling, alas, continues. The Cairngorms saw strange sights during that second world war. They saw, as I have already mentioned, bearded Indians riding across their foothills, and up to their high tops; they saw Norwegian ski-troops, hardy and bronzed, on their high plateaus at mid-winter; they saw British expert climbers of the Mount Everest expedition camping in blizzards which, they said, exceeded in fury anything they had experienced on Everest: they saw mock battles with live ammunition fought on high ground with the eagle and the ptarmigan as the only spectators; they even, perchance, heard the famous order given that tanks should traverse the Lairig Ghru from Aviemore to Braemar. It is said that the tanks did indeed set out, and their track through Rothiemurchus was visible for many a day, but they had to confess themselves beaten on the higher rock-strewn slopes of the pass. A Zeppelin flew over the Cairngorms during the first world war, and no doubt German planes were often over these hills during the second. One of our own planes met disaster on Ben MacDhui and its crew were killed. The Oxford was ill-fated, for twenty feet more of altitude would have seen it safely over the hill. It crashed so close to the summit that it actually slipped across the watershed. There was close mist at the time; indeed the accident was not discovered until the cloud lifted and a climber saw a small column of smoke ascending into the sky near the hill-top. Another air disaster was not discovered until months later. An aircraft manned by a Czech crew crashed near the summit of Ben A'an in very lonely country during a winter blizzard. It was late in the following summer when the victims were found and were buried at the head of a wild corrie— a fitting resting-place for airmen. The bodies were later exhumed, a difficult task, and were taken away.

I met a Norwegian at the Juvasshytte, beside Norway's highest hill, Galdhöppigen (8,200 feet), in the summer of 1947, and he told me that he did much of his army training on the high Cairngorms during the war, and looked back with great pleasure to his days on skis on the high plateaus 4,000 feet above the sea, where the snow lay yards deep, the lochs were invisible beneath ice and snow and the conditions were truly Arctic. Many of our allies have pleasant recollections of the Highlands of Scotland, and of the friendliness and hospitality of their people. Our own war-time soldiers, many of them city dwellers, also have these good memories. Some of them will remember with pride in later years of life that they trained under Lord Rowallan, now the Chief Scout, in one of the Cairngorm glens, on an intensive course for potential officers. Lord Rowallan asked me if I would take some of these young soldiers up to the high Cairngorms to tell them of the plants, flowers and birds to be found there, and we did a number of climbs, in magnificent weather. We nearly caused strained relations with our Norwegian allies on one occasion by driving up to their headquarters, where we were told by an irate officer that we had no business to be there. The Norwegians shared a shooting lodge with a deerstalker, who on several occasions was held up because he could not give the pass-word, but with true Highland independence he refused to submit to these infringements on his liberty—and he had his way. This reminds me of the predicament of two officers who were walking to dine with the King and Queen at Balmoral Castle. The Lovat Scouts were at the time guarding the castle, and the two officers—who, needless to say, were not Lovat Scouts—had been given the pass-word, which they had forgotten. They were challenged by the sentry, and, since they could not give the pass-word, he insisted on their being brought before the officer of the guard—to the detriment of their smart uniform and burnished shoes, as they had to walk through long wet grass. When they arrived at Balmoral, late for dinner, it was necessary for them, in order to explain matters, to give an account of the incident which, rumour had it, greatly amused their royal host and hostess.

During those war years something like a spy mania swept over certain districts of the Highlands. One day the Registrar-General for Scotland, a keen mountaineer, alighted at Aviemore platform during the change of engines at that junction, and was enjoying the view of the Cairngorm hills when the stationmaster, seeing him studying a map, politely but firmly escorted him to his office, and it was not until he had been shown the suspect's identity book and visiting card that he consented to release him.

One of the great deer forests of the Cairngorms, Glenmore, has now become a National Park, and it is likely that other areas in the district will follow, as Aviemore can be reached easily from the cities and towns—one can leave Euston or King's Cross in the evening and have one's breakfast in Aviemore in the morning. The highest point in the Forest of Glenmore is Cairngorm, 4,084 feet above the sea. It is an easy hill to climb, and a path takes the climber to the summit cairn.

One day in late March, when a friend and I drove to Aviemore from the south, the mist was low on the hills of Drumochter, and wet snowflakes were falling on the white plumage of the whooper swans that fed on the water weeds of Loch Alvie, as we passed that loch. We crossed the Druie river at Coylum Bridge in Rothiemurchus, and as we came in sight of Loch Morlich saw that, although the war was over, tree-felling operations continued. Some of the finest Scots pines which remained were now being felled and woodcutters' huts had appeared on the north shore of the loch. The clouds were lifting as we reached Glenmore Lodge, and Cairngorm was now revealed. A few days before, a warm wind from the south-west had cleared the winter snowfall from the ridges of the hill, and these ridges had that morning been whitened by a thin coat of fresh snow, which had melted on the low ground as it fell. The defile of Lairig Ghru cut deep through the hill range, the dark rocks of Creag an Lethchoin above it contrasting with the snowy slopes of Ben MacDhui which rose beyond them. In the foreground the cone of Carn Elrick was snow-powdered. On the brow of Cairngorm rested the great snowfield, Cuithe Crom, the Bent or Crooked Wreath, which on summer days is seen from a great distance. Wind flurries swept across Loch Morlich; a goosander rose from his fishing and flew low over the loch; from the old pines crested tits scolded and chattered huskily. To the north-west the sky cleared and showed blue above the Monadh Liath. One's thoughts turned to the old name of the Cairngorm range, Am Monadh Ruadh (the Red Hill Range) as contrasted with Am Monadh Liath (the Grey Hill Range) which rise from the north side of the Spey valley.

I have mentioned that Cairngorm is climbed usually by the well-trodden right-of-way from Glenmore Lodge, yet there is a more interesting ascent from the neighbourhood of Revoan (Ruighe a' Bhothain, Shieling of the Bothy), some three miles along the old drove road beyond the lodge. Plantations of spruce and Douglas fir are now growing tall where the old Scots pines stood forty years ago, but these ancients still rise in stately grandeur on the slopes of Meall a' Bhuachaille, the Herdsman's Hill, so widely spaced that the heather grows long beneath them. The track passes beside Lochan Uaine, the Green Tarn, whose clear waters of pale greenish-blue lie in the cold shadow of Creag nan Gall. Old pines overshadow Lochan Uaine, and among them are juniper bushes which seem also of great age. Perched on one of these bushes a hedge accentor sang vigorously. The head and throat of this dunnock were pale grey—an unusual colour. The singer moved his head in an animated manner, and threw a high-pitched, thin song from wide-open beak to the keen, cold air. A short climb through long, wet heather where hailstones lay brought us to the ridge which was the beginning of four miles of wind-swept land leading to the summit of Cairngorm. We could see that in the Spey valley the sun shone, and lighted the snowy slopes of Ben Rinnes, but hail and snow squalls were forming over the Monadh Liath, and soon one of these squalls approached. When it had reached Loch Morlich it seemed to hang there without movement, as though to gather fresh energy for its assault on Cairngorm. It now approached the airy slope up which we toiled, and the hail in its breath poured aslant upon us and drifted smoke-like across the face of the hill. The squall passed, the view was restored, and for a time the sun shone from a blue sky. Two male ptarmigan in snowy winter plumage flew fast across the hill slopes. One was in strong pursuit of the other: a hen bird, the cause of the dispute, flew a short distance behind them. The ptarmigan rocked as they flew, moving at great speed at a little height above the drift that swept like the smoke of a fire across those exposed slopes. Dark chocolate-coloured clouds formed to windward, quickly increasing in size. Despite the strong wind they approached slowly, all the time becoming more formidable. The light faded and the mist descended on the hill-top which we were now nearing. We walked in a sombre, snow-swept country, a contrast to the Spey valley far below, where the sun still shone and the smoke of a heather fire drifted eastward on the wind. From this Arctic twilight on Cairngorm we saw, in the direction of the Moray Firth, the sky a delicate blue and partly overspread by the white, fleecy clouds of fair weather. Where we walked the wind was so strong that small pebbles were blown over the newly fallen snow which lay upon the old snow-fields, margined with solid ice where the recent thaw had begun to melt them. Now a north-west wind had replaced that softer wind current from the south-west and full winter had returned to Cairngorm. One walked over the snow to the accompaniment of a crunching noise; so hard was the snowy surface that one's footmarks scarcely showed in it. We entered the cloud, and saw small cairns rise from the snow—the guiding cairns to the hill-top. The mist thinned and now the large cairn marking the summit was seen ahead. We reached the cairn and sheltered in its lee; the cold was intense and one's jaws were stiffened so that speech was not easy. Suddenly the mist curtain was roughly torn aside by the gale, and before it was again drawn across the hill-top there was revealed a transient view of Beinn Mheadhon, the great rocks on its summit snow-encrusted, and beyond that hill the cold, dead-white upper slopes and plateaus of Beinn a' Bhuird and Ben A'an. During those fleeting moments a steel-blue sky showed at the zenith. More speedily than can be related, the mist-curtain once again hid the view, which had been phantom-like and grand in the extreme. The wind increased with the mist, and the snow drifted more densely. We descended, along the line of guiding cairns, and when we had reached the edge of the cloud saw that the view was very clear westward, where the sun shone on high hills more snowy than the Cairngorms: a golden light flooded those hills which rose near the birthplace of the Spey. That evening beside Loch Morlich the curlews were silent except for an occasional long-drawn melancholy whistle, low-toned and plaintive. The birds had not as yet tuned their full song, for spring is late in arriving at this country. Towards sunset the squalls of hail and snow became more dense and drew closer upon the Monadh Liath. Cuithe Crom, the snow bed on Cairngorm, reflected on its white expanse the pearl-grey of the sky, and in the waters of Loch Morlich the old pines were darkly reflected as the first star shone near the zenith and roding woodcock flitted across the forest clearings.

A summer climb on Cairngorm at the end of June gave strange varieties of weather. At midnight the low moon, rising golden behind the long ridge west of Cairngorm summit, gave the illusion of sunrise. When the sun did shine, the light was very clear, but before we had begun the climb dark thunder clouds had formed above the Monadh Liath, and it could be seen that torrential rain was falling on those hills. The curlew were now in full song, and oystercatchers piped shrilly beside Loch Morlich. The climb beneath the midsummer sun was more tiring than under the wintry conditions of March. The area had recently been acquired by the state as a National Park. Below Glenmore Lodge was a notice "CAMPING GROUND," and here were to be seen motor-cars parked, and a number of small tents. One party had erected a rain-proof passage between car and tent, a wise precaution under the prevailing unsettled weather conditions. Halfway up Cairngorm we were passed by a hiker who was travelling at speed. He said that he had left London the previous evening—he was certainly losing no time in getting on to the high grounds. We left the path at 3,500 feet and crossed the short alpine herbage to look down at the curious "pocket" of snow in Ciste Mhearad or Margaret's Chest. There are several legends concerning the Margaret who gave her name to the place; in one legend she is a woman who herded goats here in summer. It is curious that on the Glen Feshie ground, on the north-west slope of Carn Bàn Mór, there should be a corrie with a similar name and similar traditions. The Ciste Mhearad of Cairngorm is a rather deep hollow with steep sides, into which the snow drifts and is packed closely. The snow often remains here throughout the year, and by late summer has become stained by peat dust and almost as hard as ice. Here *Gnaphalium supinum* grows to the edge of the snow, but at the lowest level of the hollow there is no plant life, for the period of exposure to sun and air is too short to support it.

One of the highest wells on the Cairngorms is not far from this snow-holding "pocket." It is the Marquis's Well, and is said to have received its name from the Marquis of Argyll who was defeated at the battle of Glen Livet in or about the year 1594. There is an Argyll Stone on Sgoran Dubh. It is more likely that the well is named after the Marquess of Huntly, for at the time of the battle of Glen Livet Argyll was an Earl, not a Marquis. A short distance south-east of Cairngorm summit, and almost as high as the hill-top itself, is an out-crop of rock from which Loch A'an can be seen 1,500 feet below, the river A'an flowing from it. On this June day a dark thunder cloud was creeping up from the east and threatening to envelop the hill-top as we looked down upon the loch. On Ben MacDhui beyond it much snow still lay, gleaming above the bed of the Garbh Uisge which dropped in a white cascade into the head of Loch A'an. To the west-ward, we could see the figures of men standing on the summit of Braeriach. The cloud now pressed in over the plateau, and the hill-top where we stood began to steam. Behind us a small rainbow appeared, and the hill-top assumed a peculiar beauty during the few short minutes before the cloud finally covered it and hid the sun. There was an almost complete absence of bird life that day, but when the rain which later fell had turned to sleet and a lifting of the cloud westward showed that the storm was passing, we came upon a hen ptarmigan with a very young brood. She was near the Cuithe Crom, which was still an extensive snow-field and so hard that one could with difficulty walk across it by reason of the combination of hard snow and steepness of slope, and even Dugie the collie hesitated to run down it.

The most characteristic flower of the high Cairngorms is the cushion pink; the most characteristic insect is the black burnet moth, a sun-loving moth which feeds largely on the nectar of the small red *Silene acaulis* flowers. On this day of June the moths were unusually numerous from 3,000 to 4,000 feet above sea level; they rose ahead of us and flew easily and lightly on the wind, which was travelling at a slightly faster rate than we were walking. The flowers of the cushion pink are honey-scented and their scent is not unlike that of the ling. This plant has two environments which suit it—wind-swept ground near sea level and the high hills. On this day—June 22—it was in full blossom on the top of Cairngorm. On a knoll in northern Skye beside the waters of the Minch I had seen it the same season flowering in mid-May. On the high Cairngorms, where the ground has been covered with snow drifts that have been long in melting, I have on occasion seen the plant in full flower as late as August. In some places, as on the plateau of Braeriach, it is the only plant found in growth over considerable areas. It has a long and strong tap root which anchors the plant during the heaviest gales and ensures a supply of moisture in dry weather. Although the Cairngorms are often a country of rain and storm; of sleet, hail and even snow at mid-summer, there are seasons when the sun shines for days and even weeks at a time. There is no shade of any sort, and under the intense sunlight, accompanied often by a drying wind, the plants experience conditions of extreme drought, so that a strong root system is essential. The cushion pink has flowers usually of pink or red; they are sometimes pale pink, almost lilac, and sometimes a very lovely dark red. Occasionally a white-flowered specimen is found. On one occasion I sent its seeds to Kew Gardens, and the staff there raised a number of white-flowering plants from them. I used often to see a handsome cushion of the white-flowered variety at the head of a narrow, wind-swept pass, but it has now died: it would be interesting to know the average life of a "cushion" of *Silene acaulis* in its natural environment. Abroad I have seen it in all its beauty on the lower ground of Iceland at the end of June, and also, but more sparingly, on the tundra of Spitsbergen, where its place is largely taken by *Saxifraga oppositifolia*, the purple mountain saxifrage, a plant that is rare on the Cairngorms since it is not at home on a granite formation: to see this plant at its best one must climb to the high corries of the Cuillin of Skye, notably to Coire Ghrunnda, where in April the ground is purple with its flowers.

CHAPTER II

THE WESTERN CAIRNGORMS

LAIRIG Ghru divides the Cairngorms. The chief hills rising to the west of that pass are Braeriach (4,248 feet), Cairntoul (4,241 feet) and, of hills between 3,500 feet and 3,900 feet, Sgùrran Dubh, in English the Black Rocks (sometimes named Sgoran Dubh), Monadh Mór, and Beinn Bhrodain. If you accept the legend of the naming of Loch Bhrodainn in Gaick Forest, you will probably agree that Beinn Bhrodain is named after the same supernatural hound.

Of the western Cairngorms Braeriach is greatest in extent, as it is in wildness: it may even be said to be a hill range. There are not many places on Deeside from which Braeriach can be seen, but its summit and north-facing corries show up well from Strathspey. These north corries are, from east to west, Coire Beanaidh, Coire Ruadh and Coire an Lochain. Coire an Lochain, as its name (Corrie of the Lochan) implies, holds in its hollow a tarn or lakelet Arctic in character. It is almost always frozen across, with thick, firm ice, until May, sometimes until June. I have seen ice-floes upon its cold waters in early July. It was on Braeriach that I saw the total eclipse of the sun, on June 29, 1927. My wife and I climbed from the lower bothy in Glen Eanaich (both the lower bothy and the upper bothy have now disappeared, almost without trace) by way of the north-west slope of Braeriach, skirting the high rocks of Loch Coire an Lochain. The morning was fine, and the sky partly clear of cloud, when we left Aviemore at 3 a.m. A thrush and a reed bunting were already in song, and the air was fresh and calm after heavy rain in the night. On the shoulder of Braeriach before the eclipse the air temperature was 38 degrees Fahrenheit. During the eclipse it fell to 33 degrees; in a few minutes at the passing of the shadow it rose to 35 degrees. At the onset of the eclipse the sunlight gradually became dim, and a chill air blew across the hill. The sun became sickle-shaped and the light, the strong light of midsummer of the high hills, was replaced by twilight. At the moment of totality the sky resembled that of a winter's night beneath a full moon: the margins of the clouds might have been moon-kissed and the heavens were strange and mysterious. As the sun reappeared the light quickly strengthened. Life returned to the earth. Ptarmigan bestirred themselves. That season was cold and late. At the end of June ptarmigan had not begun to sit. Nowhere was the cushion pink in flower, and the creeping azalea, which is sometimes in flower before May is over, was now only in bud.

On Braeriach is a considerable plateau, perhaps the most truly Arctic of any in Scotland. From the west top to the main summit is a distance of a mile and a half, and the average altitude over this distance is just over 4,000 feet. Character is lent to the plateau by the Wells of Dee, a number of strong ice-cold springs. The young river they give birth to meanders slowly eastward over the plateau, a shallow, slow-flowing and crystal-clear stream, before quickening its pace and falling in a number of cascades (which are often hidden beneath the snow until midsummer) to the depths of the Garbh Choire, 1,000 feet below. If the climber arrives at the Braeriach plateau from the west and follows the Dee until it falls to the corrie beneath, he has then to ascend a gentle slope to the hill-top, which is marked by a cairn. To give an instance of the weather conditions which may prevail here in spring, when a friend and I crossed Braeriach on the third day of April, 1925, we searched in vain for the summit cairn, although we knew its location and the weather was clear. It was buried beneath the snow-cap, and for the time being had literally disappeared without a trace. There must then have been an average depth of at least 8 feet of snow on the hill-top, and the snow was frozen so hard that one walked upon it as upon firm ground, one's footsteps scarcely making an impression on these snowy lands, brilliantly white beneath the April sun.

The corries on the north slopes of Braeriach are impressive although in grandeur they are inferior to those on the south side of the hill. Here is that magnificent corrie known as the Garbh Choire (in its anglicised form Garrachory), the Rough Corrie, forming the abyss separating Braeriach from Cairntoul. Immediately beneath the summit of Braeriach is Coire Bhrochain, which may mean either Corrie of Gruel, or Corrie of Porridge (*brochan* is usually gruel, but in some districts it means porridge, according to Professor Watson). It is a corrie of grandeur, and is paved with blocks of granite stone which have fallen from the hill-top in a past age when some upheaval shook the mountain. In a previous book I have mentioned the curious tradition of the naming of the corrie, as told to me forty years ago by old Donald Fraser, deer stalker at the Derry, but the story will bear retelling. Donald said that long ago certain cattle, perhaps from the summer shielings in Glen Eanaich, perhaps beasts which had strayed from the drovers on their way through Lairig Ghru when being driven to the Falkirk tryst, had fallen over the precipice from the hill-top to the depths of the corrie beneath, and by their impact with the rocks had been crushed into gruel or porridge. For many years I looked upon his derivation of the place-name as interesting but fanci-ful—indeed until one summer morning in or about the year 1927 when a companion and I were in the corrie searching for the nest of the elusive snow bunting. We then saw, lying on rough, stony ground, what appeared to be parts of the skeletons of two deer. Being familiar with the tradition, my companion sent one of the jaw-bones to an expert for identification. The reply came that it was the jaw-bone of an ox, thus corroborating in a remarkable manner the legend of the naming of the corrie. An additional point of interest was that it would have been impossible for cattle to have walked to the place where the bones were lying, and the beasts must therefore have fallen over the precipice, where their bones for half the year are protected from weathering by a covering of snow.

I have looked down into Coire Bhrochain at most seasons of the year, but the most impressive occasion was when Bob MacBain of Achnahatanich and I stood here on May 29 in the year 1923. The month of May that year had been remarkable; it had brought one snowstorm after another on a wind that blew day after day from the north and north-east, bringing the breath of Polar lands to the Cairn-gorms and even to the glens that lie beneath them. We had climbed from Rothiemurchus to discover how the ptarmigan, which that spring were very numerous, had been affected by the unusual con-ditions. Even the grouse that year had been compelled to lay their eggs on the snow, for their nests had been drifted up, and on this particular morning, within a month of the longest day, an average depth of three feet of snow covered the ground from an elevation of 2,200 feet onwards. We found the ptarmigan population in a state of unrest, for the snow had obliterated the nesting territories of the various cocks, and fights and pursuits were frequent. Even when we had entered the cloud cap the glare from the unbroken snow was trying to the eyes; had the day been sunny we should never have been able to reach the hill-top without suffering from snow-blindness.

We reached the summit of Braeriach in early afternoon, during a brief lifting of the cloud. The scene here was remarkable and probably unprecedented in living memory. Beyond the hill-top a snow cornice projected into space over the precipice a distance of some 30 feet; it was level with the plateau, and in thick mist the climber might have walked unsuspectingly upon it. Coire Bhrochain was white, and even its boulders, rocks and stones were hidden below the snow; indeed the whole world in our view was white. A snow tunnel hid the river Dee where it flowed eastward through the Garbh Choire; nowhere in its course through the corrie, or where it fell from Braeriach, were its waters to be seen. Lochan Uaine of Cairntoul was invisible. Indeed a stranger looking upon it for the first time would have found it hard to believe that a loch was buried here beneath many feet, perhaps many yards, of snow. Across Lairig Ghru Ben MacDhui seemed weighted down by its great snow mantle; since the snow blizzards had come from the north-east there had been an even heavier snowfall on that hill than on the western Cairngorms. Where, here and there, the summit of Braeriach had been drifted bare of snow by the strength of the wind, the rocks were covered with feathery ice-crystals. They grew to windward on the stones, showing delicate and varied patterns. Ptarmigan that year did not hatch their eggs until mid-July, but strong broods even at that late date resulted.

The most westerly corrie of Braeriach is named on the Ordnance Survey maps An Garbh Choire Mór, the Great Rough Corrie. It is a high, cold corrie, scarcely touched by the sun even at mid-summer, and here lies one of the very few so-called perpetual snow-beds in the Highlands. The question, "Are there perpetual snow-fields on any hill in Great Britain?" is from time to time asked. My reply would be that there are at least two snow beds which lie unmelted almost always throughout the year and melt perhaps once in thirty years, when a snowless winter is followed by a warm, and I would add rainy, summer and autumn. The year 1945 saw these exceptional conditions. The first part of October brought record temperatures, and the last fort-night of the month mild and heavy rains, which have a disintegrating effect on old, hard snow. What was more remarkable, the autumn snowfalls, which normally arrive by mid-October and cover the old snow, delayed their coming until late in November. On November 20 a friend and I set out from Aviemore at five o'clock on a moonlit morning on the long walk by way of Lairig Ghru to An Garbh Choire Mór and back, a distance of perhaps 30 miles, in order to see whether the snow had melted from the corrie. The snow lies immediately beneath the cliff; it faces north-east and in late summer and autumn the sun does not reach it. West and south-west from the cliff-top, unsheltered, wind-swept country extends, and during westerly and south-westerly gales (winds from this quarter usually bring rain to the lower slopes but at 3,500 feet above sea level the rain falls often as dry, powdery snow) the snow is drifted for long distances until, sweeping over the top of the cliff, it comes to rest at the foot. The gale may roar through the rocks above, yet there is almost always a profound calm where the snow lies; this is an important factor in the duration of the snow-bed, for it is shielded from the mild winds of summer, which would disintegrate it, as witness the great snow-field north-east of the summit cairn of Ben MacDhui, which frequently disappears although in early summer it may be of great depth and very great size.

The Braeriach snow-field as the summer wears on breaks up into three smaller snow beds, each snow-field then lying in a gravelly depression, which is not seen at the beginning of summer when the field of white is extensive and entire. I have visited the snowy corrie on many occasions, before the arrival of the new snow, and have never seen it without snow, although it was said that in the autumn of the year 1936 the snow-beds did indeed melt. As, two hours before dawn, we walked through the Forest of Rothiemurchus high clouds, scarcely moving, were silver-edged in the light of the full moon. Among the green, feathery pines here and there birches rose, gaunt and leafless. The moon was hidden from the forest by a cloud layer, but the high northern corries of Braeriach, on which the first winter snows had fallen, were flooded in bright moonlight and seemed apart from the earth and belonging to a brighter and more glorious world. Low in the eastern sky shone a planet; below us, a thin frosty haze rested above the Spey valley. No owls called in the forest; the only sound was the murmur from Allt Dhru as its limpid waters flowed towards mother Spey. Cloud descended on the radiant corries of Braeriach, and Stygian darkness and cloud filled the mouth of Lairig Ghru.

As the forest track ascended, the old pines, now wider spaced, seemed less gloomy and the pale light of dawn in the east imperceptibly replaced the moonlight of the night hours. At the edge of the forest at five minutes to seven a grouse crowed; fifteen minutes later a second cock grouse saluted the approaching day. Shadowy forms of stags crossed the path ahead of us, or stood on the heathery hillside, and the dawn silence was shattered as a hoarse challenge was thrown out by a stag and answered by another at a distance. Gradually came full winter daylight and the cloud that wrapped close the heights of Sron na Lairig stirred uneasily. Where Allt Dhru broadened to a miniature tarn a dipper was standing on a stone beside the water, preening her white breast on her mountain perch 2,200 feet above the level of the sea. We approached, very slowly it seemed, the mouth of Lairig Ghru, and now entered the country of the mist. Through the funnel of the pass drifted a breeze from the south-east, damp and chill. Against the snowless ground ptarmigan in their white winter plumage were conspicuous when they rose and flew up the pass.

The weather for long had been rainless, and the Pools of Dee were at their lowest ebb. Near them a young stag stood, guarding zealously his two wives. We could see that the mist was low in Glen Dee ahead of us. Cairntoul was hidden almost to the base, and cloud lay close upon the ridge of Carn a' Mhaim and upon the rounded cone of the Devil's Point. We left Lairig Ghru and, striking westward, entered the Garbh Choire by a deers' track. A single flower of bell heather held its pink head to the sombre light of a late November day. Through thick mist we climbed, and at last reached the head of the corrie and struck up a steep slope where, invisible in cloud, the "pockets" which hold the snow seemed to mock us to discover them. Discovery indeed would have been difficult unless one had been very familiar with the ground, but at length, as we moved through a mysterious world, where visibility was reduced to a few yards, we found ourselves standing beside the first "pocket," and for the first time in my life I saw it empty of snow. The snow bed on Ben Nevis had that autumn melted for the first time in living memory, and I now thought that the Braeriach snow had also gone, for the lowest part of the second "pocket" is invisible from the first by reason of an intervening ridge. When we reached that second "pocket" we found that the snow of Braeriach was undefeated—a small snow-bed, iron-hard, lay here. Its length, carefully measured, was $17\frac{1}{2}$ feet; its width 12 feet, and its depth approximately 30 inches. The altitude of the snow-bed is 3,650 feet above the sea; we had reached the snow line at 3,400 feet and rather more than an inch of fresh snow covered the stones and rocks, and lay upon the surface of the small snow-bed, the only old snow anywhere in the Scottish Highland on that twentieth day of November in the year 1945. The thunder of a small avalanche broke the silence and stillness, and rocks, snow and ice fell from the invisible hill-top alarmingly near us; the noise of their fall was heard when the avalanche was as yet invisible in the cloud. It is not easy to avoid a falling rock when it hurtles unseen from the mist cap which covers its place of origin. The thick mist rendered the scene mysterious, so that familiar landmarks were unreal—even the new snow was grey and unlike itself. At a little distance below the snow-bed a musical chirping drew near and a snow bunting appeared on the wing; a little later we saw its mate perched on a boulder. Here it was surprising to see fronds of the delicate parsley fern still green on stony ground and the flowering spray of a hill grass green and vigorous.

It was noon when we were at the snow "pocket," yet the light was scarcely stronger than at sunrise. One could picture the conditions here in the darkness of a winter night when a snow-bearing gale from the west hurries the snow over that high and shelterless land from Glen Feshie across the long miles of Moine Mhór and pours it, without ceasing, over the rocks of Garbh Choire Mór, and an ever thickening white blanket covers the grass, the rocks, the boulders, so that when lagging daylight arrives the world here is of unrelieved white.

A long walk of fifteen miles lay before us. We reached the edge of the mist, and remarked on the verdure of the lower reaches of the Garbh Choire. Here is no autumnal decay and shedding of leaves as in the wooded glens, for juniper and heather are hardy and xerophytic, and in full life await the snowy covering that will protect them through the months of frost. Yet prolonged frost unaccompanied by snow will kill juniper, turning its green needles to a rich red-brown. The late winter and early spring of 1947 were fatal to much of the hill juniper, both in Scotland and in Norway. A stag had been rolling in the moss beside the burn flowing through the corrie, to cool himself after the rut. Among the green sphagnum plants one saw some of a rich brown that was almost red. Is this reddish tone assumed as a protection against frost, just as the leaves of the blaeberry sometimes become reddish after strong, cold winds in summer at high altitudes, or is the red sphagnum a distinct species? We found the lower Garbh Choire mist-free, but as we approached the watershed of Lairig Ghru we once more entered the cloud. Here we were cheered by a small flock of snow buntings. The birds rose in the twilight one after another: as they spread their small, white wings they gave movement and beauty to a scene austere and dark.

When we had crossed the watershed we entered a different country. The mist thinned, and the setting sun shone red on the rocky slope of Creag an Lethchoin ahead of us. At sunrise the sky above Sron na Lairig had been aquamarine, and rose-tinted with small cirrus clouds: it was now, at sunset, pale blue. Brief glimpses were had of high rocks and buttresses which, as at sunrise, had attracted the clouds. Before we had reached the first pines we looked back and saw that Braeriach was free of cloud to the summit: the mist of drifting snow, dry and powdery, softened the sharp outlines of the ridges. In Rothiemurchus the air was still and the full moon, which had travelled far since, at dawn, we had lost its light, now rose in the east and touched the clouds with glory.

The neighbourhood of the Garbh Choire snow-beds is interesting country for the botanist. He will not find rare plants here, but he will have an object lesson in the effect prolonged burial below the snow has on plant life. He approaches, let us suppose, the snow-bed in July, before it has broken and while it is still extensive, white and gleaming. He will find that no heather is growing near that great snow-field, for heather needs a long summer exposure to air and sun in order to complete its life cycle. Various hill grasses need a shorter snow-free period, and these he will find in abundance, to the edge of the retreating snow. He will see, too, how quickly they grow once the snowy covering frees them and they feel the warmth of the summer air. Let him return in October, when the snow is at its lowest ebb. He will find then the plants which survive a snowfall of approximately ten months in the year. He will see, growing almost to the edge of the snow, *Gnaphalium supinum* and, even nearer the snow-pockets, isolated leaf rosettes of *Saxifraga stellaris*. At their nearest approach to the snow, neither of these species has time to form seeds, or even flowers, yet both are healthy. To the edges of the snow mosses extend. These evidently do not require to see the light each year in order to live. They may be buried for several years, perhaps half a dozen, perhaps even longer, yet when the snow melts from them they then make the best of two or three weeks of freedom, not in summer, mark you, but in autumn when the air at 3,600 feet is cold and when most of the alpine plants at that elevation are already preparing to die down for the winter.

144

CHAPTER III

ROTHIEMURCHUS AND BRAERIACH

I HAVE mentioned that heather does not approach the Garbh Choire snow-beds. Lower down in the corrie it grows well, and here I once found a ptarmigan sitting on her eggs in quite long heather. This was unusual, for ptarmigan nest normally above the heather line, or at all events where the heathy covering is short and wind-swept. The stock of these attractive and beautiful birds reached a very low ebb during the years of the second world war and those immediately following it. In 1946 I walked for a whole day on the Cairngorms without seeing a single ptarmigan, and two other walkers had a similar experience that autumn. A decrease in grouse stock is usually accompanied by a decrease in ptarmigan stock, and never in living memory were grouse stocks so low as in the years around 1945.

In peace-time, grouse disease attracts considerable attention: in war-time, it passes unheeded and even unobserved. I believe ptarmigan to be subject to grouse disease, or at all events to a disease closely akin to it: they sometimes decrease in number in a short time in a remarkable way. During the war years the Cairngorms were invaded by British and allied forces. There were tales of ptarmigan being shot on the nest, and even if those tales were exaggerated there is little doubt that the birds supplemented the war rations of the troops during that period. The crack of rifles and the rattle of machine gun fire must often have alarmed them. Their enemy the fox greatly increased, and during the war years on ptarmigan ground I saw, on a number of occasions, the marks of a fox's "kill"—a fox's killing is quite different from an eagle's killing, and the "kills" of wild cats on the Cairngorms are few. At the close of the second war there were not above ten per cent. of the average number of ptarmigan on the Cairngorms. The years 1947 and 1948 saw an increase, despite a cold and wet nesting season in June and the first half of July of 1948.

When I was on the Cairngorms at the end of June in 1948 I had remarkable evidence of the swimming powers of ptarmigan. I was sheltering from a heavy rain squall on the screes near Lochan Uaine, Jack Harrison, the bird artist, being with me. A ptarmigan and her

145   K

In the Cairngorms

young, the chicks being rather more than a fortnight old, rose and flew, or attempted to fly, across an arm of the loch. Young ptarmigan are strong on the wing at a very early stage (they are more precocious than young grouse), but a squall struck the brood and some of them fell into the water at a considerable distance from land. We then saw a remarkable sight. Far from being dismayed, the young ptarmigan swam fast and confidently shoreward, looking like young duck. They reached the shore in a very short time, scrambled over the rocks, and disappeared, as if swimming was an every-day affair. One might have thought that the birds, finding themselves in the water for the first time, would have been bewildered, but these young ptarmigan without a moment's hesitation struck out for the shore.

Ptarmigan are often photographed in summer plumage, but I have never seen a really good photograph of this bird in winter, when its plumage is white as the surrounding snows, nor would such a photograph be easy to obtain, unless in a mild winter when the birds are white against a dark background. They are then at a disadvantage, for they are most conspicuous, and are seen by the eagle at a great distance. On the first appearance of an eagle they fly to any snow-field which happens to be near, and crouch on it until danger is past. A fox, too, must locate a ptarmigan more easily under snowless conditions.

Ptarmigan are the only birds of the Scottish hills which remain, summer and winter, on the high tops and in the high corries. There is a slight variation in their habitat in winter, for those individuals which in summer have their haunts on the high plateaus at 4,000 feet descend perhaps five hundred feet at midwinter when the snow covers the plateaus, sealing off their food supply. The lowest nesting level of the species on the Cairngorms is 2,500 feet and the highest 4,000 feet. Personally I have never found a ptarmigan's nest above 3,900 feet, although I have seen dotterel nesting higher than this. The nesting season is regular unless, as in 1923, the birds are upset by abnormal snowfalls. The first eggs are laid around May 20 and the full clutch of six to seven eggs is incubated around May 27. During the week when the eggs are being laid the hen ptarmigan covers her nest, but is not found near it. She sits closely from the start. The closest sitter among ptarmigan of my experience was a bird which allowed me to lift her in one hand. While I held her, free to fly if she wished to do so, in my outstretched hand she remained quietly, and when I set her on her eggs again she at once brooded them, nor could she be induced to move. The male ptarmigan is usually on guard near the sitting hen, and he rises into the air on the approach of danger, uttering his snorting croak that is unique among bird calls. The only time that a cock gave me the clue to the whereabouts of the nest was at the first ptarmigan's nest I ever found. On flying away, this bird crossed a little depression and for a moment alighted on its farther side. When I went to this place, a hen ptarmigan rose from her eggs where he had alighted. The eggs of the ptarmigan resemble those of the red grouse, but are some-times rather smaller, and more brightly coloured. They take four days longer to hatch than the eggs of a grouse. When the ptarmigan brood leave the nest, which they do a very few hours after hatching, the male ptarmigan usually leaves his mate to rear the family unaided. The cocks then flock, and lead a bachelor existence, being often seen on the high plateau of Braeriach during July. I do not say that *all* ptarmigan leave their wives, but the majority of them do. The hen ptarmigan is a devoted mother, and a trick that anyone can play on her is to whistle in a high-pitched key, when by her behaviour she shows she has a brood near. She is taken in by that whistle almost always, and will run up to you, trailing her wings on the ground, and will continue to run around you until she begins to have suspicions that she is being hoaxed. Even if you do not practise that deception on her she will do her best to lead you away from where the young are crouching, invisible or almost so, on the ground. She stumbles and falls, and spreads her white wings as though gravely injured, and if you quicken your pace, or run after her, she reacts still more violently, for it is her hope, by her play acting, to lead you as far as possible from her brood. When she thinks she has decoyed you a sufficient distance from her young her behaviour abruptly changes. No longer is she the wounded bird, but she now rises on her white wings (a ptarmigan's wings remain white throughout the year) and flies over your head to where her brood await her. This play-acting is practised chiefly for the benefit of the fox, and I have wondered whether a fox is taken in by such tactics. I have mentioned that ptarmigan are able to fly at an early stage. I have seen a brood of young ptarmigan, scarcely bigger than larks, rise from the rocks at the edge of the Braeriach plateau and fly over the precipice. Their wing power presumably is sufficient to land them somewhere, but they scatter so widely that it must be a difficult matter for the mother bird to get them together again, although presumably they are able to hear her call from a considerable distance.

Ptarmigan and golden eagle do not often nest near each other, for the eagle's nesting haunts are at lower levels than those of the ptarmigan. Yet on one occasion I found a ptarmigan's nest within a couple of hundred yards of an eagle's eyrie. This ptarmigan's nest was under a rock, and I have never, before nor since, seen a ptarmigan nest under shelter. That nest was so carefully shielded by the rock that it was invisible from above. I do not think the eagle's nesting had caused the ptarmigan to seek shelter, but common gulls were often on the ground, and there is no worse egg thief. It is not generally known that common gulls on occasion nest on the shores or islets of a lochan in ptarmigan country, where, during their nesting season, I have seen many sucked eggs of ptarmigan in the shallow water. I have no doubt the gulls carried the eggs from the nests of their owners, and sucked them where they could wash them down with a drink. The grey crow also takes his eggs to water to eat them. This ptarmigan nesting under a rock was one of the few which hatched off their eggs that season. A wire fence, bounding high sheep ground, was apparently fatal to one ptarmigan, for I found her, warm and headless, beside the fence although I did not actually see the accident happen. That reminds me of the incident I witnessed many years ago. A covey of partridges were flying down wind at high speed. Just as they reached me, one of the birds struck a telegraph wire. The bird fell like a stone, and a second after it had touched the ground a small object fell—its head, which had been cut clean off by the wire.

In the late Duke of Fife's day stags used to be driven out of the Garbh Choire and shot by the rifles as the animals breathlessly emerged on the Braeriach plateau, but normally stags do not frequent ground so high. In summer in fine sunny weather hinds often feed right up to the Wells of Dee, and on one occasion I came on a "form" of a mountain hare containing leverets a short distance above the Wells, in a tussock of wiry grass—a truly high-born family. I have often wondered whether deer calves may not on occasion be born on the Braeriach plateau. I came upon a newly born calf one morning in June at a height of 3,600 feet on the west face of Braeriach. It had not yet stood on its legs, and at first was in great fear of me, and stretched its head on the ground, laying back its ears and half-closing its eyes. After a time its confidence returned; it raised its head and cocked its ears, finally rising unsteadily to its feet. Like the deer calf I recorded as lying down beside me in the Forest of Gaick, it wished to accompany me when I left the place and I was able to elude it only by running ahead of it and hiding behind a rock. When the little fawn reached where it thought I should be, it looked hopefully around for a time, then, feeling weary, lay down, and I was able to leave my hiding-place without being seen. If a deer fawn follows you too far there is a danger that its mother may not find it again.

West of Braeriach is a great tableland, most of it 3,000 feet and more above the level of the sea. Its name is A'Mhointeach Mhór, the Great Moss, and in summer it is the feeding ground of many of the red deer from the forests of Glen Feshie and Mar. The deer are wary here, and take alarm easily, yet when a thunderstorm of great violence developed over the Cairngorms on the eighth day of July in the year 1923—the date is worth recording because of the vehemence of that storm—those deer continued to feed apparently heedless of the blinding flashes of lightning and the deafening reverberations of the thunder, even when a particularly violent thunder-clap caused the ptarmigan to rise in alarm from the ground. I have often sat on the west face of Braeriach on a fine July day and watched the big herds of stags, consisting of hundreds of animals, feeding on the Great Moss several miles away, the magnification of a stalking telescope bringing the animals near. The horns are then in velvet, and the stags seem to be magnificently antlered. I have seen the deer lie down on the wet peat, ceaselessly moving their long ears as the cleg or biting horsefly attacked them. The cleg never comes so high as the plateau of Braeriach; the highest I have seen a specimen is 3,750 feet, and it probably accompanied deer which had moved up to that elevation, and which made off downhill at my approach. That view westward from Braeriach with A'Mhointeach Mhór and its deer herds in the foreground is one of exceptional charm. Distant hills rise on the western horizon. The snow-fields on Ben Nevis gleam on the blue horizon; Ben Lawers, also with its snow in July, is prominent, and on very clear days I have seen Cruachan above salt Loch Etive, home of Deirdre and Naoise. South-west in very clear weather I have seen Ben More and Stob Inneoin above Crianlarich, and Ben Vorlich above Loch Earn. Rather north of west are the Sisters of Kintail.

On the west face of Braeriach is a corrie with a curious name. It is an English name, Horseman's Corrie, and is said to have been given it because a certain Mr. Horseman, who was tenant of Glen Feshie Forest after the Duchess of Bedford, used to frequent it when stalking. Near the head of this high corrie a large snow-field is usually found at midsummer, and the hinds, but not the stags, spend much of their time here, luxuriating in the coldness of the snow when the sun shines with great power and the hill air is so heated that the breeze is perfumed by the aromatic crowberry plants. The honey scent of the flowers of the lowly cushion pink does not permeate the air; you must kneel down in order to smell the fragrance of this lowly plant.

I have said that common gulls sometimes nest high and steal the eggs of ptarmigan. I have not often seen them on the Big Moss, but in fine summer weather, especially in times of drought, the table land is visited by large flocks of black-headed gulls which fly up from Strathspey and hunt the ground with great thoroughness, usually on the wing but sometimes on foot. They are, I think, feeding on crane flies, which are always abundant here in fine weather, sometimes being seen in their hundreds of thousands. Do they hatch here, or do they, like the gulls, fly up from the glens and valleys? The gulls continue to feed here until near sunset, then rise on white wings and fly towards the north-west. A quarter of an hour's flight and less would see them once more over the Spey valley, and I have sometimes envied them their wing power when a long walk has lain between me and my base.

I have mentioned the small scented flowers of *Silene acaulis*. There is another flower of the Cairngorms resembling it in that it is small and lowly, with pink or rosy china-like flowers. This is the creeping azalea—*Azalea procumbens*—and it is found usually on the ridges on gravelly soil. It does not, like *Silene acaulis*, extend to the high plateaus, and I do not remember having found it higher than 3,500 feet. The leaves of *Silene acaulis* are grown afresh each summer; those of *Azalea procumbens* are perennial, and are strongly xerophytic. The buds open rather slowly, and when in the bud stage the flowers are of an unusual beauty, being a deep, rich red. The scent of the flowers is not so pronounced as in those of *Silene acaulis* and they do not attract to the same extent the black burnet moth which sips the honey from the cushion pink.

In the deep hollow between Braeriach and Sgoran Dubh lies Loch Eanaich, a loch over a mile in length, and 1,650 feet above sea level. At the head of the loch is the site of the old summer shielings of the people of Rothiemurchus. There are trout and char in Loch Eanaich. On the hill face on either side of the loch are two rocks shaped like pillars: they go by the names Am Bodach—the Old Man—and A' Chailleach—the Old Woman. West of Sgoran Dubh is Carn Bàn Mór, which slopes away toward Glen Feshie. South-east of Loch Eanaich are the two outlying hills of the Cairngorms, Monadh Mór (3,650 feet) and Beinn Bhrodain (3,797 feet). Since they are off the track of mountaineers, these two hills are perhaps less frequented than any others of the Cairngorm range. Seen from the west, they are not impressive, but both have wild and impressive corries on their eastern sides, that of Monadh Mór holding snow sometimes throughout the year and always until after midsummer.

Near Monadh Mór is the small loch named on some maps Lochan Suarach, the Insignificant Loch, on others Loch an Stuirteag, Loch of the Black-headed Gull. It is unlikely that the original form of the name will now be known; it has been obscure too long. As showing how a "ghost name" may become fixed, let me mention the alternative name for Sgor an Lochan Uaine, a spur of Braeriach. Forty years ago I used to be told, no doubt correctly, by the old Mar stalkers that Alexander Copeland, a keen mountaineer who sketched and published, if I remember rightly, the first panorama outline of the Cairngorm Range, had named it the Angel's Peak, in order, as he told my informants, to "keep the Devil's Point in its place." Twenty-five years later George MacPherson-Grant of the Ballindalloch family, who own Glen Feshie, told me that he used to hear the Glen Feshie stalkers refer to the hill as Sgor an Aingeil, the Gaelic translation of the Angel's Peak, and he was greatly surprised to hear my account of the naming of the hill. Whatever its origin, the name Angel's Peak is now firmly established. There are innumerable Gaelic place-names which have now English equivalents, but this must be one of the very few English names to become Gaelicised.

The Grants of Rothiemurchus have owned their lands, which extend to the summit of Braeriach, from the sixteenth century; before that time the Shaws possessed the district. It is on record that the last of the Shaws was outlawed for the murder of his step-father about the year 1570, and the chief of Clan Grant then purchased the estate, or rather the right to hold it if he could, and gave it to his second son, Patrick, whose direct descendants are the Grants of Rothiemurchus. The castle of Loch an Eilein, on which the osprey used to nest, was a ruin even when the Grants succeeded the Shaws, but was repaired and fortified by Patrick Grant, since he apprehended that the Shaws would not submit to his ownership of their country.

About fifty years before the Shaws were ousted by the Grants, Lachlan Macintosh of Dunachton, chief of the clan, had been murdered in the castle by a near kinsman. One account states that three men were responsible for the chief's murder; the murderers were tried and found guilty: one of them, the instigator, was sentenced to be beheaded and quartered, and the other two were punished with almost equal severity, their sentence being that they should be hanged and their heads fixed on poles at the scene of the crime. It must have been long after this that the ospreys first colonised the tower but, so far as I know, there is no record of their first appearance.

On the south side of the Cairngorms the original landowning family were the Earls of Mar, whose title is one of the most ancient in Scotland, their ancestor on whom it was conferred being a natural grandson of the Scottish king. His father was the Wolf of Badenoch; his mother Mairead, daughter of Eachann. Later, the Farquharsons played a leading part in the affairs of the district. Balmoral, of which one of the earliest spellings is Bouchmorale (1451), was Farquharson property when it was bought by Queen Victoria. Before the Earl of Fife acquired Mar Lodge the MacKenzies of Dalmore owned that property. One of the Dalmore MacKenzies had wrested some of their loot from the Lochaber raiders, on their return westward after despoiling the low country. This treasure he hid first in the remote Garbh Choire, and subsequently beneath the old pine which still lives and is named Craobh an Oir, the Tree of Gold, spreading its green branches on the slopes of Carn Crom not far from the waters of the Luibeg burn. Tradition says that he moved his treasure a second time, and buried it on Carn Geldie, where it now awaits discovery.

Throughout the Highlands, there is scarcely a glen, now deserted, that does not show traces of former human habitations. The glens of the Cairngorms do not show this depopulation so markedly as some western districts, but even here old ruins tell of human rural life in former days. Much has been written of repopulating the Highlands. The idea is an admirable one, yet those who are enthusiastic about it do not sometimes realise the difficulties in the way. It is true that evictions of the people, to make place for sheep and deer, were sometimes carried out in the most heartless manner, and had it not been for these evictions many a Highland glen would have a greater population at the present day than it actually has. But few people among the descendants of those who were evicted, could they be sought out throughout the world, would now come back to their ancestral glen. In the days of the evictions the standard of life was lower than at the present time: men and women worked harder than they would work today, and the fruits of their unremitting labours were meagre.

Throughout a large part of the Highland area there are still evidences that the people in former times were accustomed to live during the summer months on the higher lands, taking with them their stock, in order that their home pastures might have a period of rest. The grass-grown ruins of the small dwellings of the people— summer shielings they are called—are in many parts of the Highlands visible to this day. They are built, often in a cluster, beside a stream, in order that a supply of water might be handy, and although many of them have not been inhabited for more than a hundred years they are still unmistakable, and, covered as they are with grass and protected from the weather, may remain with little change for centuries longer. There is curiously little evidence of summer shielings in the Forest of Mar, nor have I heard traditions of this custom there. We know that the people of Rothiemurchus used to summer at the head of Loch Eanaich, yet there is no tradition that the people of Mar went to the high glens of the Cairngorms. There are, it is true, small ruinous buildings here and there in those glens, but if their history be investigated, it is found that they are bothies used by shepherds or deer watchers. I have never in Mar come across clusters of grass-grown shielings such as I have seen in the high glens of the west, and in the Isle of Skye. Neither have I seen remains of shielings in the glens of the eastern Cairngorms, where there are likely places for them. The lower glens of the Cairngorm country were less densely populated than the glens of the west, and there may not have been the same necessity to conserve the pasture. The custom of going to the summer shielings was a picturesque and romantic one, but it had a sound, practical basis, since, unless the pastures of the lower lands were left ungrazed for a period in summer, there would not be sufficient food for the cattle in winter.

What is the future of the Cairngorm area? It is, and has long been, one of the main Highland haunts of the red deer, but there would appear, in these days following the second world war, to be little likelihood of deer forests becoming popular once again. Certain of the hills are suitable for sheep, and some of them are indeed once more under sheep, after many years. The general feeling is that the whole of the Cairngorms will in time become a great National Park, for, as I have already mentioned, a part of that area is already a National Park. If the whole area were to be acquired by the state, what would be the effect on the wild life of the Cairngorms? Would the rare birds, eagle, dotterel, snow bunting, greenshank, crested tit, receive adequate protection? Many more people would then wander over the hills and through the glens than roam here at present, and protection of the nests of the birds would be by no means easy. This is a matter which should be kept in mind if a great National Park should be created here. It would entail the employment of a considerable number of watchers, good naturalists, on the ground. It would be necessary to build bothies in order that these watchers might live for some months each year actually on the ground where the rare birds nest, in order to have them under constant observation. Unless care is taken and adequate funds for the purpose are allotted, eagle, dotterel and snow bunting may soon share the fate of the Loch an Eilein ospreys, and live only in tradition—a tradition that, where these banished species are concerned, is each year becoming more nebulous.

Chapter IV.

WINTER EXPERIENCES

In the last two chapters I mentioned the Lairig Ghru pass which traverses the Cairngorms. I have crossed the pass during most months of the year. On one occasion, a great many years ago, my friend Dick Crewe and I, accompanied as far as the Pools of Dee by Bob Mac-Bain from Rothiemurchus (he helped us with our loads as far as this point), carried a weight of over 100 lb. each for a week's stay in the bothy at Corrour. There was hard frost at the time, and the wind was cold, but there was not much snow on the pass that January day. In order that we might have music during the long evenings, I carried my bag-pipes, and in their wooden box they were a considerable extra weight, as I found to my cost. But they seemed even heavier when I carried them up Ben MacDhui when we later left the Corrour bothy on our way down to Braemar.

Aviemore station is approximately 800 feet above the sea, and the pass at the watershed is approximately 2,800 feet. The ascent of 2,000 feet is spread over rather more than nine miles, so that it is scarcely felt. Whitewells in Rothiemurchus is the last house passed; for the next fifteen miles there is no house in sight, until Luibeg Cottage and Derry Lodge in the Forest of Mar are reached. As you climb southward you have on your right hand the corries of Braeriach, and on your left those of Cairngorm. When the last stunted Scots pine has been left behind you see, bounding the pass ahead of you, the high rocky slopes of Creag an Lethchoin, Rock of the Half-dog or Lurcher. The place-name commemorates a great hunt in the Cairngorms. The hunt (some say a deer hunt, others a fox hunt) began at Revoan on low ground east of Loch Morlich, and ended on Creag an Lethchoin, where one of the lurchers in the eagerness of pursuit fell over those high rocks. A herd of wild goats used to be seen here; I have not observed them now for many years. A number of deer forests on the west coast have wild goats, but these animals were always scarce on the Cairngorms, and I have not seen a single individual for a long time in any part of the range. They are able to descend in safety to ledges inaccessible to either sheep or deer.

Allt Dhru, which later becomes the river Druie, rises near the head of Lairig Ghru and for the first part of its course flows in places deep underground. In past ages great upheavals have brought down from the heights above the pass landslides of screes and earth, through which the young river has tunnelled its way, and through which it continues to flow unseen. At the head of the pass ptarmigan are almost always heard and seen, but I have not for some years noticed the golden eagle which used to enjoy chasing the ptarmigan here, wheeling round them as they flew terrified high in the air, and seeming to play with the birds, and not attempting to capture them.

Almost at the watershed, rather to the south, lie the Pools of Dee, several pools or lochans with water so clear that their depth is deceptive. There are small trout in these pools, and they may be sometimes seen, on a day without wind, cruising near the surface or rising to the flies and moths which alight on the water in fine summer weather. Yet the diet of these trout is spartan, and none of them grows to a weight exceeding a couple of ounces. There must be little food available for them from October until May and they probably spend at least half of the year lying lethargic out of sight below some of the many granite stones and rocks. It is remarkable that the Pools of Dee never freeze; even during the most severe winter and during the longest-sustained frost they have never been known to have a film of ice upon them, nor is their water, even on the hottest summer day, anything but icy cold. It is rare for birds to alight on them, but on one occasion I saw a small flock of teal, evidently on migration, resting on the largest of the pools. However heavy and prolonged the rainfall, the young Dee is always clear, for there is no peat to discolour the water. The Pools of Dee are sometimes said to be the source of the river, but the highest source and headsprings are on the plateau of Braeriach, 4,000 feet above sea-level. This branch of the river flows over the rocks at the edge of the plateau and falls in a series of cascades into the depths of the Garrachory (An Garbh Choire, the Rough Corrie), joining the Dee in Lairig Ghru at the entrance to that corrie.

As you walk southward from the Pools of Dee the view ahead is stern and impressive. To the east the slopes of Ben MacDhui rise steeply; almost ahead is the imposing outline of Cairntoul, while away toward the west are the fine corries of Braeriach, perhaps as wild as any in Scotland. A short distance beyond Cairntoul rises, prominent and unmistakable, the Devil's Point, and it is at the foot of this hill that the Corrour bothy stands. It is the last of the Cairngorm bothies. In my own lifetime both bothies in Glen Eanaich have disappeared; the Corrour bothy, made more durable and strong, remains, but has greatly deteriorated. At the time of the winter expedition I have mentioned earlier in this chapter the bothy was in a good state of repair. It was used during the stalking season by a deer watcher, who lived in it from Monday to Saturday. On Saturday he was accustomed to walk down to his home at Inverey, a walk of some eleven miles which included, at its beginning, the fording of the Dee, sometimes none too easy in times of rain. I often used to stay in the bothy while studying and photographing snow bunting and ptarmigan, and of the watchers who lived here in summer I have special memories of two—Charles Robertson and John Macintosh—he who was known in Mar Forest as the Piper. Charles Robertson was old when first I knew him, but made light of the long walk each week-end. He had remarkable poise, and used to leap from one boulder to another when crossing the turbulent and flooded Dee, to the admiration of nervous spectators half his age. I often wonder what happened to the large Cairngorm crystal which he passed one day on Monadh Mór when driving the deer for King Edward VII and other rifles. He had no time to stop, but made a mental note of the place, and returned at his leisure. Yet, neither then, nor at any subsequent time, was he able to locate the crystal, nor have I had more success. Cairngorm stones are crystals of quartz, usually sherry-coloured. The finest crystals lie generally in a bed of clay. One of the largest Cairngorms ever found weighed approximately 50 lb. It was discovered by James Grant, of Revoan, and was sold to Queen Victoria for £50. There is another Cairngorm crystal of almost equal size in Invercauld House, Braemar.

Charles Robertson used to spend much of his spare time digging for crystals; he was also a keen fisherman. He was most hospitable and used to invite the traveller into the bothy for a cup of tea. In those days sweetened condensed milk was not a luxury, neither was sugar rationed, but everything had to be carried up on one's back from Braemar, so his hospitality was admirable. He lived to be a very old man, and was over ninety when he died. John Macintosh the Piper, who succeeded him, was a powerful man, slow and deliberate in thought and actions, a good naturalist and a keen piper. He used to have his pipes with him at the bothy, and sometimes on a dark night I was guided to his door by the strains of "Donald Cameron," his favourite tune, which sounded loud and clear through the glen. I have pleasant memories of his piping, as I sat beside a roaring fire of peat and bog fir, very grateful after a long walk on the hills. John Macintosh was an adept at kindling a fire swiftly. However early in the morning a start had to be made from the bothy he had the kettle boiling and a good breakfast ready. It was a cheery wee room with its box bed; those who know it now, half ruinous and without privacy, can form little idea of what it was like in the days when it was a real home. But on the January afternoon when my friend and I, heavily laden, approached the bothy, we knew that it was shut, but the key was ready for us, and we soon had a fire burning from the store of peat and bog fir. It was either the next day or the day after that the most severe blizzard I have ever experienced struck the Cairngorms. There was little that afternoon to tell that the blizzard was near, but as we climbed to the corrie above the bothy we became aware that the ptarmigan, of which there was a large stock on the hills at that time, were behaving in an unusual manner. The birds were arriving, some flying, others running, from the higher grounds. Later in the day when we returned we found ptarmigan crouching for shelter in our foot-marks in the snow, where our feet had broken through the frozen crust.

The blizzard was near when we reached the bothy. Snow was already falling and drifting, but it was not until darkness fell, and was soon dispelled by the moon, that the storm was at its height. No words can adequately describe the scene at this time. In the moonlight the Lairig was almost as light as day. The snow had ceased to fall and overhead stars could be seen, but across the ground, and up to a height of six feet and more, snow, white and solid as a blanket, was drifted furiously by the frost-laden gale out of the north which now swept through the pass. We piled the fire high with fuel, yet in that small room a basin of water, placed on the table beside the window, perhaps eight feet from the fire, froze. Next morning the storm abated. Everywhere snow lay deep; the river was invisible. Snow had been drifted over it, and when half-melted by the water had frozen as a sheet of ice, which again had been covered by fresh snow. The weather gradually improved, yet on the morning when our stay at the bothy ended and we were to walk down to Derry Lodge we were uncertain whether to go by the pass, or to climb over Ben MacDhui, rising cold and white as a high hill of the Arctic. We decided to go over the hill-top. We had less weight to carry than when we arrived, but my pipes in their case were not handy things to transport up a steep icy slope. We climbed by way of the Tailors' Corrie, and when we saw the Tailors' Stone thought that the tailors who perished there might have been the victims of a storm such as we had so recently experienced in the shelter of the Corrour bothy.

Coire nan Taillear—the Tailors' Corrie—takes its name from Clach nan Taillear—the Tailors' Stone. The stream which flows through the corrie is Allt nan Taillear—the Tailors' Burn—and it was near this burn, now entirely hidden below the snow, that we climbed. Near the top of the corrie the plateau of Ben MacDhui falls away in a steep, scree-strewn slope, in places almost precipitous. During storms from the north-east the snow is drifted heavily into this corrie, and even in early September I have seen the fresh snow lying deep here. Successive storms drift the snow to a great depth, and in early summer a snow-field of great size always lies at the head of the corrie. The slope is so steep that when the hot weather comes the snow sometimes breaks away as an avalanche; one summer day when I was passing beneath the corrie this actually happened, great blocks of frozen snow hurtling down the hillside with the noise of thunder.

On this January day, a day of west wind when the clouds at times lightly touched the hill-top, the ground was covered with snow so hard-frozen that it bore the human weight and showed scarcely a trace of the impression of the human foot. In the corrie were ptarmigan in snow-white plumage, but when we had stepped out on to the summit plateau we might have been polar explorers completing our journey. We were in a dead-white world, a world where no life stirred. The depth of snow was so great that even stones and boulders were hidden. This made walking easier, yet the cold was intense and the frost-laden wind bitter. That was before the time when a mountain indicator had been placed on Ben MacDhui summit, to the disgust of the purists, who held that a mountaineer ought to be able to identify hills from a map and from his own knowledge, without being spoon-fed. In my time, I have seen mountain indicators spring up on Loch-nagar, on Ben MacDhui, and I am not sure that there is not one on Ben Nevis now, although there was no hint of it when last I stood on that hill-top. They destroy, I think, a certain amount of the benefit of having to find things out for oneself, although that does not detract from the honour due to those who made many arduous ascents to those high hills in order to satisfy themselves what distant peaks could be discerned on the clearest days. Had there been a mountain indicator on Braeriach it might have destroyed the old myth that the Cuillin range in the Isle of Skye are visible from that hill.

On that winter day of many years ago there was no mountain indicator on Ben MacDhui; indeed had one been in position it would have been invisible, for the large and solid cairn was encrusted with snow and ice: ice extended to leeward from the stones, firmly cemented to them by the breath of the frost. As I had perforce carried my pipes up to the hill-top it seemed necessary to play, or attempt to play, a tune there, but one's fingers in a temperature of fifteen degrees of frost and in a frost-laden wind of perhaps thirty miles an hour are apt to be stiff, and not in their best form for executing the more intricate grace notes of a pibroch. Except my friend, who was leniently disposed toward me, there was no living thing within ear-shot—the ptarmigan were in the shelter of the corrie below, and even the eagle, king of birds, was in a more sheltered and less airy site.

Writing thus of piping at 4,300 feet above sea-level in winter recalls to my mind an experience I had more recently when crossing Ben MacDhui on a walk from Aviemore to Mar. My companion on that occasion was not the friend who had been with me on that January day, but one who had at times curious psychic impressions. We were crossing the plateau and had passed beyond the hill-top when, a short time before coming in sight of Lochan Uaine, he said that he distinctly heard the sound of the pipes coming from the south. I replied that this was unlikely, since there was no house for many miles, yet he persisted in his assertion and when the sound of that ghostly pipe died a few minutes later he was visibly upset. I had experienced, a few minutes earlier, a psychic impression of my own, and there are those who say that Ben MacDhui is a fey hill; that strange footsteps have been heard, loud and menacing, here, and that the ghost known as the Fear Liath Mór—the Big Grey Man—has from time to time been seen.

The ascent of Ben MacDhui that winter's day had been arduous; the descent in places was still more formidable. We were without ice-axes, and the strength of the recent blizzard had been such that

The River Dee dropping from Braeriach to the Garbh Choire

it had swept all the new snow from the exposed slopes, leaving the old snow, which had been frozen and thawed until it was glass-like. Extreme care had to be exercised as we descended these icy slopes which ended sometimes in rocks, or in a precipice. This unorthodox winter mountaineering of a piper did not on that occasion end in disaster, and we reached, weary but intact, the hospitable home of Donald Fraser, who then lived at the Derry. I recall that when we knocked at the door, and Mary Fraser opened it, her first astonishment at seeing two wayfarers on a winter night was succeeded by mirth which surprised and disconcerted us. When we entered the house and stood before a mirror the cause of her merriment was apparent. We had not seen ourselves for a week and of course had not thought of shaving. We were impressive in our week's beards, but the colour of our faces was still more mirth-producing, for they were black as those of an African, from the peat smoke which had most of the time filled the bothy.

Those were happy days. The Cairngorms have not changed, nor have even the old pines in Glen Luibeg during the last forty years (this seems to show that they are of a great age), yet the people of the glens, the old hillmen who knew by name each knoll, hollow and streamlet, have gone never to return. Houses are ruinous where courtly highlanders lived, and those who remain are fast losing the old tradition. This is the tendency everywhere in the Highlands, but it is specially marked in Mar. Think of old Charlie Robertson lighting his fire before dawn in the Corrour Bothy in order to walk through Lairig Ghru fifteen miles to Aviemore to catch the morning train to Inverness, so that he might hear the leading pipers compete at the Northern Meeting, and of Sandy MacDonald who made that long walk partly in order to see the Moray Firth. Think of the hill ponies, carrying the stags shot near the Wells of Dee, traversing by the light of the moon, or in inky darkness, the Lairig Ghru, from the outlying beats of Braeriach where no rifle has been fired these many years. The old stalkers have gone, and with them the Gaelic language which survived in Mar until after the close of the first world war, and which still lives in the place-names of hill and corrie.

The birthplace of the River Dee,
Plateau of Braeriach

CHAPTER V

SUMMER DAYS WITH THE SNOW BUNTING

B Y the old right-of-way through the Lairig Ghru pass the distance from the Corrour Bothy to Derry Lodge is between five and six miles. Despite the marching of armed men, with their laden mules, through the Lairig during the years of the second world war, the small stone set on end beside the track, marking a distance of four miles from Derry Lodge, remains. It is a cheering thing to see after a long walk on the hills. Often at dusk when returning through the Lairig I have found this stone elusive, and have been almost sure that I had unintentionally passed it, when its welcome form appeared, perhaps in the last of the sunset glow, perhaps in the light of the moon (how often have I blessed the moon for guiding me over these last four miles). As the stone is reached, the waters of that small and lonely tarn, Lochan Feith na Sgor, are seen. There are ancient tree stumps in these waters, although no tree at the present day grows in sight of them.

On an August evening of long ago my friend Malcolm Barclay Harvey and I were saved the long walk down to the Derry, for John Macintosh the piper had told us that we could put up at the bothy of Corrour, he himself having gone down to Mar Lodge for the night. I should mention that in those days a wonderful excursion train left Aberdeen each Wednesday and Saturday at one o'clock in the afternoon, and ran to Aviemore, returning the same night, the first-class return fare being half a crown! That was in the days of the Great North of Scotland Railway, which lost its soul when it was amalgamated with the L.N.E.R., which in its turn has parted with its identity and is now unrecognised among "British Railways." That afternoon excursion to Strathspey from Aberdeen was really a remarkable achievement. The first stop was Craigellachie, which is sixty-eight miles from Aberdeen and was reached in eighty-five minutes —anyone consulting a modern time table will at once see how much slower that journey is at the present day. On that occasion we had received permission to ride in the cab of the locomotive, and I remember how worried the driver was as we rushed through Kintore thirty-five seconds late! I was on the foot-plate as far as Craigellachie, and Malcolm then took my place as far as Aviemore. Incidentally he (now Sir Malcolm Barclay Harvey of Dinnet) later wrote the *History of the Great North of Scotland Railway*. After travelling at high speed non-stop to Craigellachie, the train was booked to call at most of the stations along the Spey and, leaving the Great North of Scotland Railway at its terminus at Boat-of-Garten, the engine and carriages then travelled the extra distance of five miles to Aviemore by permission of the Highland Railway (which later became part of the L.M.S. system). When at Craigellachie, my friend changed places with me in the cab of the locomotive, I seated myself in the first class compartment he had just left, no doubt depositing soot and grime on its dark-blue cushion.

Having for the sum of half a crown been carried from Aberdeen to Aviemore first class—for which privilege we should now have to pay several pounds and should spend a whole day on the journey—we set out in the late afternoon on our walk through the Cairngorms by way of Lairig Ghru. The day was fine, and there was little or no wind. In the forest of Rothiemurchus the blaeberries and the cowberries were ripening, and the sun was drawing the resinous scent from the pines. Darkness had come when we passed near the Pools of Dee, and I recall the light of a bright planet reflected in the still waters of one of the pools, and a cloud, borne low on the rocky slope of Cairntoul, that imperceptibly grew. The ptarmigan, aroused by our passing, croaked sleepily. The Lairig at the watershed is stony, and the path in places difficult to follow. A hundred years ago there was a certain amount of trade between Strathspey and Braemar, and as ponies sometimes crossed between the two districts the path at the stony watershed was kept clear, but for more than half a century nothing has been done to it, and in darkness it is not easy to follow. It was after midnight when we reached the neighbourhood of the bothy. The small cloud on Cairntoul had by now flowed into Lairig Ghru, and through the cloud we walked, knowing, by the land-marks on the track, when was the correct moment to strike off the path, reach and cross the river, and then climb the short distance to the bothy. So close was the mist, we were able to locate the bothy only by the murmur of the burn that flows down from Corrour (Coire Odhar) close to the small building. The hiding place of the key of the door had been revealed to us, and I remember that we groped our way into the one small room and lit the candle set ready for us on the table. The peat fire had to be coaxed into life, water fetched from the spring, and the kettle boiled. The bothy in those days was kept clean, so clean that we slept on a mattress on the floor. It was then a place of happy memories. The wee room had a homely and hospitable feeling such as no other room I have lived in, either before or since. How changed is its aspect, even the atmosphere that pervades it, at the present day! It was good to hear the grouse crowing outside the bothy when one awakened early in the morning (there was no artificial Summer Time in those days) and saw the sun shine on the green ledges of Carn a' Mhaim so that they seemed to glow, intangible, in mystic light. I have a clear memory of opening the bothy door on that particular August morning. The air was still and silent and dew lay thick on grass and heather. The whole air was perfumed by heather blossom, not the strong scent of heather in sunlight but an aroma very delicate and pure such as I never remember having experienced either before or since. The great hills—Cairntoul, the Devil's Point, Ben MacDhui—seemed near and friendly. All the world was at peace and it was good to share the peace which lay at the heart of nature. I have stayed many times in the Corrour bothy, at all seasons of the year from early summer to mid-winter, and I have never left it without a feeling of regret; yet that particular morning stands out in my memory, among happy hours spent in that remote habitation which now stands derelict, the last of the bothies of the Cairngorms.

It was from the bothy, which I usually made my base, by permission of the owner of Mar Forest, that I used to climb to Ben MacDhui, to Braeriach, and to Cairntoul, to study the rarest bird of the Cairngorms—the snow bunting. The more I have seen of this Arctic songster, in this country a frequenter of the highest Scottish hills, the more convinced I have become that there are times when the resident stock dies out, or almost dies out. Then a resident cock, or perhaps a resident hen, persuades a migrant mate to remain with him, or with her, instead of flying north to Iceland or Greenland in early summer; fresh blood is introduced, and the race of Cairngorm snow buntings increases for a time. On an early summer morning of the year 1909 I first heard the song of the snow bunting at close quarters, although in 1906 I had heard it come from a great distance, from the depths of a wild stony corrie a thousand feet below where I stood. There is an elusive quality in the snow bunting's song which, in this instance (the song varies greatly), was sweet and flute-like. In the twilight of an early July night, with drifting showers of fine misty rain through which the full moon, low in the south, shone golden and several times that night lighted a ghostly lunar rainbow which spanned Lairig Ghru, I had climbed through mist to a height of nearly 4,300 feet and heard, at earliest dawn, the sweet unmistakable song of the bird for which I was searching, and with which, years later, I was to become familiar in Spitsbergen. I think at that time my greatest ambition in life was to find the nest of the snow bunting. The song came from the far slope of the hill. It had an elusive quality, due perhaps to the songster turning his head as he sang perched on a boulder, but at length I tracked it down, and my delight was great when I saw, on the screes at the edge of the mist cap, the handsome black and white form of a cock snow bunting. He sang sometimes softly, sometimes loudly, his song, as noted by me at the time, consisting of six clear whistles, beginning in a low key and quickly rising. The last two notes were the loudest and most clear part of the song, and at a distance were the only two that were heard. After I had for some time watched the snow bunting singing in this wild corrie before sunrise, he flew lightly down from the great boulder on which he was perched, and began to pick up insects from the ground. This done, he flew a little way across the screes, and where he had alighted a young snow bunting ran up and with open bill and trembling wings stood expectantly before his father, who at once fed the chick and then proceeded to feed a second member of his family. The young bird he had first fed permitted me to approach to five feet; it had probably left the nest only the day before. While I was photographing this young bunting the mother bird flew up fearlessly, and endeavoured to persuade the chick to fly off with her, hopping beside it and encouraging it with soft twittering notes. Although I was only a few yards from them, she fed her family with complete confidence. On the far side of the corrie a second snow bunting was in full, wild song. He was strikingly plumaged in black and white and could be seen at a considerable distance. This bird sang not only from his boulder, but in the air, into which from time to time he rose almost vertically, then sailed quickly to the ground, the while uttering his song. This cock bunting fed two young ones, fairly strong on the wing, while I watched him. His song was audible at a distance of approximately seven hundred yards, and in a still dawn might, I think, have been heard a mile off. Besides these two pairs of snow buntings with families, I saw that morning, on the same ground, two more pairs of birds. The following summer (1910) I was often in the corrie, yet never saw more than one pair, and have often wondered what became of the stock, which must, including old and young, have numbered at least a dozen at the close of the nesting season of 1909. I do not think any young were reared in 1910, and by 1912 the race had entirely gone—not a single snow bunting frequented the corrie that summer.

During the summer of 1911, a week before taking my honours degree at Oxford, I travelled up from that city to Aviemore with Malcolm Barclay Harvey, who was my contemporary at the University. We left on a Friday evening, reached Aviemore the following morning, and were conveyed by the celebrated Mr. MacWilliam in his "machine" to the upper bothy at Loch Eanaich. We then climbed, by the stalking path, through Coire Dhondail out on to the "flat," which we crossed to the shoulder of Cairntoul and then descended to the Corrour bothy. The weather had been intensely hot, and I remember that *Silene acaulis*, the cushion pink, was in full flower at 3,300 feet above sea-level on June 5, more than a fortnight before its time. The change from Oxford to the Cairngorms was a great one, and, the weather continuing fine, we spent the whole of the Sunday watching the snow buntings in their corrie. On the Monday we returned over the high tops to Loch Eanaich, seeing the mist fall lightly upon the far western hills on the breath of the moisture-laden south-west wind which had arisen. Our friend Mr. MacWilliam was awaiting us beside Loch Eanaich and we drove down to Rothiemurchus forest where, I remember, the birches already at the beginning of June were beginning to shed their leaves because of the long-continued drought and heat, and caught the five o'clock train, arriving in Oxford the next morning in time for the day's work.

Most of my friends thought I was mad to have obtained leave of absence for a long week-end so near my finals but, as it turned out, it was most fortunate for me that I did so. I was taking, or attempting to take, an honours degree in the School of Natural Science, my final subject being botany. I had brought back from the Cairngorms specimens of the various alpine plants we had seen, and these I showed to my tutor, learning their life histories during the week which remained before my schools. In one of the papers which was set I saw to my joy the question, "Write as fully as possible what you know about the alpine flora of Britain." On this question I wrote upwards of 2,500 words and it was this that gave me my "second." Indeed at my "viva" I soon discovered from the questions which the examiners put to met hat they considered me an authority on alpine plants, and my difficulty was to cloak my ignorance when they asked me, among other hard questions, the name of the saxifrage which grows only on Ben Lawers among British hills. I did not then know that the last stronghold of *Saxifraga cernua* was Ben Lawers, but still I got a good class in my honours degree, and I think it can be safely said that never before has a long week-end spent on the Cairngorms just before a final school at Oxford helped in the obtaining of a degree.

At the end of June, I returned to the Cairngorms to continue my study of the snow bunting. One night, in fine anticyclonic weather, I reached the high corrie a few minutes before midnight and, with the afterglow bright on the north horizon and a mystic silence enfolding the high tops, I awaited the first dawn song of the snow bunting. At 1.5 a.m. his flute-like notes were heard, and for the next six hours he sang almost without pause, usually perched on a boulder, but sometimes on the wing. His song flight was charming, for he sailed at a little height with his wings held in the shape of a V, somewhat in the same manner as a golden eagle or a hen harrier holds the wings when following the contours of a hill while hunting. I was near enough to admire his white head and throat and black bill, against the deep blue of the summer sky, for this snow bunting seemed to be without fear of the human observer who was paying him such flattering attentions. On one occasion, when I was sitting, a conspicuous object, on a granite boulder, the songster flew up from the far side of the corrie and perched on a favourite singing stone not a dozen yards from me, where he sang with great verve, time after time. His singing hours were from one o'clock in the morning until after eight o'clock in the evening. During those nineteen hours he sang his song on an average three or four times a minute, so that each day he sang approximately 3,500 songs. But there was one day too hot even for the sturdy snow bunting to sing. There was no wind, nor was a cloud to be seen over the great expanse of country between Ben Nevis and the North Sea. I waited awhile near the three or four prominent boulders on which he sang, and near his favourite singing station of all—a small knoll, moss-covered, where he was accustomed to spend a great part of his time—but he did not appear. Later in the day, on reaching a snow-field, I found my bird enjoying himself on the cold surface. I watched him there. He loved to run over the snow, cooling his head by using it like a miniature snow plough, as he pushed it, half-buried and throwing up two tiny ridges, through the snow. Thus refreshed, he sang his song from a boulder several times before returning to enjoy his winter sports beneath the summer sun. Late in the afternoon he took up his singing station at his usual haunt, the sun by this time being less fierce.

One fine day when I was watching the snow bunting, he behaved in an unusual manner. He was singing strongly from his boulder when he rose to a height of a few yards, and as he sailed earthward with his wings held V-shape he sang his song. Instead of alighting, as he seemed about to do, he suddenly shot into the air, like an aircraft when warned by a red rocket not to attempt a landing at an airport, and for several minutes flew wildly to and fro at a considerable height, calling all the time eagerly and excitedly. At last he set his course northward, and flew on and on until he was invisible even with the assistance of binoculars, nor was he seen or heard again that day. Throughout the season there was no sign of any brood.

Captain and Mrs. Nethersole Thompson, who have studied the snow bunting for many years on the Cairngorms and have on several occasions found the nest, are inclined to think that this strong and persistent singing of a cock snow bunting rather late in the summer means that he is without a mate: that the local stock has become so low that there are not sufficient mates to go round. Certainly for a number of years after watching that tame and persistent songster I did not see a single snow bunting in the corrie, and indeed I do not think the singing stations have been occupied from that day to this. Is it, I wonder, possible that certain of the snow buntings which habitually winter on the Cairngorms may, under exceptional conditions, remain there to nest? Might one or two birds decide that Scotland is as good as Greenland as a summer home? We know little of the habits of the local race of snow buntings—whether they remain on the Cairngorms throughout the year, or whether, as is more likely, they fly south at the close of the nesting season. The Ross Links in Northumberland is a favourite winter haunt of snow buntings, where they pass their time at sea-level, and I have seen them in early March feeding below high-water mark on Sandwich beach in Kent, but it is more usual to find them at a considerable height above the sea, where they feed on the seeds of the hill grasses which thrust their heads through the snow.

In Rothiemurchus Forest, Strathspey
Sgoran Dubh and Glen Eanaich, in the Cairngorms

An observer might easily be led into the error of thinking that in certain seasons a large number of snow buntings had decided to nest on the Cairngorms. One day of early May, as hot as any day of the summer, J. C. Harrison, the bird artist, whose pictures have given pleasure to so many, and I climbed to the plateau of Braeriach and found it literally alive with snow buntings. They were tame and flew reluctantly, and might indeed have been about to nest, yet I realised that this was unlikely. We returned a week later and made a careful search. Not one of those birds remained: they had evidently been migrants, and may have taken off for their flight to Greenland from this great height of 4,250 feet, which would have given them a good start on their northward migration.

Loch an Eilein, Rothiemurchus
Lairig Ghru

CHAPTER VI

A FURTHER CHAPTER ON BIRDS
OF THE CAIRNGORMS

IT has sometimes been the fashion to write in a disparaging manner of the eagle; to call it lethargic and indolent, even cowardly. But the naturalists who have written thus did not know the golden eagle intimately, for no person who has studied this, our greatest British bird, can fail to admire it. It is certainly on occasion a lazy bird, but its every movement is dignified, majestic and regal. Only a few days before writing this page I visited a haunt of the eagle, hoping to find the birds at home. It was one of those rare days of December when the sky was cloudless, the air clear, the wind at rest, and a touch of frost binding the peat bogs. The cliff which I visited faces north-east, and thus is in shade throughout the short December day, but the sun was lighting up a pinnacle which projected above the main cliff, and here, side by side, the male and the female golden eagle were perched, enjoying to the full the unaccustomed sunshine. I watched them for an hour and a half, and although one of them towards the end of that time flew away, the other was still perched on his airy pinnacle half an hour after sunset: it looked as though he intended to roost there. I was interested that the eagles showed no disposition to make a hunting excursion for their supper; it was almost certain that they would deliberately go to roost supperless that December night—and December nights are long. They may have fed well earlier in the day on a carcase of a sheep or a deer.

To see the golden eagle at his best, you must watch him on a day of storm, when his unrivalled flight is displayed; he is the only bird able to face the most severe gale which sends even the strong raven to shelter or hurls him (as I have seen it do) to the ground. Yet even in a moderate breeze his power of flight is superb. Have you ever watched a golden eagle, after its mate has arrived at the eyrie and there has been a change over on the eggs, set out from that nest, built on a ledge of a cliff, on a foraging expedition? As though realising that its presence in the air may give away the whereabouts of the eyrie, the departing eagle flies away at its utmost speed, and if there is a strong following wind that speed is literally tremendous. When the eaglets are well-grown, the parent eagles do not have the same reason for making a precipitate departure. The procedure in leaving the nesting rock is then different. The great bird sails out over the precipice, then in spirals climbs leisurely on the breeze, higher and higher. When at a height of some 4,000 feet, the eagle now sets a straight course for the hunting grounds. The plan of operations is masterly, because from its great height (which it has reached without effort), it can reach its goal with a long swift glide, perhaps over a number of miles, aided by an occasional beat of its great wings, strong and broad.

The golden eagle is affected little by a spell of severe weather, so long as prey is available. But sometimes prolonged snow may wipe out its food supply. This happened in February of the year 1947. One pair of Cairngorm eagles prey largely upon rabbits; at the end of that exceptional snowy spell the entire rabbit population had been killed, and the eagles must have been hard put to it to find food. That storm caused the eagles in certain Highland districts to nest in unexpected places. Their usual rocks were still deep in snow when the season for nest-building arrived, and the eagles in some instances nested in small rocks, low down and easily accessible.

In the western Highlands the golden eagle nests almost invariably on a rock, but in the Cairngorm area the nesting site is as often as not a Scots pine: one pair of eagles for a number of years nested in a birch tree that was easy to climb and was the home of a willow warbler which sang with complete confidence only a few feet from the eagle's eyrie. The vertical limit of the Scots pine in the Cairngorms is higher than anywhere else in the British Isles, and is the 2,000 feet contour line above sea-level. I have known an eagle build in a pine only a few yards from the foot of a glen, beside a small river, but this is the exception and the pine usually chosen is an outpost one, on a slope and affording a wide view. This notwithstanding, the cup of the eyrie is deep, and the eagle, impeded in its view by branches, often fails to see, or hear the approach of, the human adventurer. I recall one Highland stalker who used to say that he could always reach the foot of an eagle's tree unobserved. This done, he used to tap smartly on the trunk of the tree with his stick, and after one or two taps the head of the eagle would be poked over the side of the eyrie, and the great bird would glare at the intruder with an outraged expression before launching out and flying heavily away until favouring wind currents were met. This eagle was a very early nester: I have watched her for forty years, and she is still, I believe, in the district. She was unique among golden eagles in hatching on occasion around mid-April, which is approximately three weeks earlier than the usual hatching time. When a heavy snow storm covers the eagle's country at the building season those birds having their eyrie in a tree are at an advantage, since they rarely have much snow to inconvenience them, but when the nesting site is on a rock, the ledge may be drifted up and inaccessible, and the eagles may have to search elsewhere for a nesting site.

One season, many years ago, I climbed to a rocky gorge in the hills where, at a height of rather more than 2,000 feet above sea-level, a pair of golden eagles nested, although I am afraid they were never permitted to rear their young—they were too near grouse moors for that. There was at the time a snowstorm of unusual severity, and when I left the track I found a foot of snow covering the heather. The depth quickly increased as I climbed, and before I had reached the nesting place of the golden eagles I found myself walking wearily through (not over, for the snow was soft) an average depth of thirty inches of snow. Anyone who has climbed a hill under such conditions will realise that my progress that day was slow. At length I approached the gorge and saw one of the eagles rise from a rocky spur. Even the juniper bushes were invisible beneath the snow, and my difficulty was to approach the nesting ledge sufficiently near to look into it and yet avoid precipitating myself over the edge of the cliff in a miniature avalanche. I should explain that the second eagle of the pair had taken wing from the neighbourhood of the ledge, and I hoped to be able to obtain what would have been a unique photograph of the eggs with two and a half feet of snow lying all around them. At last I reached, not without some difficulty, a point from which I could look down to the eyrie. My disappointment was great when I saw that it was empty. The nesting cup was the only snow-free object in sight, and the eagle had evidently been about to lay, and had been keeping her eyrie free of snow against the laying of the first of her two eggs.

It says much for the buoyancy of the spirit of birds that the curlew that had arrived to nest on the lower slopes of that hill should have been sailing on tremulous wings in full song above a dead-white snowy expanse when I retraced my steps that afternoon. Their feeding ground had been sealed off, yet they were singing as though a soft, mild rain, such as curlews love, had been falling and the world had been a pleasant place. An April snowfall is not often accompanied by intense frost, nor do April snows lie so long as those of winter.

The Cairngorm area has not known the kite as a nesting species for the best part of a century, yet an eagle's eyrie which I used to visit was built in the neighbourhood of a kite's nest which was then still in good shape although it had not been used for more than forty years: it was built firmly in the fork of a tall pine.

The osprey survived the kite in the country of the Cairngorms, but the osprey, too, has gone. The osprey's last nesting place in this area was the ruined castle on Loch an Eilein, a beautiful loch in Rothiemurchus Forest. The last year in which the ospreys there reared young was in 1897. In 1899 two ospreys arrived on April 3, and subsequently nested. A third osprey then appeared on the scene. Much fighting followed, during which the eggs were broken and fell from the ruined tower into the loch. This was apparently the last year in which eggs were laid at the Loch an Eilein nesting site. C. G. Cash, who in Vols. IV and V of the *Cairngorm Club Journal* gives a contemporary account of the nesting of the birds, states that two ospreys arrived at Loch an Eilein in 1900, but did not nest: it was thought they had nested in Glen Feshie, as four birds later in the year were seen there. In 1901 a single osprey arrived, and was seen fighting above Ord Bàn with a golden eagle. A single bird came in 1902 for the last time. In his article C. G. Cash mentions that he used to swim in Loch an Eilein before breakfast, and the osprey at first alarmed him by flying above him as he swam, and uttering its screaming cry. This writer mentions that in the years 1842-48 a pair of ospreys nested on the ruins of the old lodge at Loch Morlich, not far from Loch an Eilein. He quotes Lewis Dunbar as saying that these ospreys moved their young to another place if they were disturbed. I have more than once heard of the golden eagle doing this.

The Grants of Rothiemurchus, on whose territory the Loch an Eilein ospreys nested, did what they could to protect the birds during the nesting season, and in 1893 John Peter Grant of Rothiemurchus and Donald Cameron of Lochiel were each awarded a silver medal by the Zoological Society of London, "in recognition of the efforts made to protect the osprey in their respective districts."

Shortly before the ospreys finally disappeared from the district a second eyrie was found in a tree on the shore of Loch Morlich, but, not being on an island, this nest could not be protected. Indeed the nest on Loch an Eilein was sometimes robbed, although the boat on the loch was padlocked during the nesting season of the birds.

The almost legendary daring of one egg collector, who swam over to the island during a spell of Arctic April weather when six inches of snow covered the ground, used to be spoken of by the old people of the district. On a night of this kind there was apparently no watch on the shore of the loch, and the would-be despoiler of the osprey's nest swam naked across the loch in the darkness, scaled the ruins of the castle and reached the nest. Here he received a shock, for he suddenly realised that he had left his cap behind on the mainland shore —the cap which, placed firmly on his head, was to be used to hold the precious eggs during the return swim. On the outward swim he had towed a rope, held by a companion on the shore, behind him, lest he should be overcome by cramp, and he now found the rope to be of service, for, taking an egg in either hand and lying on his back, he was drawn back to the shore. Half-way across he was seized with cramp, but was pulled safely ashore. One would have thought that a single experience of this kind would have been sufficient for any man, but the same nest robber in a subsequent season swam out to the island under cover of darkness and again robbed the nest. On this occasion he almost succeeded in capturing the owner of the nest, the osprey realising the danger only when his hand actually touched her.

The Highland ospreys had enemies not only at their summer haunts: they were shot in the south of England during their migration, and Highland landowners like Grant of Rothiemurchus and Cameron of Lochiel, who did their utmost to protect their ospreys, fought a losing battle. There are rumours from time to time that a pair of ospreys have reared their young on some unfrequented Scottish loch, but I am doubtful of these reports, although I realise that close secrecy is of the greatest importance if a wandering pair of ospreys should ever nest in the Highlands.

There is, for the time being at all events, a lessening of the activities of egg collectors, and eagles have not done badly in recent years in rearing their young in the Cairngorm area. It is unfortunate for them that they are most conservative of birds, and return year after year to the same eyrie, or to one of two eyries, which in course of time become well known. Were they to change their nesting site yearly like most birds they would be hard to locate in the old pine forest: it is surprising how difficult it is to find an eagle's eyrie in a tree.

A large bird whose exploits at first earned for it the reputation of an eagle had its home in Rothiemurchus in the early years of the twentieth century. I have mentioned it in a previous chapter. One day the local butcher arrived at Inverdruie with the strange tale that he had been attacked by a large eagle-like bird which, attracted, he believed, by the meat in his van, had made a determined onslaught on him and had been driven off only with difficulty. Investigation showed the supposed eagle to be a cock capercaillie, a bird of remarkable pugnacity and boldness. He (for his male sex deserves to be emphasised) attacked women and children in preference to men, at least latterly, for he had perhaps received blows from the male sex which had rendered him more cautious, but in his more reckless days he had knocked over a man, who had rolled with ignominy down a steep bank. Latterly the discriminating truculence he showed towards women as compared to men made it plain that he realised the relatively harmless character of the female sex. This exceptional bird terrorised the neighbourhood for several seasons.

The forests of Glenmore and Rothiemurchus are the headquarters of the crested tit in Scotland. This small titmouse is a firm resident, and its husky chattering cries may be heard proceeding from the old pines. Most tits choose a ready-made hole in a tree, but the crested tit almost always excavates its own nesting hole, usually low down in a dead fir.

That long-legged wader the greenshank nests in the forests of the Cairngorms, arriving at its spring haunts early in April. The call-note of the greenshank is one of great beauty, deep-toned and musical: the song is rarely heard, but is a remarkable performance and when uttered on the wing, as it usually is, is literally breath-taking. Because of the rareness of the bird and the beauty of its eggs, the greenshank has suffered at the hands of egg collectors, but is (I write in 1949) at the moment holding its own.

One of the most attractive Scottish birds to nest in the Cairngorm area is the dotterel. This is a plover-like bird, resembling on the wing a miniature golden plover, but whereas the golden plover is wild and unapproachable the dotterel is perhaps the tamest of all British birds. It is well for it that it nests on high and remote hill-tops and hill-plateaus, for it not infrequently shows you its nest, running ahead of you and sitting down on the eggs with a look of satisfaction. It is only fair to say that the bird which acts thus is a mere male—the hen dotterel takes, so far as I have seen, no subsequent interest in her three handsome eggs, richly spotted and blotched with reddish-brown markings, after they are laid.

Not all dotterel are equally tame, but a really tame dotterel can be made so tame that it has literally no fear of man. My own experience when photographing a certain dotterel was so remarkable that I remember the incidents clearly although they happened a dozen years ago. I climbed almost daily to this dotterel's nest, in order to determine the exact incubation period. Most birds would have resented this and would have become gradually wilder; not so the dotterel. Among many incidents two stand out clearly. One was that morning when a cold west wind was sweeping the hill-plateau 3,000 feet above sea-level. The eggs were chipping, but were chilled when I reached the nest, and there was no sign of their owner. This worried me, and when a hail shower swept the hill I sat to windward of the nest, sheltering it, and placed the eggs against my arm pits in order that the fledglings within might be warmed up. Soon, to my relief, I saw the dotterel running towards me at speed. Without pause or hesitation he approached, and I had only just time to replace the eggs in the nest when he arrived, settled down to brood them, then looked up at me with a friendly look in his bright eyes, saying, as plainly as possible, "Good morning. I got back just in time, didn't I?" The second incident which stands out in my mind is of sitting watching the dotterel, in full view of him and perhaps three feet away. After a time I saw that he was eyeing me intently, and with obvious interest. He rose on his nest, ran swiftly to me, looked up at me, again with his friendly glance, picked a "daddy-long-legs" from my arm, swallowed it, then returned to brood the eggs. It was the more remarkable that he had no fear of me because he did not extend that trust to my collie Dara. I used to tell Dara to lie down a couple of hundred yards away, but sometimes she became bored, and when the dotterel rose in alarm and ran from the nest I knew, even before I looked round, that I should see the form of Dara on the sky-line. When I told her to lie down, and she obeyed, the dotterel at once returned to the eggs. He mistook her, I think, for a fox.

Loch A'an and Ben MacDhui

CHAPTER VII

THE EASTERN CAIRNGORMS

BEN A'an and Beinn a' Bhuird may be said to form the eastern
boundary of the Cairngorm hills; near them are Beinn Mheadhon,
a hill remarkable—as Ben A'an is remarkable—for the dark granite
warts on its summit, and Ben Bynack. None of these hills reaches a
height of 4,000 feet, although Beinn a' Bhuird and Ben A'an closely
approach it. Ben A'an is unmistakable even at a great distance because
of its vast size, especially its length, and its granite warts. I have seen
those warts when flying over the Cromarty Firth at Invergordon, and
they are visible in clear weather from a ship at sea off the coast near
Aberdeen. Ben A'an takes its name from the river A'an, or Avon,
which rises in Loch A'an and flows through Strath A'an to join the
Spey at Ballindalloch. Hear what Timothy Pont writes, before the year
1600, on the A'an: "Avin river, which cometh out of Strath-Avin
. . . yea more clear and pure than anie river in Scotland whatsoever."

Professor Watson has pointed out to me that Ath-fhinn, or A'an,
means Very Fair One.* This might well apply to the river itself, but
the tradition, which is mentioned in the old *Statistical Account*, is
that the name Very Fair One, was actually the name of the wife of
Fingal, leader of those super-men the Fingalians, whose era is generally
supposed to be the fourth century, and whose deeds of prowess and
daring are still remembered in the Highlands of Scotland and in Eire.
Fingal, or Fionn as he is usually spoken of in the Highlands, had one
day been hunting, Ath-fhinn his lady wife with him. When crossing
the A'an at the end of the day, near the Linn at Inchrory, she slipped
and was carried away by the swift stream. Two miles below the linn,
at a place called Bogluachrach, her body was recovered and her grave
is still pointed out. Fionn in his grief then spoke the following qua-
train, set down in the old *Statistical Account*:

> Chaidh mo bhean-sa bhàtadh
> Air Uisge Bàn nan clachan sleamhuinn;
> 'S bho chaidh mo bhean a bhàtadh,
> Bheirmid ATH-FHINN air an abhuinn

* In an old poem in Turner's collection (1813) Strath A'an is spelled
Strath-Thamhuinn. The title of the poem is "Glacadh Mhoirir Hunti."

M

Balmoral Castle

My wife has been drowned
On the Fair Water of the slippery stones;
And since my wife has been drowned,
Let us call the river ATH-FHINN.

It is elsewhere noted that before the event the river had been called
Uisge Bàn—Fair Water—and that its name was then changed to
Ath-fhinn—Very Fair One. The ford on the A'an below Loch A'an
is to this day known as Ath nam Fiann—the Ford of the Fingalians.

When Timothy Pont wrote of the exceptional clearness of the
A'an he may have been thinking of its upper reaches, where the
purity of its waters renders their depth deceptive, as I have found
when fording the river at Ath nam Fiann. Farther down, in times of
rain, I have seen the Burn of Loin flowing into it with peat-stained
waters which coloured the main river amber. Yet in normal times the
A'an is colourless, and I have been told that salmon which run up it
retain their silvery colour until late in the season.

There is no road along the upper reaches of Strath A'an beyond
Inchrory, but a rough walking track. When Loch A'an is reached,
some of the grandest country of the Cairngorms is seen, the north-
east face of Ben MacDhui rising abruptly from the head of the loch.
Here is in view the great snow-field I have mentioned in a previous
chapter, a snow-field which often remains unmelted throughout the
course of the year.

There are few of those who climb on the Cairngorms who have
not visited the Shelter Stone (its Gaelic name, Clach Dhion, has
almost been lost), a great boulder standing near the head of Loch A'an
above its southern shore. In a past age it fell from the high precipice
above, and now rests on other lesser boulders in such a way that a
recess is formed. Here is the "shelter," which has been used by hunters
of the red deer for centuries, and, more recently, by those who love
to wander over the Cairngorms.

It is a memorable experience to spend a summer night beneath the
Shelter Stone, especially if the weather be fine. The evening when my
wife and I descended by the Garbh Uisge from Ben MacDhui was
one of the warmest of that summer, and the July sun was melting the
snows quickly, so that in the evening the Garbh Uisge was a foaming
torrent of snow water. During the night hours one heard the sound
not only of this stream, but of others which fell from the high ground
into Loch A'an, itself 2,600 feet above the level of the sea. Until the

178

gathering darkness hid them, trout could be seen rising on the loch, and a goosander which flew in from the east and at once began to fish must have had good sport among them. Mist flowed up Strath A'an during the night, and as we returned over Ben MacDhui we could hear unseen hinds bleating near us as we walked through thick cloud. We climbed above this low cloud and had the unusual experience of watching a thunderstorm gather from a high cloud layer, and in the clear zone between that upper cloud and the lower mist, of seeing swifts hawking insects. Swifts habitually visit the highest of the Cairngorms: the sound of their wings has been heard by a mountaineer as he rested on the summit cairn of Cairngorm in June. The distance from Aviemore, where a considerable population of swifts have their nests, to the Cairngorms is an easy flight for the swift. It could reach the top of Cairngorm, or the plateau of Braeriach, in a quarter of an hour. During fine summer weather there is sometimes more insect life on the high tops than at lower levels, and it is only in fine weather that the swifts ascend to the high Cairngorms. From time to time one hears reports that the swift is nesting in the precipices of these hills. A swift once was seen on Lochnagar at a height of 3,600 feet with a straw in its mouth, and there was a similar report from Ben Wyvis, yet I think it unlikely that a bird that is an insect feeder would nest in a country where, in fine summer weather, insect life is indeed plentiful, but where on days of mist and rain (and these can be frequent) no food would be available without a long flight to the glens beneath. In early June I have seen swifts migrating north across the Cairngorms; the birds were moving steadily in a flock at a considerable height.

Writing of migrating birds on the Cairngorms recalls to my mind a remarkable sight I once saw, very early in the morning, near the Pools of Dee when crossing Lairig Ghru. The sun had gilded Cairntoul, but had not reached the depths of the Lairig. I saw what for an instant seemed a serpent-like creature approaching at an incredible speed. I had not recovered from my astonishment when I realised that this was no strange terrestrial being, but a flock of migrating swallows, moving south through the pass in line and travelling so close to the ground that I could look down on their blue backs as they passed me. It was late August, or early September, and they were on their migration south, having perhaps spent the previous night in Strathspey. In April, 1947, I saw a single swallow migrating northwards over the foothills of the Cairngorms. It was a terrible day with torrential rain and sleet, sometimes mixed with dry snow, yet the swallow was travelling easily, flying low over the heather, although he would have found no single insect to relieve his hunger for many miles. I once found a robin dead, on deep snow, at the Pools of Dee, and on another occasion found a lapwing mummified high on Ben MacDhui. I have no doubt that in mist and driven snow birds on migration lose their bearings when crossing the Cairngorms and, blinded and suffocated by the blizzard, fall exhausted in the snow. Ptarmigan are supposed to burrow beneath the snow during a heavy storm: do the snow buntings, I wonder, also allow themselves to be covered?

I have mentioned that there is a ford on the A'an, by name Ath nam Fiann, near where the river leaves the loch. A century and more ago, it was a ford of considerable importance, for the Lairig nan Laogh—the Calves' Pass—crossed the river here. This pass was used by drovers when they were driving young cattle from the northern Highlands to the markets of the south, hence the name Calves' Pass. The pass left the low ground near Revoan, and ascended to no great elevation as it wound beneath Ben Bynack and then dropped to the A'an. From the A'an it climbed to the Dubh Lochan or Black Lochs, which lie in the pass between Beinn Mheadhon and Beinn a' Chaoruinn, and rather more than a mile south of them reached the march between the counties of Inverness and Aberdeen. It then descended into Glen Derry, and followed the Derry Burn down to Derry Lodge, where it was joined by Lairig Ghru. Although it is long since cattle were driven through Lairig nan Laogh their tracks remain, and it can be seen how the beasts spread out where the surroundings were dry and more or less level—as, for example, when passing beneath Ben Bynack. It shows that when the ground is hard and has been well-trodden it takes very many years for hill vegetation to grow: the ground is presumably pressed too hard for the seeds of heather to germinate.

In Glen Derry can be seen some of the finest old Scots pines of Mar Forest. The root system of these veterans must be of extreme strength. The gales which from time to time sweep the glen in winter are of great violence, yet it is rare, even after an outstandingly severe gale, to find a pine tree which has been uprooted. Lower down, where the woods have been planted, such a storm leaves a tale of destruction, yet the old pines, which have ample space in which to anchor themselves, are able to withstand the strongest gusts. I wonder whether my readers have walked through a wood during the height of a storm when trees were falling like ninepins? I have only once done this. It was not far east of Mar Forest, during the second world war, when great fellings were taking place in the old pine forest. This was the first strong gale since the outpost trees had been felled, and the scene was remarkable. It had been a stormy day, but up to sunset (it was midwinter, when sunset comes early) the force of the wind had not been remarkable. After sunset the wind veered to north-west, and snow squalls drifted past on the gale which quickly increased in violence. There was a young moon in the clear sky when I went out of the house where I had been having tea, and the ground was already frost-bound. Snow was drifting over the surface of the ground, and as I approached the wood through which my path took me I quickly realised the might of the storm. Trees were swaying in the most remarkable way. Some of them bent until they were almost horizontal, yet slowly recovered without losing their roots. But all around me was the menacing sound of trees crashing; they could be seen falling ponderously and the noise of their doom rose above the loud, continous roar of the gale as the wind rushed through the canopy of pine needles. Next morning the road which passes along that wood was blocked by fallen tree trunks.

I have said that the old outpost pines are able to withstand the most severe gale. Yet that is not strictly accurate, for a storm which swept Glen Quoich, in the eastern Cairngorms, almost immediately below Beinn a' Bhuird, in December of the year 1893, created havoc which is now (1949) noteworthy even at first glance, fifty-six years afterwards. I have met no one who was near, or in, Glen Quoich on that day. Anyone who had chanced to be there at the height of that gale would have witnessed a scene which he would have remembered throughout life. The trees here were not sheltered woodlands, but were those strong, noble pines such as the golden eagle nests in, centuries old, with strong root systems. Yet in the gale of 1893 they were helpless, and were blown down like seedlings. These fallen trees are bleached by summer sun and winter frost, yet disintegration has scarcely begun, and their height and girth are well seen as they lie there, all facing south-east, showing that the storm that uprooted them came from the north-west. Not all were uprooted: the root-holds of a few of them defied even that storm, but this was of no avail, for the tree was then snapped clean across by the pitiless wind. Thus in a few minutes one part of the glen lost almost all its trees, yet higher up little havoc was caused, for here it seems that Beinn a' Bhuird broke the full violence of the storm. Beinn a' Bhuird—Hill of the Table— or as it might be more aptly translated Table Mountain, has an unusually level summit. From the south top to the north top is a distance of two miles, and a mountaineer reaching those tops from the west would have little idea of the tremendous precipices which fall from the summit plateau on its east side.

The plateau of Ben A'an is more broken, and the actual summit of that hill is a granite rock 30 feet high—the rock which can be seen from vessels far from land in the North Sea. At one time there must have been a yellow stag who had his summer home high on Ben A'an, judging by the place-name of a shallow hollow near the hill-top. This is named Leabaidh an Daimh Bhuidhe—Bed of the Yellow Stag. The tradition of this Yellow Stag has been entirely lost. Had Scrope, deerstalker and chronicler of deer, ever stalked on Invercauld Forest, or Inchrory Forest (these forests march on Ben A'an) he might have had something to say of the yellow stag. His book *Days of Deer Stalking* treats mainly of the Forest of Atholl, and although he writes shortly about Invercauld he is evidently unacquainted with that district.

Ben A'an is one of the few places which give a view of Loch Etchachan, a high hill loch which lies rather less than a couple of miles south of Loch A'an and 500 feet higher than that loch. It is probably the highest sheet of water in the British Isles to hold trout. At one time a boat was used on the loch, but it has long ago disintegrated: I do not know whether any record was kept of the numbers and weights of trout taken here. The trout which I have seen caught in Loch Etchachan were very thin, as might be expected from the absence of bottom feeding in this clear hill loch, and the scarcity of insects, even in summer. I do not think there is any loch or stream in the Cairngorm area which holds good trout, though many hold small trout in great numbers.

Chapter VIII

STRATHSPEY EAST OF AVIEMORE

AND ACROSS THE HILLS, TO BRAEMAR AND PITLOCHRY

TIMOTHY Pont described the A'an as the most clear and pure river of Scotland: he might have described the air of upper Strathspey as being more clear than in any, or almost any, other Highland district. The moisture-laden winds from the Atlantic have lost most of their dampness by the time they have reached Aviemore, and the air from that place eastward is sometimes of a remarkable clearness. A like purity of atmosphere may perhaps be said to be found above the upper reaches of the Aberdeenshire Dee, here separated by no great distance from the Spey. On upper Deeside, and on Strathspey is to be found what most closely approaches the continental climate in the Scottish Highlands—a warm summer followed by a cold, frosty winter, with snow covering the ground during long periods.

The Cairngorms have their own climate, and the grey plumes of driven snow may be seen waving in the sky to leeward of Braeriach and Cairngorm when in the Spey valley there is no snow on the ground. But the snow can lie long in the Spey valley, and there are years when February gives place to March and still the arrival of spring seems as remote as ever. During spring, that is throughout April and the first half of May, I watched from Aviemore during a number of years a long-sustained migration of lesser black-backed gulls moving north-eastward above the Spey valley. The birds fly usually at a considerable height, but in snowy weather, especially with an adverse wind out of the north-east, they fly low, from time to time calling as they pass. There is, I think, no doubt that these are Scandinavian lesser black-backed gulls, moving towards the Moray Firth, thence across the ocean to Norway, where the species nests abundantly on most of the lesser, uninhabited islands of the Atlantic coast. The birds have perhaps moved up the west coast of Scotland from their winter quarters off the coasts of Spain, Portugal and Africa, or it may be that they have flown by way of the east coast, and have followed the valleys of Tay and Tummel northward, as the wild geese do in April and early May, flying high with musical clamour above Pitlochry, and calling bird lovers to their windows, or into their gardens, to look skyward with eagerness in the hopes of discerning the high-flying geese which produce those wild and musical sounds.

The Spey as it flows through Aviemore and Kinchurdy is still slow for a Highland river, although faster than on its sluggish course through the Drowned Lands above Loch Insh. Five miles below Aviemore it flows through Boat of Garten, where a bridge spans it. The name Boat of Garten commemorates the era when there were no bridges spanning the Spey, and when the crossing of the river was made by boats. Besides Boat of Garten, the place-names Blacksboat, Boat of Cromdale and Boat of Insh tell of the sites of former ferries. The boat at Boat of Garten continued to transport passengers until the year 1899, when the present bridge was built. The Boat of Cromdale was no longer used when, in 1881, a suspension bridge was built over the river. Two years earlier the Boat of Insh had made its last crossing when a bridge was constructed where Spey leaves Loch Insh. In an account of the Spey valley, written in the year 1723, the following Boats are mentioned, beginning with Boat of Spey at Fochabers: Boat of Budge, Boat of Fiddich, Boat of Aberlour, Boat of Delnapot, Boat of A'an and Boat of Cromdale. Shaw in his celebrated *History of Moray* names the "passage boat of Gartenmore," where stood the house of Cumming of Glenchernich, "as yet called Bigla's house, because Bigla, heiress of Glenchernich, married to the Laird of Grant, was the last of the Cummines that enjoyed that land." Shaw continues: "A current tradition beareth that at night a salmon net was cast into the pool below the wall of the house, and a small rope, tied to the net and brought in at the window, had a bell hung at it, which rung when a salmon came into and shook the net." It must have been worth while to have been aroused from sleep in the small hours when a clean-run salmon, waiting to be hauled ashore, was the cause of the disturbance.

The moors east of Aviemore support much bird life, although I do not think birds are so numerous here as they were twenty-five years ago. On the banks of the river itself, oystercatchers arrive early in March, and are joined in mid-April by many sandpipers. The sandpipers remain near the river, but the oystercatchers before the nesting season spread out over the low moors which extend for some distance toward the north from the river's shore. On these moors, in May bright with the flowers of the creeping bearberry, golden plover, oystercatcher and curlew nest on the same ground in sight of the stone circles of Granish, a place of associations with the Druids. There are small lochs and tarns which support a considerable black-headed gull population and there is, or was, at least one fighting ground of black-cock here. This was a heathery knoll, where each morning at dawn blackcock were accustomed to gather for their "lek" or display, a strange ritual such as is practised by no other bird in the British Isles, except perhaps by the capercaillie and that very rare bird the ruff. This sparring, fighting and displaying is not, as might be expected, carried on only during the spring months before the nesting season— I have watched the birds performing on the snowy frost-bound moor on a morning of December as the warm light of the moon was gradually replaced by the cold brightness of a winter dawn. The "lek" or display of the blackcock has been so often described that I need say little of it here, except that the birds showed no fear of the canvas "hide" from which my wife or I so often watched them: on occasion a bird would display excitedly on the roof of the hide, his eager "rookooing" notes sounding very loud when heard at a distance of only a few inches from the observer's head.

A bird which has returned to its ancestral haunts on Upper Spey-side during the last twenty years is the raven, which was unknown here when we lived at Aviemore in the years around 1925, although ancestral nesting places were then pointed out on certain rocks. It has now returned to the district, and also to the Braemar district across the Cairngorms, where it had been unknown for much longer than twenty years. It has so far been able to hold its own, but a much rarer bird, the hen harrier, which also returned to Strathspey during the years of the second world war to nest where it had not been known for perhaps a century, was greeted by a hostile reception, the birds being shot and the nests destroyed.

I have mentioned oystercatcher and sandpiper as being birds of the Spey. The goosander is not common on the main river, although it is on some of its tributaries, but its relative, the red-breasted mer-ganser, is a characteristic bird of Spey, nesting often in a rabbit burrow beside the river. The goosander, on the other hand, usually nests in a hollow tree—often one of the old Scots pines which have died and become hollow. The goosander may nest so far down the hollow of the tree as to be almost invisible, and it has sometimes been wondered how the young ducklings are able to make their way out of the hole—

it has been suggested that they are carried out by the mother bird. In order to observe how the escape from prison was effected my wife on one occasion had a goosander's nesting tree under close observation, and made the interesting discovery that the ducklings, armed with long, very sharp claws, were able to climb up the inner walls of the hollow trunk without difficulty; they then fell perhaps a dozen feet into the heather below with no ill-effect, and were shepherded by the mother to a nearby stream, on which, being water-borne, they were immediately in their element.

The river Dulnan flows almost parallel to the Spey for a time. This river rises in the Monadh Liath hills, flows past Carr Bridge (the old Wade bridge here spans the river above the present bridge) and enters the Spey near Dulnain Bridge. In old days the Dulnan was renowned for its run of autumn salmon. Hear what an old account has to say of the fishing (it should be explained that the word Kipper occurring in the quotation means salmon near or at the time of spawning):

> There comes no salmon in this water, but extraordinary much Kipper, which are in such abundance, that a gentleman thinks nothing to kill 160 in a night. They used to feast the Sheriff, and so escape the fine, but the Commonalty pay some little thing.

The water of the river Dulnan is almost always peat-stained; it rises fast after rain, and the Celtic scholar MacBain gives its name as Tuilnean, from *tuil*—flood.

I have mentioned Kinchurdy, east of Aviemore. On the south bank of the Spey near Kinchurdy stands the historic church of Kincardine. It is a small church, and was a ruin until 1897, when it was restored. It had been without a roof since the fifteenth century; ever, indeed, since that day when it was set on fire by the Grants and the Stewarts of Kincardine to exterminate their enemies the Cummings who, when fleeing from them (they had murdered the chief of Grant), had taken refuge within the church. The pursuers shot a burning arrow into the thatched roof of the church and those within were consumed. The walls have remained: in the south wall is a small opening, the Leper's Window. This was a not uncommon adornment in old churches; through it lepers were able to watch, without exposing those within the church to infection, the celebration of the Mass. In the burial ground is a laburnum tree, centuries old, which may have been in its youth on that day of long ago when the church was fired. The goshawk then doubtless nested in Glenmore and Rothiemurchus and the kite with it, and perhaps the osprey also.

In those days supernatural beings lived with mortals. Most of the old Highland families had a being of this kind closely attached to them. It is said that the Shaws of Rothiemurchus sheltered a sprite named Bodach an Duin—the Old Man of the Doune. When the Grants took possession of the property Bodach an Duin left the house and the warmth of the wood fire, and from that time onwards guarded the tomb of the Shaws in Rothiemurchus burial ground. The Grants of Tullochgorm had also their tutelary being, in the form of a small boy. His name was Mag Molach, the word Molach meaning Hairy, because his left hand "was all over hairy." On a dark night Mag Molach, or Meg Mulloch as his name was sometimes written, would hold a candle before the Goodman, and show him the way home. He was an autocratic being, for if the Goodwife was dilatory in going to bed he "would cast her in beyond him."

Near Loch Morlich was the haunt of a more formidable spectre, he who was known as Bodach Lamh-dhearg—Red-handed Spectre. Lamh-dhearg was accustomed to challenge those who passed through his territory. There is an old undated account of this dreaded being in MacFarlane's *Geographical Collections*, vol. III. Hear what the writer has to say of Lamh-dhearg:

> There is much talking of a Spirit called Ly-Erg that frequents the Glen-More. He appears with a red hand in the habit of a Souldier and challenges men to fight with him, as lately in 69 he fought with three Brothers one after another, who immediately dyed thereafter.

From other incidents mentioned in this old account, I take it that "69" refers to the year 1669. It is possible that it is 1569, but the spelling I think points rather to 1669. Sir Walter Scott mentions the spectre in *Marmion*, and quotes as a foot-note the account which I have quoted.

It is long since the last appearance of Bodach Lamh-dhearg was chronicled, although he, or at all events his tradition, was well known to the Spey floaters—that hardy race of men who floated the pines felled in Glenmore and Rothiemurchus down the Spey to the distant Moray Firth. The felled timber was dragged by ponies to the banks of the main streams flowing through the forests, and when all was ready the sluice gates on Loch Morlich, or the sluice gates on Loch Eanaich, were opened, the logs were thrown into the flood waters, and were guided on their downward course by men of the district armed each with a long pole having a sharp hook at the thin end. When the logs reached the Spey their course was arrested, and they were now in the charge of the Spey floaters, who fashioned them into rafts equipped with oars. The floaters manœuvred these unwieldy floats through the rapids of Spey and over its broad, quiet pools until they had reached Arndilly near Craigellachie, where a sunken rock in mid-channel usually necessitated local help, given by families of the district. A Hull merchant, William Osbourne, in the year 1785 purchased from the Duke of Gordon the forest of Glenmore. In the space of 22 years he felled the forest, and with the timber built at the mouth of the river Spey a fleet of 47 ships. The largest of these vessels was one of 1,050 tons, and she was from the first in the service of the East India Company. The forest was felled at a cost of only £70,000.

Fifteen miles down the Spey from Aviemore is Grantown-on-Spey. The town is on the north bank of the river; above it, on rising ground, stands Castle Grant, once named Freuchie. It has been for at least six centuries the home of the chiefs of Clan Grant—ever since Sir John Grant in the thirteenth century received as a gift from the King of Scotland part of the lands of Strathspey formerly held by the Cummings. It was first named the Castle of Grant in the year 1694. The towers of the castle are the oldest part of the building, and are believed to date from *circa* 1200. One of the towers, Lady Barbie's Tower, is said to be haunted by the ghost of Lady Barbara or Barbie, who was walled in alive here. In the castle is a striking portrait of the family piper, dated 1714. It is said that this piper marched, playing all the way, from Inverness to Castle Grant, a distance of more than thirty miles, perhaps for a wager. He was approaching Castle Grant and was already being acclaimed by those who had gathered to see his arrival, when he staggered, his pipes wailed their last, and he fell dead.

Opposite Grantown-on-Spey, on the south bank of the river, the road to Tomintoul and Braemar leads over the hills. It is one of the most mountainous roads in the Highlands and is snow-bound and usually impassable until late in the spring. At Tomintoul, which village shares with Braemar the doubtful honour of being the highest village in Scotland (it is built high above the river A'an), a sign board is erected in snowy weather where the road to Balmoral and Braemar continues south over the Lecht, 2,090 feet above the sea. If the motorist sees the ominous words "ROAD AHEAD IMPASSABLE THROUGH SNOW," he must abandon the idea of proceeding. I remember one day in late May reading this notice beside the road. It wanted less than a month to the longest day, and I wondered whether it was possible that even this mountain road could be snow-bound at that date. Petrol at the time being severely rationed, I realised the risk of proceeding and being held up in a district where houses are non-existent and turning places are few and far between, and therefore returned to Tomintoul to make further enquiries. My appearance caused something of a stir, for it recalled to the "powers that be" that the notice, which had been put up at the time of an early May snowfall, had been forgotten and, but for my enquiry, might have remained there all summer.

From the highest point of this mountain road there is little view, but half-way down the steep descent to the Don valley an impressive prospect is obtained westward of Cairngorm and Ben MacDhui, the extensive snowfield a short distance below the rounded summit of the latter hill at once catching the eye during the summer months when it gleams white beneath the strong sun. The road drops more and more steeply until, in the valley 1,400 feet above sea-level, it crosses the river Don, here a small stream. Above the river stood the Allargue Arms inn, now a private residence, the landlord being at one time a retired coachman named George Morrison, a man of singular charm and quaint mannerisms. Although himself not a native of upper Strathdon, he was enthusiastic about the strength and purity of the air at his hospitable inn. On one occasion I recall that he told a certain distinguished admiral, "Oh admiral, when I cross the hill to Deeside, I can scarce *breathe*, the air is that stuffy." The admiral, a staunch supporter of Deeside, was "not amused" by the remark. Opposite the former inn is the ruined castle of Corgarff, used, it is said after the rising of 1715, as a garrison.

The road across the hills leaves the Don valley after two miles and crosses to the valley of the Gairn, the high moor between Don and Gairn being prolific in juniper and indeed excellent red grouse country. On this stretch there is a good view down the valley to the hill of Morven, on which I had, many years ago, one of the most memorable nature experiences of my life. I was on the hill-top one winter day at sunset. It was a day of great beauty which increased just before the sun set. At this time a flight of ptarmigan came up the north face of the hill. They were in deep shadow and as they reached the summit ridge their white plumage of a sudden was flushed with a rosy glow which created in them an almost unearthly beauty as they passed on strong wings close to me. From the Gairn, the road crosses yet another hill range and descends to the Dee valley at Balmoral, 900 feet above sea-level. Here it joins the main Deeside road, opposite the royal castle of Balmoral, built on the site of the old residence of Farquharson of Balmoral. Queen Victoria bought the property and for some years resided in the old castle, before building the present more imposing edifice. One of the first forms of the word Balmoral is found in 1451. It is Bouchmorale. This change from 'Bouch' to 'Bal' is seen also in Balquhidder.

During the descent to the Dee valley Lochnagar, rising to a height of just under 3,800 feet above the sea, dominates the view, its precipices holding snow until late in the summer, and on occasion throughout the year. I heard recently from an old stalker how he had found a red grouse sitting on eggs within two hundred yards of the summit cairn of Lochnagar. This must, I think, be the highest grouse's nest recorded in the Highlands. Although he was positive that the hen bird was a red grouse, he did not see the cock, and I have wondered whether this was one of the rare occasions on which a ptarmigan cock had mated with a hen grouse. The only record I have of this happening was given me by Frank Gordon, for many years head stalker on the Balmoral Forest.

West of Balmoral the road to Braemar passes through a part of the old pine forest of Ballochbuie, one of the last haunts of the kite in the Scottish Highlands. Old people remember the pine marten roaming the forest, but this creature, too, has disappeared from Ballochbuie. The Balmoral and Invercauld beats of the Dee give excellent salmon fishing, although the early spring fishing is now non-existent and it is April before the salmon arrive in any numbers, and sometimes even May. Yet I recall the old fishermen telling me that in their youth the river here was full of fish at the opening of the season in February. The salmon have changed their habits—but why? I have read, and heard, many explanations; the most likely being that in old days the Dee was netted as far up the river as Banchory, eighteen miles above the tide. Now the nets have been bought off, and operate only in the tidal reaches. The netting of the river presumably exercised a disturbing effect upon the salmon, and caused them to run through to the upper reaches; the pools, too, must have been kept as clear of stones and rocks as possible, in order that the nets might be worked, and the salmon therefore had comparatively few "lies." When the nets were bought off, the fish were undisturbed and their "lies" in time reformed in the pools. Soon a generation of gillies and fishermen will arise with no memory of the great fishing days on the upper reaches of the river Dee in February, when the river was half choked with ice and the line froze to the rings of the rod.

At Braemar, eight miles farther up the river Dee from Balmoral, is held each September the celebrated Braemar Gathering. This reached the height of its glory—I use the word "glory" advisedly—in the years prior to the first world war. It was always a large gathering, but was a more homely affair than it now is, for these were the days before long-distance motor tours, and buses and char-a-bancs come from Glasgow and Edinburgh, Manchester and Liverpool. The clans then were in their pride. In those days three clans paraded and marched round the gathering ground with pipes playing. The first to enter the arena were the Balmoral Highlanders, followed by the Duff Highlanders, and by the Invercauld Highlanders. Each clansman was in full Highland dress, and each carried some war-like instrument. There were humorous episodes, as when an old clansman saw a halfpenny on the grass, stooped with Highland thrift, slowly and painfully, to pick it up, and thereby held up the whole march-past. There was more whisky then than there is now, and some of the veterans towards the close of the proceedings walked stiff and straight, but steered a devious course. I remember one of them after the march past coming up to me and, waving grandly towards the sky, saying "Eagles [a long pause], eagles, Mr. Gordon, *hundreds* of them."

In those days the Duff Highlanders were led by a large pipe band, their acting pipe major being Colin Cameron, the Duke of Fife's piper. He was a distinguished man, with white beard and martial air. He was besides a very fine piper, who came of a famous line of pipers. His brother Alexander (usually named Sandy) was perhaps more renowned than Colin. The clans, with their bands, made two appearances on the gathering ground. In the morning they marched round bravely, and after the King and Queen had arrived they marched round still more bravely, for they had been fortified by an excellent lunch. I remember on two occasions, when I was one of the judges of the piping competitions, an amusing episode occurring—amusing, that is, for the spectators, but not for those more closely concerned. Pipe Major George MacLennan of the Gordon Highlanders, a renowned piper, was in the midst of his pibroch, "The Desperate Battle," when the sound of approaching pipes was heard, and to the horror of the judges the clansmen of three clans appeared in the offing, with their massed bands. As they approached the platform where Geordie MacLennan was playing, the noise became almost deafening. We were in a quandary. Should we stop the piper, who was playing very well, or allow him to proceed? We, as I think rightly, chose the latter course, and by sitting on the platform and actually at the piper's feet, were able to hear his faultless playing above the turmoil. Geordie was apparently unmoved, and finished his tune as well as he had begun it, winning, if I remember aright, the first prize. "The Desperate Battle" was an appropriate pibroch to be played under these strange conditions. Some years later the same predicament occurred. The piper on this occasion was Pipe Sergeant J. D. MacDonald of the Scots Guards. He was playing his best when the ominous sound of the pipe bands was heard. As they neared the lonely competitor Sir Douglas Ramsay, who was the King's Commissioner and in command of the Balmoral Highlanders, saw what was happening, and stopped his pipers as they passed the platform. But the pipers of the two other clans, who followed, continued to play their hardest, and one of the judges, being strange to that gathering and not knowing what had happened on a previous occasion, took it upon himself to stop the piper, wrongly as I think. It was a decision that was unfortunate for J. D. MacDonald, for when he played the second time his perform-ance was not so good as it had been on the first occasion.

King George V was much interested in pipe playing; indeed there were few non-pipers of that time who took so much interest in the classical pipe music as the king. He always used to send for me at the close of a competition, and ask me the history of the various tunes, and who composed them, and how his own pipers were playing. He was interested when I told him that the Prince of Wales, as he then was, used to play on my pipes at Oxford. The day of the Braemar Gathering was always a memorable one, and the stalkers in the out-lying glens for some days previously scanned the sky anxiously.

Corran Ferry, looking across to Ardgour

On one occasion I crossed the Cairngorms the day before the meeting, and after judging at Braemar walked back through the hills during the night to judge at the Kingussie Gathering the next day. I tried unsuccessfully to persuade some of the competing pipers to accompany me, but they preferred to travel the easier way, by bus and train, rather than cross the hills a distance of twenty miles in the dark. The second occasion on which we did this, my friend and I had so dark a night for our walk that we could scarcely see our hands in front of our faces. King George sent me a letter through his equerry after that walk. It ran, "When the King heard the rain in the small hours of the morning His Majesty hoped that you were enjoying yourself." The Braemar Gathering, although shorn of some of its former splendour, still attracts great numbers of spectators, among them many visitors from overseas.

Braemar Castle, leased by many years by Princess Alexis Dolgorouki, a Scottish lady with great kindness of heart, who did much good to the district, was, like Corgarff Castle, built as a garrison after the Jacobite risings.* Rather more than a mile from it is the site of Kindrochaid Castle, a residence of Malcolm Ceann Mór and no doubt of other Scottish kings. The country west of Braemar has been denuded of its trees, great areas having been felled during the years of the second world war. West of Braemar is Mar Lodge and near that residence, but on the south side of the river Dee, the Ey flows down from the south.

At the Linn of Dee the river flows through a narrow gorge, sheltered by old Scots pines. Here many salmon may be seen in late summer and in autumn leaping the formidable cascades and appearing to have little success. Yet success they must have, for the salmon fishing above the Linn is excellent if the season is right and the water in good order. The road, as a public highway, ends at Linn of Dee, but a track continues to the Bynack, and across the boggy watershed to the upper reaches of Glen Tilt in Atholl.

* Invercauld House is on the opposite side of the Dee from Braemar Castle but a great rock face, named the Invercauld Charter Chest, is on the same side. This received its name because the Invercauld charters were concealed on a ledge of the rock during the Jacobite rising of 1715. The Farquharsons of Invercauld—the family is now extinct in the male line—were much respected by their tenants. John Stoddart records that when he was there about 1799 each tenant brought the Laird a lump of coal, carrying it on foot all the way from Aberdeen, nearly sixty miles distant. The same writer at Invercauld House saw a Cairngorm crystal nearly 2 feet in length; it was found on Beinn a' Bhuird.

Corpach with Ben Nevis in background

The main Deeside road, after passing in view of Invercauld House, the childhood home of Lady Anne Mackintosh who supported Prince Charles Edward at the memorable Rout of Moy, and winding close to Braemar Castle, leaves the valley of the Dee in Braemar village and climbs south steadily until at the Cairnwell, or more correctly Cairnwall, it reaches a height of 2,200 feet above sea-level, the highest road in Britain. Here the golden eagle may be seen sailing overhead; here ptarmigan may rise actually from the side of the road. The renowned zig-zag known as the Devil's Elbow has been improved, yet the gradient, which is a down-gradient coming from Braemar, still is formidable. The road now descends to and traverses Glen Beag, which soon joins Glen Shee, the Fairy Glen. In Glen Shee is a strong tradition of that great warrior band, the Fèinne or Fiann, sometimes referred to in English as Fingalians. We have only to refer to the old *Statistical Account* to know how strong was the tradition. Let us hear what the parish minister, the Rev. Allan Stewart, writes concerning it:

A hill at the head of Glenshee, called Beinn Ghulbhuinn, is distinguished by having been the scene of a hunting which proved fatal to Diarmid, one of the Fingalian heroes. Here are shown the den of the wild boar that was hunted, a spring called Tobar nam Fiann, the fountain of the Fingalians; a small lake, called Loch an Tuirc, the boar's loch; also Diarmid's grave, where he was buried by his comrades. . . . The eminence where Diarmid was buried is called Tulach Diarmid, Diarmid's Hill, whence the late proprietor of the ground was called, Fear Tulaich Diarmid, laird of Diarmid's Hill.

The scene of the death of Diarmid is located in many places. It is on Tiree in the Hebrides, in Sutherland, in Ross-shire (both Easter Ross and Kintail), in Brae Lochaber, in Knapdale in Argyll, and in Skye, but the strongest and most circumstantial tradition of them all is in Glen Shee. The tales agree that Diarmid was killed by a poisonous bristle from a boar piercing his heel (in one version entering beneath his toe nail), the only vulnerable part of this great hero, most handsome of the Fèinne. In one version of the tale the boar slain is one of the herd of magic swine owned by Balar, the Fomorian giant, famed for his evil eye. When slain, this boar provided a week's food for a hundred warriors with their hounds. Diarmid, as the boar's poison began to take effect, made the request for a draught of water from Fionn's

magic cup of healing. Fionn refused, for he had not forgiven Diarmid
for eloping with his young and beautiful wife Grainne.

The hills at the head of Glen Shee are more pastoral than those
on Deeside and give grazing to many sheep. Below the inn named
Spittal of Glenshee there is good arable land, although crops ripen
late, since the elevation for eight miles down the glen continues to be
1,000 feet or more above the sea. In Glen Shee the boundaries of the
counties of Perth and Angus closely approach one another, although
the glen itself is in the county of Perth. As you cross from Braemar,
you leave the county of Aberdeen at the watershed, where Carn an
Tuirc (perhaps named after the boar from whose poisonous bristle
Diarmid met his death), Cairn na Glasha, and Glas Maol rise magnificently to the east on the county march. These hills are a grand
ski-ing ground when, after a long storm from the south-east, they are
sometimes buried yards deep in snow. In the early months of the year
1947 in particular these high hills had a depth of snow on them so
great that they resembled hills of the ice-cap of Iceland or Spitsbergen
rather than British mountains.

The road through Glen Shee travels near the river that is first
named the Water of Shee and lower down the Black Water: it reaches
Blairgowrie and there joins the main road to Perth. A second road
leads across country to Kirkmichael, and thence over the hills to
Pitlochry. I recall driving across this road on a day of late April when
a strong west wind was blowing. From the high ground above Pitlochry there is, in clear weather, an impressive view of Ben Lawers
far to the west. On this afternoon the westering sun was near Ben
Lawers, and the whole of the hill was haloed in gold and silver. The
wind, on those high slopes blowing with gale force, was lifting the dry
powdery snow and carrying it forward in clouds which rose a hundred
feet and more, and caught the sun's light with impressive effect—the
whole hill seemed to be alight with mystic fire. Here we were beneath
Ben Vrackie, a distinctive hill of majestic appearance. At the summit
of Ben Vrackie I once watched a hen ptarmigan fashioning her
nesting hollow. Both cock and hen birds were feeding, and after a time
the hen settled down in a brooding attitude among the short heather
and blaeberry plants. When she had risen and walked away I gave the
birds time to feed some distance from the place, then went to it. Where
she had brooded, I found a nest ready for eggs. I returned very early
in the morning on May 20, two days afterwards, hoping to find an

egg in the nest, but there was no egg, neither was there any sign of the birds themselves—I had no opportunity of going at a later date to see whether eggs had been laid and hatched in the nesting hollow.

The usual ascent of Ben Vrackie (Beinn Bhreac—the Speckled Hill) begins at Moulin. The high rocks above Moulin were, since time immemorial, the nesting place of a pair of peregrine falcons which, because of their use in falconry, were under the special protection of the Scottish king. One year, so the old tradition has it, just as the falcon was preparing to lay her first egg an old raven came from the haunted Forest of Gaick in Badenoch, and drove the falcon from her eyrie and from her rock. The falcon had given long battle against the raven, but when at last she was defeated she rose higher and higher into the air, then set a course southwards and was seen no more. Seven days went by, and then the falcon was seen flying in from the south. She had with her a slim, long-winged white bird, and the stranger flew at once at the raven and killed him at a blow, at the same time losing a single feather from his own wing. He watched, as he circled, the falcon take possession of her ancestral eyrie, then flew swiftly southwards, being never seen again. The feather was picked up, and was found to be so hard that it could cut a shaving from the hardest oak plank. No one had seen the like of that bird of supreme swiftness, strength and beauty, but all were agreed that it was the King of Birds, to whom the falcon had flown for help. During the second world war the rocks above Moulin saw each evening a gathering of ravens, sometimes scores of these birds, which flew in from every direction to roost on the high ledges. They remained until May, at which time the local ravens had hatched their eggs and were tending full-fledged young in the nest. Can this assembly have had anything to do with the upheaval in the bird world caused by the northern front, in Finland and in Russia? The gathering of ravens grew with the war years, quickly became less, and is no longer seen here.

PART IV

THE CALEDONIAN CANAL

CHAPTER I

BEN NEVIS AND LOCH ARKAIG

FROM Fort William in the west to Inverness in the east the Caledonian Canal cleaves its way across the Highlands, through a district known as the Great Glen. The ships that use it (it is passable only for vessels of a comparatively small tonnage) are saved the long passage round the north of Scotland and through the stormy Pentland Firth. Steering in from the Atlantic to the entrance of the Caledonian Canal, a vessel enters the upper reaches of Loch Linnhe at Corran. East of Corran the sea loch is now named in Gaelic an Linne Dhubh—the Black Pool—but the old name was Loch Abar, a name from which the well-known west Highland district of Lochaber takes its name. At the end of the Corran—the word means a low, pointed cape—a lighthouse stands. Near the Corran is the house of Ardgour, where the Macleans of Ardgour have lived (the property descending from father to son in unbroken succession) for over 500 years. From the heights above the house a stream falls in a succession of white cascades. In wet weather the falls are imposing. They have long been named Maclean's Towell, in Gaelic Tubhailt mhic 'ic Eoghainn. A couple of miles east of the Corran is a low skerry not far from the south shore of the sea loch. Here, when the tide is low, the seal population of the district congregate. They climb out of the sea, and bask in the summer sun, lying with great happiness on sharp-edged rocks to which their thick blubber renders them impervious, acting as a cushion so that they rest there as comfortably as a human being on a feather bed. I have sometimes watched those seals; for its size, the rock is more crowded than any I know. It is possible that one of the members of this seal club—for that is what it is—may have been the hero of an incident which took place on a neighbouring river one autumn day, when, as I have related elsewhere, an angler who had played a salmon and had in triumph dragged it on to a shingle bed, had it seized and carried off by a seal under his very eyes. On a sunny afternoon in early summer I watched the seals' skerry for some time. More and more seals climbed heavily from the sea loch, until there did not seem to be room for another—and still they came. They were of all sizes, small

199

common seals, round-headed, and large Atlantic seals with long retriever-like heads. They lay, close-packed like sardines, dozed and then slept soundly. From time to time a seal would awaken, yawn hugely, or wipe its face with a flipper with a human-like gesture. This sun-bathing dried the seals' fur, and it became loose and shaggy like a dog's. When the tide began to encroach upon the skerry the seals, thoroughly warmed and still sleepy, were reluctant to move. They allowed the water to wash over the ledge on which they lay, and it was only when they were almost afloat that they plunged beneath the surface and turned to fishing as a change from sun-bathing.

The Caledonian Canal, a lasting monument to the great Telford, is entered at Corpach, where the upper waters of Loch Linnhe, Loch Abar, an Linne Dhubh—call it what you will—bends away to the north to form Loch Eil. In 1799 John Stoddart in his book *Scenery and Manners in Scotland* describes the projected idea of the Caledonian Canal. He writes, "An undertaking of this magnitude seems justly to claim the patronage of government, and to the coasting and foreign trade it would save a most dangerous and difficult navigation." Corpach received its name in the distant past, when the bodies of the illustrious dead were rested here on the journey to sacred Iona, the journey from Corpach to Iona, or at all events from Corpach to Mull, being completed by sea. The vessel which enters the canal is lifted in a series of locks, appropriately named Neptune's Staircase, and then proceeds east, following closely the course of the river Lochy. To the south are the ruins of the castle of Inverlochy, a seat of the Scottish kings in very ancient times, and said to have been in its glory three hundred years before the days of William the Conqueror. It is perhaps most celebrated for its associations with the battle of Inverlochy, fought in the year 1645 between the Great Montrose and Argyll, Montrose gaining a spectacular victory which inspired the Gaelic poet Iain Lom to produce verses of such excellence that he received the appointment of Poet Laureate to the King. Iain Lom was a master of satire. He might have had something to say about the great aluminium works which have sprung up beside Inverlochy. The water, which has passed beneath the heart of Ben Nevis from Loch Treig through the bowels of the earth, provides power for these works. Fluorine is given off in considerable quantities, and it is held that this, being drifted over the land on the wind, is injurious to cattle and trees; teeth of sheep and cattle rot, and trees die.

Glen Shiel, Ross-shire, looking west
Inverness

A couple of miles from the old and ruined Inverlochy Castle is the modern castle of the same name. Here Queen Victoria stayed when journeying in the west Highlands; her room is still known. Below the castle is a small loch with an island. Each year a pair of mute swans arrive here in April from the salt waters of Loch Linnhe. The male bird arrives first, flies away again, and returns a little later with his wife. The nest is made on an island of the loch and when the cygnets are hatched they are led over the fields by their parents to the river Lochy, and on it are borne to the salt water, on which the family party may subsequently be seen. The cygnets are sometimes carried by the old swans on their backs during the over-land journey.

Dominating the scene here, either from the canal, the river, or the road, is Ben Nevis, the highest hill in the British Isles. Its height (4,406 feet) exceeds that of Ben MacDhui in the Cairngorms by only 110 feet, but actually Ben Nevis is much the higher mountain of the two, for its base is at sea level, whereas the base of Ben MacDhui (if this be taken at Derry Lodge in Mar Forest, where the road ends) is 1,400 feet above sea-level. The grandeur of Ben Nevis is, I think, best appreciated from Inverlochy. One looks from the castle with its sheltering trees and sees a vast hill rising, usually to the clouds. Ben Nevis recalls to me, more than any other Scottish hill, a mountain of Norway. Unlike a mountain of Norway, it has no glacier, but in its north-east corrie it bears a snowfield that remains unmelted from one year to another. During the tropical August of the year 1947, when there was an absolute drought at Inverlochy throughout the month, the snowfield gleaming high in the corrie of Ben Nevis seemed to belong to another world. The secret of its longevity is that it lies beneath the north-east precipice and is entirely sheltered from the warm breath of the south-west winds from the Atlantic which would soon disintegrate it were it on the west slopes of the hill. The only other snow drift that remains throughout the year on Highland hills is on Braeriach, one of the Cairngorms, and, as I mention in another chapter, it also lies in a site completely sheltered from winds from a south or south-westerly point.

The snow cap is unbroken on the rounded summit of Ben Nevis until the end of May—in some seasons later. It has been computed by experts that if the hill were a thousand feet higher it would be snow-capped throughout the year. When my wife and I visited Norway in the summer of 1947 we climbed Snehette, one of Norway's highest

201

hills, at the end of June. Even on that hill-top, 7,560 feet above sea-level, the snow cap had already broken by June 30, but Snehette rises inland and Ben Nevis, which had in one year a rainfull of 240 inches, recorded in the days when an observatory stood on the summit, must have a considerably heavier snow-fall than Snehette. Although there is no snow-cap permanently on Ben Nevis there is no month in the year on which snow does not fall here. The average shade temperature on the summit is 20 degrees lower than at Fort William—thus on a cold summer day with a temperature at Fort William of 55 degrees Fahrenheit, the temperature on the summit will be found to be approximately 35 degrees, which is cold enough for snow. This summer snow does not usually lie, but may sometimes be seen as a grey shower drifting over the hill. For weeks at a time the hill-top may be in mist, but when the sky is clear and the visibility is good the view from the summit will be remembered through life by him who sees it. On exceptional days—I should say less than half a dozen times in the course of a year—the hills of the North Ireland coast are visible. More often the hills of the Outer Hebrides can be seen. From one of these hills (Beinn Mhór in South Uist) I have actually seen the shadow of a cloud fall on one of the great snow-fields of Ben Nevis—and this at a distance of a full ninety miles.

I recall being with a friend on Ben Nevis throughout a July night. At that time there was a small building on the summit where it was possible to stay. We arrived late in the evening and were out on the small plateau before sunrise. The night before had been almost cloud-less, and we had seen the sun set in the north-west, behind the hills of Knoydart and the Isle of Skye. During the short hours of twilight a low cloud layer, white and woolly, had spread over Scotland from the North Sea and the Moray Firth, and at sunrise had covered all the low-lying land and the lesser hills, only the high hills emerging from the mist which, an aerial sea, became silvery and dazzling when the sun shone upon it. At sunrise the mist was salmon pink, and showed delicate shades in its slow-moving billows which moved almost im-perceptibly westward on the breath of a light wind. As the sun gained in strength rifts appeared here and there in the mist and there were glimpses of lochs and rivers, and of the sea. Overhead the sky was deep blue, that glorious unclouded blue which is seen only on the high tops, and, even there, only in fine weather. At a little distance from the summit a small colony of plants of *Saxifraga stellaris* were beginning to open their flower buds, their small white flowers, each with a yellow spot at the base, the only alpine blooms to be seen in the neighbourhood: growing as they do at a height of 4,300 feet above the sea, they are the highest flowers in the British Isles. I remember looking that morning across to the Cairngorms far to the east, where the sun was shining on the corries of Cairntoul and Braeriach, and then across the abyss of cloud-filled Glen Nevis to where two stags stood, sharply outlined against the sky, on the ridge of Sgùrr a' Mhaim, small dark figures against a background of glowing mist, white as snow and more white than the lingering snowfields which lay in the corrie below the stags. There was here no twittering song of snow bunting—a song which I had listened to almost throughout the night on the high Cairngorms a few weeks before—nor was there the hoarse croaking and snorting of ptarmigan; one seemed to be in a world above even that of the birds.

On another day, this time in early summer, a friend and I found the snow cap still unmelted on Ben Nevis, and when we reached the plateau, we saw the roof of the observatory just appearing above the snowy level. Many insects crawled upon this snowy surface; they were the only life to be seen here, on the highest ground in Scotland. The observatory on the summit of Ben Nevis was opened in October, 1883, and was closed, through lack of funds, in October, 1904.

A record of the life at the observatory is given in W. T. Kilgour's book, *Twenty Years on Ben Nevis*. Some of the winter storms were tremendous. On November 22, 1898, the wind force was estimated as 150 miles an hour. The drifting was then so fierce that the dry powdery snow was forced into the observatory through the tiniest chink. In the morning fully a ton of snow was lying in the lobby and passages, and the kitchen floor was snow-covered to within a yard of the stove, which was always alight day and night. That morning, although a bright fire was burning, the temperature of the office fell to 27 degrees, and a thermometer hanging 6 feet from the fire in the kitchen fell to 2 degrees below freezing point. That particular snowstorm and tempest came at a bad moment for the observatory. There was only a slight covering of snow on the hill-top and the walls of the building were bare, so that the snow drifted through the crannies. The snowfall gradually increased during the winter and spring months until on one occasion an average depth of 12 to 14 feet of snow lay on the summit. When a depth of snow of even half that figure lay on the mountain, the rooms of the observatory were warm and cosy however wildly the storm raged without. On one occasion a temporary observer at the weather station almost lost his life in a blizzard. As he left the tower door to take one of the hourly readings the gale was at its height. He was told to grasp the guide rope, but did not do so, and at once was a plaything of the wind. Losing his bearings he shouted feebly for help. He was located after several unsuccessful attempts and dragged inside. He was unable to utter a word, for his features were covered, and his mouth was sealed, with frozen snow.

It is strange that, while observatory records show that a sun temperature of 130 degrees was not uncommon at midsummer, the snow in the gully beneath the observatory should remain unmelted from one year to another. There is a tradition—I have never seen it confirmed in writing—that by an ancient charter the owner of Ben Nevis holds his lands only so long as there is snow to be found on the Ben. If that were so, one would imagine that the property would have changed hands in the year 1945. The snow-beds were small at the beginning of October, and that month was mild and rainy. The rain melted the snow, and during the first days of November, as I have in another chapter recorded, mountaineers who looked from the ridge to the east of the main hill into the snowy gully beneath the precipice saw that it was entirely free of snow.

The derivation of the word *Nevis* is unknown. The Celtic scholar, Alexander MacBain, whose *Place Names in the Highlands and Islands*, published in 1922, is still a classic on the subject, inclines to the belief that "the nymph Nebesta gave her name to, or found her name in, the River Nevis, and gave her name to Glen Nevis, and it again to the famous Ben, which again renders Inverness-shire unique, not merely among Scottish but among British counties, by having, as one of its glories, the highest hill in Britain. Loch Nevis also lends proof to the argument that Nevis denotes water originally."

From the Caledonian Canal in clear weather there is a good view of the snow-field lying in Observatory Gully of Ben Nevis. It is noteworthy that this snow-bed should remain from one year to another while, only five miles as the eagle flies, the climate is, even in winter, moist and warm, and in some seasons the winter may pass without a single snow-fall.

About eight miles from the sea the Caledonian Canal broadens into Loch Lochy, a long and narrow loch some eight miles in length, with water deep enough to afford a passage to the *Queen Elizabeth* if she could pass through the canal. Into Loch Lochy flows the river Arkaig, a short river of rather more than a mile in length with its source in Loch Arkaig, which was one of the last haunts in Britain of that rare and beautiful bird the osprey. At Achnacarry beside Loch Arkaig is the home of Cameron of Lochiel, whose ancestor, sometimes known as the Gentle Lochiel, lost his lands but won immortal fame and renown through placing himself and his clan at the disposal of Prince Charlie in 1745. The Lochiel of the rising of 1715 did not so greatly distinguish himself, and it was said that as a baby his foot was too large for the silver shoe which Lochiel's eldest son always wore at the christening: this was held to be a bad omen. At Achnacarry is to be seen a memorial to the Gentle Lochiel of the Forty-five such as he would have loved—a stately avenue of beech trees growing very close together. At the time when Lochiel took up arms for the Prince the young trees had been laid temporarily in the ground, to be planted elsewhere, and spaced more carefully when the time was opportune. Then came the rising of 1745, the campaign which ended with disaster on Culloden Moor, and the dispersal of the clans. Lochiel escaped to France. His castle at Achnacarry was burned to the ground by Cumberland's troopers, and not a vestige of it remains. Lochiel died a fugitive in France, and the trees grew and flourished as they were temporarily laid in the ground. There are still older trees near the avenue; in some of the trunks hollows were cut by the Hanoverian troops, so that a beam might be held in position at a little height from the ground, either end of the beam resting in slots cut in two neighbouring trees; on the beams were hung the kettles and pots of Cumberland's soldiers. On a wooded hill near the castle stood the hut which Lochiel used when in hiding, and to which I refer later on in this chapter; no trace of it remains.

The present castle at Achnacarry was built near the site of the old. Here is the snuff-box given to Lochiel by the Prince, and the standard that was carried by Cameron of Coruanan at the battle of Culloden; another relic is the targe carried by Lochiel at the battle of Harlaw in 1411.

Loch Arkaig is a beautiful loch, a forest of ancient Scots pines growing to the west and oak woods to the east. Like Loch Ness, it has, or had, its monster. Lord Malmesbury records it in his *Memoirs* (1857) as follows:

My stalker, John Stuart at Achnacarry, has seen it twice, and both times at sunrise in summer, when there was not a ripple on the water. The creature was basking on the surface; he saw only the head and hind-quarters, proving that its back was hollow, which is not the shape of any fish, or of a seal. Its head resembled that of a horse.

This record is of singular interest, since most of those who have seen the Loch Ness Monster agree that its head resembles the head of a horse.

On the north shore of Loch Arkaig grew, or perhaps still grows, the oak tree associated with a tragedy enacted after the Forty-five. The story was given me by a descendant of one of the chief actors in that tragedy. After the suppression of the rising of 1745 a Lochaber man, Dugald Roy Cameron, sent his son to Fort William with his arms, to be delivered up to the government troops, pursuant to the order regarding the surrender of weapons in the possession of the Highlanders. This lad was proceeding along the road by the north shore of Loch Arkaig when he was met by an officer named Grant who was conducting a party of soldiers through the hills to Knoydart. Grant seized young Cameron and, since he was carrying arms, flatly disbelieved his tale that he was carrying them to be delivered up—and had him shot there and then. When the lad's father heard of this ruthless act he vowed to be revenged, and to take the officer's life. It was not difficult to distinguish Grant from his brother officers because he rode a white horse. Dugald Roy took up his position on a rocky knoll which overlooked the Loch Arkaig road and grimly awaited the rider on that white horse. Now it happened that on the morning of Sunday, August 31, 1746, Captain George Munro of Culcairn decided, for some reason, to borrow Grant's white horse for a tour of duty. As he was returning from it, Donald Roy saw at last the sight he had long been hoping to see—a white horse in the dusk rounding a bend of the road. He took careful aim at the rider of that horse and shot him dead.

Thus did tragedy follow on the heels of tragedy. A widespread search ensued for Dugald Roy Cameron, when suspicion later fell on him, but at the time the fatal shot was fired Colonel Grant of Moy was walking along the road with his gun on his shoulder, and he was the first suspect. He was arrested, and was taken to Fort William, but was later declared innocent and was set at liberty. Dugald Roy evaded capture and later enlisted in the British army, where after a time his identity was discovered but he was allowed to go unpunished. It is traditionally said that the retainers of Munro of Culcairn were confidently expected to join in the hunt for the man who had killed their chieftain: they refused to do so, saying that, although the deed had brought them bitter sorrow, they could not avenge it, because the man who had shot Culcairn had done so in error.

There is a belief that French gold and treasure were concealed somewhere in the neighbourhood of Loch Arkaig during the time of the 1745 rising. Search has been made on more than one occasion for the Loch Arkaig Treasure, and under this name it has achieved considerable notoriety, but nothing has been discovered, and indeed its exact whereabouts is unknown.

Near the lower end of Loch Arkaig, on its north shore, is Achnasaul. It was in a broken-down shieling above Achnasaul that Prince Charles Edward, while "skulking in ye Highlands," spent the night after fording the river Garry in flood at the hazard of his life. The next day two of his party went to repair a small hut in which Lochiel had hidden for some time. As they approached the hut they saw a deer feeding near it. They shot the deer, which provided the party with much-needed food, and, having found the hut in good condition, the party lodged there the night.

It is likely that the osprey in those days nested on Loch Arkaig, although it is doubtful if the oak on the small island where the birds latterly nested was then sufficiently grown. I photographed the nest in the autumn of 1909. At that time only one of the birds was returning each spring to that old eyrie, its mate having in all probability been shot, and I do not think the nest was afterwards occupied although it was then in a good state of preservation. A few years before my visit those pioneer naturalists, Richard and Cherry Kearton, had visited the island and had obtained a striking photograph of the osprey perched on the oak-tree top beside its eyrie. This photograph would hold its own in comparison with even the best nature photographs of the present day and is a valuable record of the osprey's life in the Highlands, for the species has, alas, long been extinct except as a passage migrant, although there are often rumours that a pair of ospreys have been nesting on some remote loch. The rarer the osprey became, the more enviously were the eyes of egg collectors fixed on the Loch Arkaig pair. All that could be done was done to protect the nest. The boats on Loch Arkaig were kept under lock and key, and entanglements of barbed wire surrounded the island, yet collectors swam out, surmounted the obstacles, and stole the eggs. There was in addition a danger to the birds themselves, for being migrants, they twice each year ran the gauntlet of gunners on the south-east coast of England. Stuffed pairs of ospreys, probably Highland-nesting birds, may still be seen in collections in that part of England. It may be remembered that at a later date an attempt was made to reintroduce the osprey to Loch Arkaig by liberating a pair of American birds there, but, perhaps naturally, they did not return to the district. It might be possible to fly a clutch of osprey's fresh eggs to Prestwick from northern Scandinavia, where the species still nests, and transfer them to a buzzard's eyrie in the neighbourhood of Loch Arkaig. I think the buzzards would successfully rear the young ospreys, and birds reared in the district would be more likely to return to it than young birds brought from overseas to a country that is foreign to them. Lochiel tells me that he remembers one memorable season when there were seven ospreys on Loch Arkaig. Two pairs had nested, and one of these pairs had reared two young; these were beside an unattached old bird. One pair nested on the mainland that year but their eggs were taken and in their place was found in the nest a pebble of the shape and size of an osprey's egg. I hoped that the experiment might be made on some of the ancestral nesting lochs of the osprey in the Highlands of placing a cart wheel horizontally at a height of a dozen to twenty feet above shallow water. It has been found, in countries where the osprey still nests, that a cart wheel is an attractive nesting site. The osprey in Scotland nested often on the island of a loch, usually in a tree. It also nested on ruined castles, as Loch an Eilein Castle in Rothiemurchus and the old MacLeod stronghold, Ardvreck Castle, on Loch Assynt in Sutherland, both of which nesting sites I mention elsewhere in this book. Ospreys are still seen from time to time in April and early May in the Loch an Eilein district, and in autumn not so many years ago an immature osprey broke its wing by striking a telegraph wire in Strathspey. Hopes on these occasions have arisen that the old nesting place might be occupied once more, but the birds are apparently on migration, to Lapland and other northern countries, and have not shown any intention of remaining to nest. It is said that the Loch Arkaig ospreys never fished in Loch Arkaig but crossed to the salt water of Loch Eil for their food.

CHAPTER II

LOCH LOCHY AND GLEN GARRY

I HAVE recorded the now little-known record of the monster of Loch Arkaig. I do not think Loch Lochy has its monster; if it has, the creature lies low and does not advertise its presence. Loch Lochy is separated from Loch Oich by no more than two miles of land. Loch Oich, a much smaller loch, has no great depth of water, and during the remarkable February of the year 1947, when no snow, nor even a single shower of rain, fell throughout the month, and when a prolonged frost sealed many of the springs, the loch shrunk to such a low level that vessels could no longer pass through it and the Canal had therefore to be closed for a time.

Halfway down Loch Oich, on its north side, are the ruins of Invergarry Castle, the ancestral fortress and home of the MacDonells of Glengarry. It stands on Creagan an Fhithich—the Rock of the Raven—and from time immemorial the slogan of the MacDonells of Glengarry has been "Creagan an Fhithich." It is believed that two earlier castles stood where the ruins of the present castle stand. The first castle was destroyed by General Monk, who had been sent by Cromwell to reduce the Highland chiefs. The second castle was completed before the battle of Killiecrankie in 1689, the masons employed at the work being paid at the rate of 2d. a day.

It will be remembered that the massacre of Glencoe took place because MacDonald of Glencoe delayed taking the oath of allegiance to the king. Glengarry also delayed, but he apparently came in just before the end of the period of grace. He was nevertheless ordered to leave his castle, which by autumn of the same year was garrisoned by government troops. Lord Stair about that time wrote to Colonel Hill as follows:

> I wrote to you formerly that if the rest were willing to concur, as the crows do, to pull down Glengarry's nest this winter, still the garrisoning of his house will be fully as acceptable.

The garrison remained in the castle from 1692 until 1715. In that year, when the gathering of the clans for the first Jacobite rising took place, Glengarry with 500 men marched to his castle, and took the garrison prisoners. But the rising ended in the defeat of the Highlanders, and in April Glengarry surrendered to General Cadogan in Inverness and a garrison was once again sent to the castle. In August of the same year the castle was again burnt down, some say intentionally by the garrison. The castle was rebuilt, and at the time of the rising of 1745 Prince Charlie was on two occasions a guest in it—on the day before he and his men crossed the Pass of Corriearag to surprise Cope, and later as a refugee after the fatal day of Culloden. It was very shortly after this, on a dark and tempestuous night in May, 1746, that a party of soldiers arrived from Inverness at Invergarry, with orders to demolish the castle. It was set on fire there and then, and has ever since remained a ruin. Invergarry House, which stands near the ruined castle, had its Brownie. This being forsook the place on being scalded by one of the servants. Everything went wrong in the house for some time afterwards.

At Achadrom, sometimes spelled Achadron, about three miles west of Invergarry, is the watershed between the east and west coast. As an old MS. written *circa* 1630 puts it:

> It is alleadgit be ancient men that this Achadron is in the midst of Scotland in lenth. And there is one stone in a plaine ground . . . it is called the stone of the Ridge of Scotland, and so the strath is named the mid part of Scotland. . . . There is a litle burn fra the hill syde that divides, one branch runs to the Westsea into Lochlohy and the other branch runs to the Eastsea through Lochoich.

In olden times the people of Achadrom used to pasture their goats on Creagan nan Gobhar, a hill with a wide view rising from the canal on its east side. The tradition of the glen is that when MacDonell of Glengarry wished to summon his clan for some war-like foray he kindled a beacon on the tower of Invergarry Castle. When this was seen, the men of Achadrom hurried to the top of Creagan nan Gobhar, and there kindled a beacon that could be seen from afar, both east and west. Achadrom in olden days was a place celebrated. Here the old deeds were signed; here was held an annual fair; on a gallows here those who had been judged guilty were hanged. But, perhaps at the making of the Caledonian Canal, the renown of Achadrom has departed, and now even its name is known to few. The first skirmish of the campaign of 1745 was fought in this district. A body of the

MacDonalds of Keppoch and three companies of government troops came in contact near Spean Bridge. The regulars retired on Fort Augustus. When they were passing through Achadrom the Glengarry men showed themselves; they barred their way and called on them to surrender, which they refused to do. After a time they ran out of ammunition, when the Highlanders charged with the sword and took them prisoners, eighty-two being carried off to Lochiel's residence at Achnacarry.

One of the MacDonells of Glengarry is commemorated in a fine composition of classical bag-pipe music, the "Lament for Donald of Laggan," the composer being Patrick Mór MacCrimmon. Donald of Laggan was born in 1543, succeeded to the estates and title of Glengarry in 1574 and died, at the great age of 102, on the day of the battle of Inverlochy, February 2, 1645. He was always referred to by the people of the glen as Domhnall an Lagain (Donald of Laggan), because during his father's lifetime he lived at Laggan, Achadrom, and even after his accession to the estate he continued to be known by that name. His son having died before him, his grandson, Angus, succeeded him in 1645. It is interesting to note that up to 1660 the MacDonells of Glengarry always signed their name "MacDonald"; it was Angus who, raised to the peerage in 1660, took the title of Lord MacDonell and Aros. Since then, this branch of the MacDonalds have signed their name MacDonell. Lord MacDonell was accused of idolatry in that "he had a painter in Lochcarron (which then belonged to him) painting images; that he worshipped the image of St. Coan, called in Edinburgh Glengarry's god, which was burnt at the cross."

That a great Skye piper should have composed the famous lament above mentioned may at first seem strange, as the districts of Glengarry and Skye are far removed, but there was a close connection between the MacLeods of Dunvegan (whose pipers the great Mac-Crimmons were) and the Glengarry family. The daughter of Donald of Laggan was the wife of Sir Rory Mór MacLeod of Dunvegan and the mother of Sir Norman MacLeod of Bernera and Sir Roderick MacLeod of Talisker, both of whom were knighted for bravery at the battle of Worcester. This lady exceeded in age even her long-lived father, for she died at the great age of 103. It is said that for several years before her death she was lulled to sleep by Patrick Og MacCrimmon (who had by this time succeeded his father as piper at

Dunvegan) who played, in an adjoining room, this beautiful lament. She could not close her eyes in sleep unless she heard it.

The district of Achadrom is now largely under the control of the Forestry Commission. There are large nurseries and plantations here. The hills rise steeply southward, hiding the winter sun, but the trees grow well, for the district is sheltered from the sea winds and the rainfall is heavy.

East of Achadrom is Loch Oich. The dredging of Loch Oich during the construction of the Caledonian Canal proved difficult and costly, as great oaks lay deeply embedded in the peaty bottom: it was supposed that they had, perhaps many centuries before, been carried down the Garry during times of spate and had lain there, protected by the peat. They greatly exceeded in size the oaks which at the present day grow in Glen Garry, and it is on record that some of these old trees were 12 feet in diameter when taken from the loch.

North-east of Loch Oich the Caledonian Canal reaches its highest level, 104 feet above the sea. Vessels are lifted to that considerable elevation gradually as they steam east, by a number of locks. The river Oich, which, as the Garry, has flowed down Glen Garry and through Loch Oich, runs near the canal until it enters Loch Ness. Salmon reach Loch Oich early, and are frequently caught here on January 15, the opening day of the fishing. These January salmon are beautiful fish, usually around 20 lb. in weight, strong and fierce in their playing when hooked.

The main road from Fort William to Inverness crosses the river Oich where it leaves the loch. Here is Druineach Teampull, where were buried the Frasers of Foyers who were slain at the battle of Blar na Leine. About a mile to the north-east of the bridge crossing the river, the road passes near what is known as General Cope's Rampart. It was opposite this rampart that the Great Montrose set out with his mobile army across the hills, to descend into Glen Roy and, pressing on to Glen Nevis, to attack with ferocity the garrison of Inverlochy who, taken by surprise, suffered an overwhelming defeat. The place where his army left the Great Glen can be identified by one oak tree growing on the face of the hill, among the birches.

Let us, before reaching Fort Augustus and sailing, or motoring, or walking, down Loch Ness, retrace our steps to Invergarry on Loch Oich and travel through Glen Garry to the west, to Shiel Bridge, and to Kyle of Lochalsh beyond it. As we approach Glen Garry from the east we see the distinctive and impressive mountain Ben Tee, in Gaelic Beinn Sihdh—the Fairy Hill, or rather the Hill of the Fairy Dwelling. This hill has looked down on strange and often grim doings in the low country beneath, but surely none more grim than Iain Lom the bard, he who was made Poet Laureate by Charles II, hurrying to Mac-Donald of Glengarry with the seven heads of the murderers of MacDonald of Keppoch and his brother, "slung by the ears to a withy." He washed the heads in a well near Loch Oich (the memorial commemorating the deed is seen from the road) and since that day the well has been named Tobar nan Ceann—Well of the Heads.

Loch Garry, alongside which the road to the west winds, is a most beautiful loch; the birches reach their Highland perfection here, and in spring, when the first film of green overspreads them, and again in autumn, when their leaves turn to orange and flaming gold, they delight the eye of the traveller. There is sometimes a flash of red among the birches as a greater spotted woodpecker flits through the trees, and a quickening of life when a black-throated diver flies high overhead with harsh quacking cries. At Tomdoun, beyond the head of the loch, the main road to the west branches off to the right, or north: the lesser road, to Kinloch Hourn, continues west, by way of Loch Quoich, and drops steeply to the sea above Loch Hourn.

The road to Shiel Bridge and Kyle of Lochalsh passes near Loch Loyne, which was probably the last Highland loch where the osprey nested, then climbs an ascent to a height of 1,424 feet. From the high part of the road the view of the peaks of Glen Quoich Forest is impressive. This is a rain-swept land, and the traveller must hope for a wind out of the east or north-east, which usually gives fair weather, the south-west wind being almost always rain-laden. During the descent north-westward the former Cluaiaidh Inn, which had excellent brown trout fishing on the loch of the same name, is seen below. The house is still occupied, but is no longer an inn, which is a loss to the many anglers who used to frequent it.

The road now leads westward to Glen Shiel, following near the old road made by General Wade, and the traveller sees the great plantations which the Forestry Commission have set in the ground. At the foot of Glen Shiel the salt water of Loch Duich is reached at Shiel Bridge.

CHAPTER III

LOCH NESS

LOCH NESS is, I suppose, the most celebrated of Scottish lochs throughout the world because of the creature, or creatures, which make periodic appearances on its surface. Every schoolboy has heard of the Loch Ness Monster: some no doubt believe in it, others do not, yet perhaps wish they did. There is, to my mind, no doubt at all that the creature exists; too many reputable witnesses have seen it for them all to be classed as liars. It has been drawn, and even photographed; one of the last persons to see it (I write in 1949) was Mr. MacKillop, for many years clerk to the Inverness County Council, and a most respected citizen of Inverness, besides being a Commander of the Most Excellent Order of the British Empire.

Although everyone has heard of the Loch Ness Monster, few people realise that its appearance is no modern thing, but goes back to the mists of old tradition. Perhaps its first description is in Adamnan's *Life of St. Columba.* Adamnan was abbot of Iona, and wrote his account in Latin. He was elected abbot when fifty-five years of age, in 675; his *Life,* therefore, was written less than a century after the time of St. Columba. He describes a visit of Columba to the river Ness, in the land of the Picts. When he reached the bank of the river he saw the burial of a man who had been seized, as he was swimming in the river, by a monster, which had bitten him severely, but had not, be it noted, eaten him. His body had been taken out of the river by a hook, by those who went to his assistance in a boat. The saint wished to cross the river, and the boat was now on the farther shore. Undismayed by the tale he had heard of the monster, he directed that one of his companions should swim across the river in order to bring the boat over. Lugne Mocumin at once divested himself of his clothes except his tunic. As he swam, the monster rushed upon him in the middle of the stream, roaring terribly. As all stood stupefied with horror Saint Columba, raising his hand, made the sign of the cross in the air and called to the monster in his clear, powerful voice (which was said to carry great distances), "Thou shalt go no further, nor touch the man; go back with all speed." As he spoke the monster had almost reached the swimmer, and there was less than the length of a spear-shaft between them, but on hearing the voice of the saint it at once turned, and swam fast away, disappearing soon beneath the waters. Lugne, believing implicitly in the power of his saintly master, continued to swim strongly, reached the farther shore, landed, and brought the boat back. Both the saint's companions, and the "barbarous heathens" who were present were struck with admiration and gave glory to God.

This event took place apparently before the saint and his companions had sailed down Loch Ness, from east to west, on their journey back to Iona, after having converted the king of the Picts at Inverness. Before he set sail in his boat Broichan the Druid asked him when he intended to depart, and when Columba said, in three days' time, the Druid then told him that he would raise a contrary wind, accompanied by a great darkness. Accordingly in three days the saint and his followers journeyed to Loch Ness. The wind now became violent and contrary, and the sky dark and threatening, and the Druids, seeing this, exulted greatly. Columba saw the great waves of Loch Ness (it can be very rough at times on this loch with a south-west wind), saw the darkness envelop the sky, called on Christ, and embarked in his boat. When the sailors hesitated, he ordered them firmly to hoist the sails against the wind. The wind then veered, to the intense astonishment of all, and the voyage down the loch was accomplished under the most favourable conditions.

Sir Archibald Geikie was of opinion that the Great Glen is a line of weakness in the earth's crust, and that the agitation of the waters of Loch Ness during great earthquakes in modern times shows that underground movements still make themselves felt along the old line of dislocation or fracture. Is it possible that the waters of Loch Ness never freeze because they are warmed by subterranean activity?

The Great Glen has been enormously denuded by ice. From the west there flowed into it the large glaciers of Loch Eil, Loch Arkaig, Glen Moriston and Glen Urquhart. Geikie believed the hollows in which Loch Ness and the other lochs of the Great Glen lie were formed by glacial erosion. That these hollows are in some instances very deep is evinced by the depth of Loch Ness, which at its deepest known point is 774 feet deep; this is opposite the Falls of Foyers. Old accounts have stressed the fact that no ice ever binds the waters of Loch Ness. In a letter to Mr. James Gregory, Sir George

MacKenzy of Tarbut, under date February 25, 1675, writes as follows:

> Our famous Lake Ness never freezes; but on the contrary in the violentest frosts, the greater clouds of steams do arise from it. And I remember that at two several times, I being at Inverness, walking in the evenings along the Bridge over the River Ness, a mist of those steams coming from the Lake and falling down to us over the River (for there was no mist in any place thereabout, but on this Lake and River only) our hair became all white, like the whiteness of a hoare frost, but it was soft and warm; and this was in the midst of summer and in warm evenings.

Another old account of Loch Ness declares that it "never freezeth and if a lump of ice is cast into it, it soon after dissolveth, its commonly thought on this account, it runs on sulphureous minerals, though it may be otherways as it is with our springs of water, which either through constant motion, pressure of the aire or the heat retiring itself in time of cold does not allow them to freeze."

Loch Ness is approximately twenty-four miles long, but it is a comparatively narrow loch, being nowhere more than two miles wide. Its shores are beautified by birches and, because the relatively warm waters of the loch keep the frost at bay, the birches are in leaf here when they are still bare as at mid-winter in the surrounding glens. Primroses grow in profusion near the loch, and broom is in its glory here at an earlier date than anywhere else in the Highlands. Along the course of the main road between Fort William and Inverness there is seen in April and May a natural rock garden bright with flowers— the yellow of the broom and the yellow of the primrose blending with the deep blue of wild violets and the white of wood anemones.

Urquhart Bay is a favourite haunt of the Loch Ness Monster, and it has been seen more frequently here than at any other part of the loch. It has been described as being a creature with a long, thin neck and horse-like head, and it has been watched through binoculars eating water weed.

After his encounter with the Loch Ness Monster, St. Columba on his return journey to Iona no doubt landed at the head of Loch Ness, at the small town which is now called Fort Augustus, after the Duke of Cumberland, he whose name is still hated in the Highlands, where he was and is known as Butcher Cumberland. The earlier name of Fort Augustus was Cill Chuimein, after the saintly Cummein, who

216

On Loch Eilt
The white sands of Morar

was one of the early abbots of Iona. The Fort was built by General Wade. Here Samuel Johnson and his friend Boswell stayed the night, and were treated with great courtesy by the governor. This was before the days of roads as we know them in the Highlands, and the garrison of Fort Augustus was supplied with provisions from Inverness by a sloop of sixty tons which sailed regularly backwards and forwards on Loch Ness. Inverness was, even in very early times, celebrated for its ship-building. One of the first vessels built there, in 1087, became flagship of the Viennese navy. The fort at Fort Augustus has gone; where it formerly stood is built the Benedictine abbey, completed in 1878. A part of the old fortress is incorporated in the abbey, and the room in which Lord Lovat of the Forty-five was confined as a prisoner is still known, and the tree planted in memory of Culloden still lives. There is an unfounded tradition that Jacobite prisoners were hanged on this tree; actually they were shot on a piece of level ground which is now the cricket ground of the abbey.

Even at the time of the Jacobite rising of 1745 the castle of Urquhart was a ruin, for in February, 1715 it is recorded that the "castell of Urquhart is blowen down with the last storme of wind." Very little is known of the early days of this great castle. In a seventeenth-century MS (MacFarlane's *Geographical Collection*, vol. II, p. 550) it is stated that the castle was supposed to have been built by the Lords of the Isles, and that it was for some time inhabited by them. The traveller Pennant writes that it was the seat of the once-powerful Cummins and was destroyed by Edward I. Cameron Lees also mentions, in his work *The County History of Inverness*, that Edward I subdued the castle. Robert the Bruce later besieged it, and after a hard siege captured the stronghold, which he held during his reign.

As early as 1509 the castle apparently needed repairs, for when James IV bestowed the Lordship of Urquhart upon John Grant of Freuchie he bound him to repair or build at the castle a tower with a rampart of stone or lime, for the protection of the lands and the people from the inroads of thieves and malefactors. He was also enjoined to construct within the castle a hall, chamber and kitchen, with all the requisite offices, such as pantry, bake-house, brew-house, barn, ox-house, kiln, cot, dove-grove and orchard. The castle is now in the care of the Ancient Monuments Department of the Office of Works.

Loch Ness is beset with hills. Of them all the most conspicuous and imposing is Meallfourvonie (2,264 feet), a hill that is conspicuous

Mallaig: a West Highland fishing port
Eilean Donnan Castle, Loch Duich

from far out in the Moray Firth. I climbed it with a friend on a fine
October day, when there was mist hanging over Loch Ness. We soon
left the mist behind us and walked through birch woods, then over
heathery ground. A golden eagle was sunning himself on the summit
cairn; when the great bird took wing he flew at a vast height across
Loch Ness, towards the hills south of the loch. Although the eagle is
rarely seen in the lower glens, I believe he often sails over, and crosses
them, but flies at so great a height (because of his well-merited distrust
of the human race and their dwellings) that he cannot be seen.

I have mentioned the vessel which plied between the Inverness
end of Loch Ness and Fort Augustus to provision the garrison there.
One hundred years earlier, at the end of 1651, when Cromwell's
troops occupied Inverness, they built a frigate to carry sixty men.
Inverness is some five miles from the foot of Loch Ness and the frigate
was dragged overland the whole way, snapping three 7-inch cables
during the journey. Four pieces of cannon were later placed aboard
of her and, thus armed, she patrolled Loch Ness to overawe the unruly
Highlanders. The frigate which succeeded her in General Wade's
time had six guns as armament; these are now to be seen in the grounds
of Glen Moriston House, the seat of Grant of Glen Moriston.

CHAPTER IV

GLEN MORISTON

HALFWAY up Loch Ness, on the north side of the loch, is Glen Moriston, through which flows the Moriston river, a good stream for salmon. The Falls of Moriston, where the river rushes in tumult between rocky banks on which old pines and stately juniper bushes grow, are some of the most beautiful in the Highlands, as indeed Glen Moriston is one of the most beautiful glens. In an old MS *circa* 1630 the writer praises Glen Moriston. He says:

> Glenmoriestoune is a verie profitable and fertill litle glen or countrie, both plenteous of corne and abundance of butter, cheese and milk, and great and long woods of firr trees doeth grow in that countrey. The river doeth transport big Jests and Cutts of timber to the fresh water Loghnes. There is very manie Deares and Raes in this Countrie, and high mountaines very bigg in everie syde of it.

In a cave high amongst the hills at the head of Glen Moriston Prince Charles Edward after Culloden was successfully concealed and fed by certain devoted men of the glen. It was said that the MacLeod militia from Skye did more damage to Glen Moriston than even Cumberland; no doubt they were acting under strict orders, for, like all the people of the Isles, they were at heart adherents of the Prince.

On the river bank, near the large shooting lodge named Ceann-na-croc, the grave is still visible of one who was the hero of a singularly brave action. He was Roderick MacKenzie, usually named Rorie, an officer in the Jacobite army, and had a remarkable resemblance to the Prince. He was seen by a party of government troops and, knowing that the Prince was being eagerly searched for at the time, may even have deliberately attracted their notice. When attacked he defended himself bravely and as he fell dying is said to have exclaimed, "Alas, you have slain your Prince." His dying exclamation confirmed the soldiers' suspicions. They cut off the head of the slain man and hastened with it to Fort Augustus, where its arrival occasioned great excitement. It was thought to be the head of Prince Charles Edward, and it was some time before the true identity of the hero was discovered. During this time the hunt of the Prince slackened, and he was thus given most valuable days of grace. This noble deed, one of the most striking in the campaign, is commemorated by an inscription on a cairn beside the road.

Ceann-na-croc Lodge, a large building standing by itself far up a lonely glen, is a nesting place of many birds. I recall visiting it one June day of fine, warm weather. Many house martins were nesting beneath the eaves, and swifts were also nesting in this large house. These far-travelled birds were wheeling and dashing backwards and forwards, at varying heights, and the scene was an animated one. Here is probably the most westerly nesting place of the swift in this part of the Highlands, for I do not think it nests either in Glen Shiel, or in the district of Kyle of Lochalsh and, farther west, I am sure that it does not nest in the Isle of Skye, or the Outer Hebrides. Why the swift should be averse to western districts has not been explained, for insect life is numerous here: the heavier rainfall may be distasteful to it. It passes along the west coast both on north and south migration, but these swifts are, I think, Scandinavian birds, for they travel north in June, when the resident Scottish swifts are already nesting, and go south in September, when the resident swifts have already left the country on their passage to their winter quarters.

The river Doe which enters the Moriston at Ceann-na-croc flows from the high hills through Corrie Doe (Coire Dhoth). Near the head of this corrie Prince Charlie was in hiding about the time that Roderick MacKenzie literally laid down his life for him. It was high in Coire Dhoth that the Seven Men of Glen Moriston, in whose care the Prince was, made a daring raid on a party of redcoats and militia, to the number of sixty redcoats and seven militia-men, with one Donald Fraser, a miller in North Uist as their guide, who were driving cattle which they had stolen. The small band of Glen Moriston men defeated this comparatively large force, and recovered all the cattle, to the number of sixty. The guide, Donald Fraser, seems to have at heart sympathised with the Jacobites; he was probably in the Skye militia as being a tenant of Sir Alexander MacDonald of Sleat, who owned the island of North Uist.

If we return to Loch Ness and travel a dozen miles down the loch, we come to the mouth of Glen Urquhart. The road traversing this glen does not run through to the west coast, but when it reaches the river Glass bends toward the south-west, up the river Affric. Strath

Glass is old Chisholm territory. It does not (according to the Celtic scholar MacBain) mean, as might be imagined, the Green Strath, but the word here is from the old Celtic, *glais*—a stream. The river Glass and the river Farrar join at Struy to become the Beauly, a river celebrated for its salmon.

In its upper reaches the river Glass is named the river Affric. It rises no more than four miles from the waters of Loch Duich, a sea loch of the Atlantic, and thus, as first the Affric, then the Glass, and finally the Beauly, flows almost across Scotland from west to east. The scenery at its upper reaches is grand and wild in the extreme, and its two lochs, Loch Affric and Loch Beinn a' Mheadhon, are among the most beautiful of Scottish lochs. On the June day when a friend and I crossed the hills from Glen Moriston to Loch Affric snow fell heavily on the high ground, covering the red flowers of the sea thrift which grew here. When the snow ceased, the high hills, Màm Sabhal (3,862 feet) and her neighbour Càrn Eite, rose white to the evening sky—a strange sight for June. Màm Sabhal is noted for its grazing, and goats formerly had their home upon Càrn Eite. At Ath nam Muileach—Ford of the men of Mull—we approached Loch Affric. It is probable that the ford takes its name from a remarkable occurrence in the seventeenth century, when a family of Macleans on the Chisholm territory were brought to trial for witchcraft with the pleasant prospect, if found guilty (as in those superstitious days they usually were), of being "strangled to a stake and their body burnt to ashes." The Macleans in their dire extremity sought help from their chief, Sir Allan Maclean of Duart in Mull. In those days a journey from Strath Glass to Mull was a formidable undertaking, and there was always the fear that it might be too late. It is likely that Donald Maclean, who was being sought for, but had so far escaped, was the one to hurry to Duart for help. As a result of his visit, and of their chief's efforts, the men and women destined to be strangled and burnt escaped that fate. As William MacKay, who narrates the incident, truly says, "In the annals of our country there is perhaps no case which illustrates better than the one now under consideration the strength of that cord of care and confidence which bound together the Chief and the Clan." It was the more remarkable in that the Macleans who sought protection had been away from their native island and on the Chisholm property for two or three hundred years. Ath nam Muileach—Ford of the Men of Mull—is on the track the hunted man or men would have been most likely to take, and it seems to me that the name may well commemorate that event of the distant year 1662, when an epidemic of witch-hunting made people lose their balance, and almost their sanity.

That evening in June when, after a long walk over the hills, we were traversing the stalking path through the old pine forest on the south shore of Loch Affric I noticed ahead of me a very old tree, white, bleached and lifeless. All that remained was the stem or trunk, broken off at a distance of perhaps 10 feet from the ground. I saw what at first I thought was a grey object swaying from the top of this tree stump, and wondered what it might be, or whether my imagination after a long and tiring walk, was playing tricks on me. Just in time, to realise that this was fact and not fiction, I saw that the object was the grey, bushy tail of a wild cat. When we reached the tree stump, we found that it was hollow, and was evidently the home of a wild cat, where perhaps she had kittens. It was late at night, between ten and eleven o'clock, and the cat had very likely been on the point of leaving its hole on a hunting expedition and, hearing our approach, had thought better of it and was in the act of retreating into the tree when I saw the last part of it to disappear—the bushy, grey tail. After a night's rest we crossed the hills again to Ceann-na-croc, and saw no sign of that wild cat but Dara the collie had a thrilling chase after a large hill fox in our full view. The snow had gone, but a strong, cold wind swept the high ground as we made our best speed over it, as my friend had to catch the London train at Spean Bridge that afternoon— which he did with a second to spare. I believe that no one previously had left Loch Affric in the morning and had caught the west Highland train on the Braes of Lochaber the same afternoon. That was before, but only just before, the second world war, when life was still good, and simple things gave pleasure.

A walk which my wife and I accomplished about the same time— on this occasion from Killilan up Glen Elchaig, then over the hills to Benula Lodge—was through a different country, yet as the golden eagle flies the distance from Affric Lodge to Benula Lodge is no more than five miles across the hills. It was late in October when we did this walk, and the weather had been wet and stormy for some time previously, as it often, indeed usually is, in the west Highlands at that season. There is an old drove road through the hills, and this we followed. In summer the walk would have presented no difficulties, but we had not been over the ground before, and had not realised the number of streams to be crossed. None of these burns was spanned by a bridge, and in some of them was a strong volume of water. When we reached the shepherd's cottage at Lungard, the shepherd was most surprised to see us, and told us that he had been isolated from Benula Lodge by the floods for a week previous to that morning: he said that if we had attempted the walk on any other day of that week we should not have been able to ford the streams. At Benula Lodge the friends with whom we were to stay at Glencannich Lodge met us in their car. As we drove slowly along Loch Mullardoch the rain began to fall, and soon was sweeping the glen in torrents—we had only just made the crossing in time.

The high hills between Glencannich and Glen Affric are of granite formation, and the small alpine azalea grows plentifully on some of them. I was fortunate on one occasion to find here a white-flowered variety of this hill plant. The white-flowered variety of *Silene acaulis*, the cushion pink, a plant of rather similar habits, and often found on the same ground, although rare is not unduly so, and at the time I did not realise the extreme rarity of this white *Azalea procumbens*. But enquiries elicited the fact that neither had Kew Gardens ever heard of a similar variety, nor had the British museum a single specimen in their herbarium. I am glad I did not uproot the rarity, for a hill plant never takes kindly to being transplanted, and it would in all probability have died, but had I realised in time its extreme rarity, I should have made a cairn of stones near it, in order that I might have returned to take some of the seeds. On one occasion I sent the Director of Kew Gardens seeds of a white-flowered *Silene acaulis*, and from these seeds a number of healthy seedlings were grown, one of which we had for some years in the garden. My impression of this plant of white-flowered *Azalea procumbens* was that its flowers were of extreme beauty: they had a pale greenish tinge, as of sea water, in their whiteness, and were not dead-white, as are the flowers of the white variety of *Silene acaulis*. Also I remember that this particular plant grew by itself, at a little distance from a ridge that was literally pink from innumerable flowers of the normal-flowering variety—it was as if that rare plant realised its worth, and was living a secluded life apart from its crowded fellows. A few minutes after coming upon that rare find, I saw a golden eagle fly over the ridge only a few yards from me; our surprise was mutual and the eagle, when he had for his part recovered from it, changed his course and swept grandly from my view.

Glen Cannich joins Glen Affric at Invercannich, and the two form Strath Glass. Glen Strathfarrar, which joins Strath Glass six miles eastwards, has a lonely loch, Loch Monar by name, near its head: west of it lies the West Monar Forest, whose high tops, Sgùrr Choinnich (3,260 feet) with its neighbours Sgùrr a' Chaoruinn (3,452 feet) and Bidean an Eoin Deirg (3,430 feet), stand at the watershed between the east coast and the west.

Beauly with its old priory, being near the coast, does not come within the province of this book. The name is mediæval French, and a curious one to find in the Scottish Highlands; it was introduced in 1232, by the Vallis Caulium monks, who founded the priory and, delighted by the pastoral beauty and fertility of the land, named it Beau Lieu—Beautiful Place—whence comes the place-name Beauly. The Gaelic name, which is not often heard now, is A' Mhanachainn —The Place of the Monks. Near Beauly is Beaufort Castle, seat of Lord Lovat.

PART V
WESTERN COASTAL DISTRICTS

CHAPTER I

MORVERN

HAVING reached Glen Affric and Beauly, it may be well, before continuing northward, to retrace our steps back to the confines of Dalriada and travel northward along the west seaboard of Scotland. The mainland district of Morvern, north-west of Oban, is on three sides washed by the salt water. Along its west and south-west shores flow the strong tides of the Sound of Mull. North, the long and narrow Loch Sunart reaches within seven miles of the district's south-east sea boundary, Loch Linnhe, which is a continuation of the Sound of Lorne. It is possible that at one time Morvern was an island, and the low-lying Glen Tarbert (Glen of the Isthmus) was a tidal strait. Morvern indeed in character is an island: the passengers and goods for its western districts travel almost entirely by sea. Each morning the mail steamer from Tobermory, in the Isle of Mull, on its passage to Oban calls at Drimnin and Lochaline, and on its return voyage in the afternoon lands passengers, mails and goods at both those places. On the voyage from Oban, Duart Castle, standing strong and firm as the rock on which it is built, and the Lady Rock, where the chief of Duart left his wife at low tide to drown, are prominent objects. At Lochaline, where the steamer makes her first call on Morvern, a new industry has arisen during recent years. At a little distance inland a deep deposit of very fine sand has been discovered, and there is a regular shipment of this sand for the manufacture of high-grade glass and the most delicate optical lenses. It is interesting to see the white sand, spilled during the loading, lying beneath Lochaline pier, pale-green in the deep water, for there is no natural sea sand on this shore; it may be that an artificial beach will in time arise here. The sand itself, laid down under pressure, is almost as hard as rock, and when it is being mined, or quarried, no supports of the rock face are necessary.

When St. Kilda was evacuated in or around the year 1929, at the request of the younger generation of that lonely island, who found life growing too difficult for them, some of the families were settled in Morvern, and were set to work tree-planting on the land acquired

227

by the Forestry Commission. No tree grows on St. Kilda, or within fifty miles of it, and the story goes that the St. Kildans, when first they were put to this, for them, novel task, planted the trees with the leading shoots in the ground, and the roots spreading out in the air.

As the St. Kildans approached Lochaline by sea, they doubtless wondered what might be the history of the ruined castle guarding the land here. This, the castle of Ardtornish, is an old residence of the Lords of the Isles, one of whom, Good John of Islay, died here in 1380. In the seventeenth century, we learn from a contemporary account, the "Castell of Ardtorrenish" was one of the strongholds of that powerful chief, Maclean of Duart.

At Ardtornish a road leads along the Morvern shore of the Sound of Mull to Drimnin and beyond it: there is also a narrow road north-east across country to Kingairloch and the shore of Loch Sunart. The south-east coast of Morvern is as wild and trackless as when the original inhabitants of one of the islands of the Hebrides, being pursued by a monster, sailed up this coast to colonise Ardgour, from which place they were driven by the MacMasters, who, in turn, were driven out by the Macleans (the MacMasters having offended the Lord of the Isles who thereupon agreed that the Macleans should dispossess them if they had the strength to do so). For nearly five hundred years the Macleans held the property in unbroken succession, from father to son.

Loch Aline, the Beautiful Loch, which penetrates two miles into the land at Ardtornish, is at its headwaters no more than five miles from Loch Teacuis, which, an off-shoot of Loch Sunart, insinuates itself into the land through two narrow entrances. It would need a rise of only 50 feet in the sea-level for a tidal stream to connect Loch Teacuis with Loch Aline. Midway between these two sea lochs lies Loch Arienas, from which the river Aline flows into Loch Aline. There are salmon and sea trout in the river and in the loch, the latter lying only 36 feet above sea-level. At the entrance to Loch Teacuis are the two islands, Oronsay and Carna. There are a number of Oronsays on the west coast of Scotland. The word is Norse, and means an island from which the sea recedes at the ebb, so that it is possible to cross to it over the land. The most celebrated isle of the name Oronsay is separated in this manner from Colonsay: the priory of Oronsay and its sculptured stones are renowned. Few people have heard of the Oronsay which guards the north entrance to Loch Teacuis. I recall that I made an expedition there by sea in October, 1914. I was then on Admiralty Patrol Service, and it may be recalled that the Grand Fleet under the command of Jellicoe was for a time that autumn based on one of the sea lochs of the Isle of Mull, only a few miles distant. There were many scares of enemy submarines at this time, and I received a message that a suspicious craft had been seen at the back of Oronsay. I accordingly chartered the small steamship "Princess Louise," owned and captained by an intrepid seaman, Captain Patterson, who knew the west coast as few men did. We nosed our way next day through a narrow sound, where assuredly no steamer had ever been before, and it was very soon apparent that no submarine could possibly have sheltered here. It was a wild day, with a southerly gale blowing, and the skipper was not sorry to regain the open sea and set course for Tobermory in the Isle of Mull. Another excitement about this time was the reporting of morse signalling by a vessel at sea as coming from the island of Ulva. The coast watchers were out all night, having armed themselves against the desperate character or characters they half expected to meet, the parish minister being in charge of these operations. The mystery resolved itself when it was discovered that a moorland fire which had burnt the previous week had set fire to the peat, which glowed when gusts of wind fanned it and apparently went out when the wind fell light. This rhythmic waxing and waning of the red glow was, not unnaturally, taken by the ship as being part of the signalling operations of some German agent who had hidden himself, perhaps after being landed from a submarine, on this large and lonely island.

The small islands in the Sound of Mull, off the Morvern coast, provide a nesting station for considerable numbers of Arctic terns, graceful and charming birds, which have come from their winter quarters far to the south. Throughout the day, during the months of late spring, summer and autumn, there is a passage of ocean birds through the Sound of Mull. It is evidently a flight-line for shearwaters, and one would give much to know whence the winged travellers had come and whither they were going. It is now realised that the shearwater flies great distances to feed during the nesting season. R. M. Lockley has shown that the birds fly regularly from Skokholm in the Irish Sea to the Bay of Biscay to feed, and it is possible that birds from the shearwater colonies on Eigg and Rum in the Hebrides, and even from those of the Faeroes, may fly as far as the Bay of Biscay: they would then, under certain weather conditions, use the sea route through the Sound of Mull.

The question is sometimes asked, How far is the red deer able to swim? The Sound of Mull averages in width two miles, its waters are cold and deep, and a strong tide almost always runs here. Yet more than once during recent years a stag was seen swimming from Morvern to Mull across the strait, and I do not think that he has ever failed to reach the opposite shore. These long swims do not take place at the mating or rutting season, but at other times of the year, as though the animal had set out with the idea of exploring a strange land, seen so often under changing conditions from the hills of Morvern.

Chapter II

ARDNAMURCHAN AND MOIDART

ARDNAMURCHAN Point has the distinction of being the most westerly land of Scotland proper, the Hebrides excepted. Its lighthouse is visible from afar, and I have seen it from so distant a view-point as Beinn Mhór on the Outer Hebridean island of South Uist. As with Morvern, so with Ardnamurchan—the sea road is the easier way of approach. Three days a week the mail boat to the Outer Hebrides slows down off Kilchoan, and a motor ferry boat puts out to her, landing passengers and mails. Now there is talk, this summer of 1949, of a converted R.A.F. launch making several trips each day between Tobermory and Kilchoan. In the days of the Norse rule Ardnamurchan formed the boundary between the North Isles and the South Isles. The ancient name for Ardnamurchan was Rioghachd na Sorcha —Kingdom of Sorcha. Nothing is now known of Sorcha; and indeed the present place-name, Ardnamurchan, has never been fully understood. In the year 1266, Norway ceded to the Crown of Scotland the Hebrides or Western Isles, and Angus Mór of Islay sent his son, Iain Sprangach (John the Bold), with a strong force to Ardnamurchan. He was successful in taking possession of the district, and his descendants, under the clan name MacIain of Ardnamurchan, held it until the strong and wily Campbells in the seventeenth century defeated them.

There is a hill with the name Creag an Airgid—Silver Rock— some four miles inland from Ardnamurchan Point. Here a battle was fought between Sir Donald MacDonald of Loch Alsh (helped by Alexander MacDonald of Islay) and Iain MacIain of Ardnamurchan. The MacIain forces were defeated with great slaughter, the chief and two of his sons being among those killed.

Near Mingarry Castle on the south shore of Ardnamurchan is a bay with an historic name, Port nan Spàinndeach—Bay or Port of the Spaniards. It was named after the following event. MacIain of Ardnamurchan was seized, some say by treachery, by Maclean of Duart, and was a prisoner for more than a year in Duart Castle. In the autumn of 1588, when MacIain was still a prisoner, one of the vessels of the Spanish Armada, scattered by strong gales, took shelter in Tobermory Bay. Maclean of Duart had her refitted and re-victualled, and in return for these services obtained the loan of 100 Spanish soldiers. With these he plundered and harried the islands of Rum, Eigg, Canna and Muck, the last two being among the possessions of the MacIains of Ardnamurchan. Duart and his Spanish mercenaries then sailed south, and landed in the bay beneath Mingarry Castle, which they besieged, but were repulsed. The bay has ever since been named Port of the Spaniards.

One of the most prominent hills on Ardnamurchan is Beinn Shianta—the Charmed or Fairy Hill. It is a noble hill, and on the clear spring day when I climbed it, gave a view of great beauty over land and sea. But it is not necessary to climb high in Ardnamurchan in order to enjoy a view; the whole country abounds in beauty—sandy bays and rocky promontories gay with the flowers of sea thrift in May and early June. There are here old churches, and the sites of still more ancient chapels. Yet there is a background of tragedy in the district, for the country has often been laid waste by strong enemies during the last thousand years. The Cave of the MacIains, for instance, on the north coast of the promontory, in a remote district, commemorates in its name the death of a number of the MacIains who took refuge here when the Campbells in the year 1624 overran Ardnamurchan, and reduced the strong castle of Mingarry. Some of the MacIains took refuge in this cave but, being betrayed, so it is said, by their footprints in the snow, were killed to a man by the Campbells, who lighted a fire at the cave's entrance, and suffocated those within. A very similar tragedy was enacted at a cave on Eigg.

The river Shiel and the long, narrow Loch Shiel from which it flows form the boundary between the districts of Ardnamurchan and Moidart, and form also the county march between Argyll and Inverness. The river Shiel, less than three miles long, is mentioned in history from the time of St. Columba onwards. It is recorded in Adamnan's Life of the Saint that on one occasion, when some of the brethren of Iona had cast their net in the Shiel and had taken five salmon, Columba told them, "Try again, cast your net into the stream and you shall at once find a large fish which the Lord has provided for me." The monks did as he had commanded, and landed a salmon of astonishing size.

The second occasion on which the brethren of Iona visited the Shiel was when, wood being needed for the repair of the monastery, twelve vessels from Iona sailed for the mouth of the Shiel to bring back oak trees for that purpose (the Shiel is still noted for the size and luxuriance of its oaks). The men had felled the trees, loaded their boats, and had put to sea on the return voyage when a contrary wind from the west forced them to shelter in the lee of Eilean Shona. Complaint was then made to Columba, and very soon a favouring wind replaced that which had been contrary, and "the sailors were then directed to raise the sail-yards in the form of a cross, and spread the sails upon them. Putting to sea thus with a steady and favourable breeze, we were enabled, without the slightest fatigue, to reach our island that same day, rejoicing in our cargo of wood, and in the company of all who were engaged in assisting us in the ships." St. Columba is commemorated in Ardnamurchan in the name of a well at Ardslignish, which is called Tobar Chaluim Chille—St. Columba's Well.

The peaceful years of the era of Columba were followed by the merciless raids of the Danes and Norsemen, during which Iona was sacked and its monks murdered. Atharacle (a modern spelling of this place-name, Acharacle, is incorrect) is said to commemorate the leader of a body of Norsemen who were slain here by the people of the district under the valiant Somerled, the place-name being Ath Torquil—Torquil's Ford. The ford is on the river Shiel below the manse. According to an article on "Place-names of Ardnamurchan" in the *Celtic Review*, it was still used on occasion in 1914, and no doubt is to the present day.

Loch Shiel, in length some fifteen miles, is one of the very few fresh-water lochs of the Highlands which has a steamer service, summer and winter, the boat sailing up the loch from Atharacle each morning to Glen Finnan, the rail-head for the district, and returning in the afternoon. The steamer passes close to a small green island having strong associations with the past. It is Eilean Fhionáin—St. Finan's Isle. This island has been for centuries sacred ground for catholics and protestants alike. St. Finan, who sanctified the isle and had his cell here, was a contemporary of Columba, and was sometimes styled Lobar—the Infirm. The old ruined chapel, which may have been built on the site of the saint's cell, has been without a roof since the middle of the seventeenth century. On the High Altar rests St. Finan's Bell, of musical voice; it is a small bell, and is said to have been brought from Eire by St. Finan, who landed at Kilchoan in his coracle and walked northward to Loch Shiel. The place from which he perhaps had his first view of the loch is named Suidhe Fhìonáin—St. Finan's Seat. The chapel on St. Finan's Isle is said to have been built by Alan MacRuairidh, one of the early chiefs of Clanranald. The burial ground beside the chapel is, as I have said, used by catholics and protestants alike, the protestants burying their dead on one side and the catholics on the other.

The old road which leads from the north shore of Loch Shiel opposite the island to Castle Tioram, the ancestral Clanranald stronghold on the coast, might well be named the Road of the Cairns, for cairns are built along its length—in one place I counted forty of them. Most of the cairns have been built beside water. They mark where a coffin was rested by the burial party; it was expected that a passer-by should add a stone to a funeral cairn, in order to show his respect for the departed.

Castle Tioram stands at the entrance to Loch Moidart: five miles up the loch is Kinlochmoidart, where Prince Charles Edward remained for several days before sailing up Loch Shiel and raising his standard at Glen Finnan, of which historic event I shall have more to say later in this chapter. John Macintyre, one of the family of hereditary pipers to the MacDonalds of Clanranald on that occasion composed the renowned pibroch, "Thàinig mo Righ air tir am Muideart"—My King has landed at Moidart. The ground of this tune was played by Norman MacRae, piper to Lochiel, at Glen Finnan in 1945, when the bi-centenary of the raising of the Jacobite standard of 1745 was celebrated; I was sorry the whole pibroch was not played. Castle Tioram, built on an island near the shore, to which it is joined at ebb tide, was burnt in the year 1715. It was only once taken by an enemy during its long history—by the Campbells of Argyll, by a subterfuge. They had besieged it for six weeks: apparently despairing of its capitulation, they sailed away in their galleys. The men of Clanranald, believing that their enemies had gone, left the castle to seek news of their wives, families and relatives, and also no doubt to replenish their stocks of food and drink, which must have been running low. That night the Campbells sailed back unseen in the darkness, and surprised and overpowered the small guard that had been left in the castle. Yet the victors were not allowed long to enjoy their success. The defenders returned in force, drove the Campbells to their galleys, and put to the sword those who did not escape. The tale of the burning of the castle is a strange one. Alan Mor of Moidart,

Captain of Clanranald, before setting out to join the Old Pretender in his rising of 1715, at which the standard was unfurled on the distant Braes of Mar, had so strong a feeling that he would not return that he gave orders for the castle to be burnt. That is the story, though it does not sound, on the face of it, to be a probable one. At all events the place was burnt, and has remained for over 200 years a picturesque ruin. It was built in one of the most beautiful districts of the west coast, where trees are able to grow and flourish almost at the edge of the tide, since the irregular outline of the coast, and its many hills, break the full force of the winds of ocean which prevent tree growth on the neighbouring promontory of Ardnamurchan. It is indeed a memorable experience to visit Castle Tioram on a day of clear weather, preferably a day of early summer when the north wind blows and sea and sky are blue. Then the view of the island of Muck away to the west is of especial charm, and the old-world atmosphere of the country, with its many associations with the past, can be sensed. Kinloch-moidart house, not far from it, stands in a deep, sheltered glen. Near the house are seen the historic beeches known as the Seven Men of Moidart, planted to commemorate the seven leading followers of Prince Charles Edward on his arrival at Moidart on his daring enter-prise, so nearly crowned with success. A younger tree now takes the place of one of the veterans, which was uprooted during a winter gale of great violence. At Kinlochmoidart, too, the Prince is commemor-ated in the Prince's Walk, beneath spreading trees, and in the clear waters of the Prince's Well.

Near the house of Kinlochmoidart is Shona Beag, an island which at low tide is joined to the mainland by a dry and muddy strait, across which the traveller can walk to the isle. Here, in a sheltered house with an old-world atmosphere, lived, at the time of my visit, Dr. Mac-Vicar, a direct descendant in the female line of the MacDonalds of Kinlochmoidart. He showed me an old bagpipe which had been given to Donald MacDonald of Kinlochmoidart by the last representative of the Macintyres, before that family emigrated to America. The Macintyres, as I have said, were hereditary pipers to the MacDonalds of Clanranald, and a branch of the family were pipers to the Menzies. The Macintyres lived at Uldary at the head of the river Moidart, and since they did not wish to take with them the old historic pipe they gave it to Kinlochmoidart, and it had, at the time of my visit, passed into Dr. MacVicar's keeping. In this pipe chanter is an extra hole, which was made on the advice of a fairy; the mouth-piece is four-sided. It is said that this pipe was played at the battle of Bannockburn. My friend and I had walked across to Shona Beag. During our visit to the isle the tide had risen, and when we were rowed back to the mainland young coal-fish or saithe were playing in the tidal stream, which now flowed through the channel over which we had walked dry-foot. It is many years since I visited Shona Beag and saw the old pipe. Its owner has now passed to Tir nan Og, and the pipe has, perhaps, found a new home.

Let us in imagination leave Kinlochmoidart with Prince Charles Edward and, passing Castle Tioram, sail with him up Loch Shiel to Glen Finnan. When he saw Castle Tioram, already a ruin from the fire which gutted it thirty years before, he was no doubt told the history of the place, and how its owner had distinguished himself in the previous Jacobite rising. As he sailed up Loch Shiel and saw its hills rise in beauty on that summer day, he may have been inspired, romantically inclined as he was, by the beauty of his surroundings (a few days previously an eagle, sailing for a considerable time astern of his ship, had been hailed as a bird of good omen), his heart full of high endeavour, as were the hearts of those who had staked their lives and fortunes in his service. Yet it is not certain that he journeyed by sea, for he may have ridden overland to Dalilea, on the north bank of Loch Shiel, where he met MacDonald of Glenalladale and Gordon of Glenbucket. Here he spent the night at Glenalladale's house and the following morning, at six o'clock, he and his followers, some twenty-five in all, proceeded in three boats to the head of Loch Shiel, landing on the shore of the loch at the spot which is now marked by a tall pillar surmounted by the figure of the Prince. He had expected to find the nucleus of an army awaiting him; instead there was no one to be seen except some of the inhabitants, who showed by their interest and astonishment at the arrival of the strangers that they knew nothing of what was on foot. Charles, disappointed and chagrined, entered one of the primitive huts, waiting for two hours in suspense. Then at last he heard the sound of a distant pipe, hurried to the door, and saw what caused happiness to replace depression in his heart—an army of kilted figures descending the glen. They were the Camerons, with Lochiel at their head. They had marched, between seven and eight hundred of them, over the hills from Achnacarry. In two columns, of three men deep each, they advanced, with prisoners they had taken between the lines. The standard was then raised on a knoll, by the Marquis of Tullibardine. It was, according to Browne's *History of the Highlands*, a full and accurate account, "of silk, of a white, blue and red texture, but without any motto." The Marquis of Tullibardine, after reading a commission from the Chevalier de St. George appointing his son Prince Charles as regent, marched to the Prince's quarters with the standard under an escort of fifty Camerons. An hour after this ceremony the sound of piping, this time from the east, was heard, and MacDonald of Keppoch, at the head of 300 of his Highlanders, arrived. MacLeod of Dunvegan and MacDonald of Sleat had refused to join what they considered a foolhardy enterprise, but that evening some gentlemen of the name MacLeod, among them perhaps MacLeod of Raasay who so valiantly supported the Prince in his campaign and saw his fortunes lost with its failure, arrived, to disassociate themselves with the action of their chief, and to offer to raise a force from their territories in the Isle of Skye. Although Prince Charles remained at Glen Finnan only one night he found himself at the head of an enthusiastic force of upward of 1,400 men when he set out on his march towards the south-east the following day. The following night the Prince passed at Fassiefern on Loch Eil, and the night after at Glengarry Castle on Loch Oich.

Let us now go forward two hundred years to that day of mid-August in the year 1945, when the bi-centenary of the raising of the Prince's standard was commemorated at an impressive ceremony. The second world war had just ended, and it seemed that men were glad to cast off that nightmare, and to turn their thoughts to an event of long ago when chivalry in war still existed—did not the Lochiel of that day entertain honourably in his own house certain prisoners whom the Jacobites had captured? At all events, an astonishingly large number of persons arrived, by car, bus and train, that August morning. Glen Finnan has the reputation of being one of the wettest places in the Highlands, but on that day there was not a cloud in the sky, and the sun shone with great power. Some of those who were there were the direct descendants of the leading figures of the Forty-five. Sir Donald Cameron of Lochiel spoke of his ancestor, without whose aid Prince Charlie would have been unknown to the present generation. Lochiel was careful to emphasise that there were at the present day no more loyal subjects of the King and Queen than the descendants of the Jacobites. When the Marquess of Tullibardine—

the descendant of the Marquis who had unfurled the Royal Standard two hundred years before—mounted the platform to speak, and, putting on his bonnet with its prominent white cockade, said that it was the very cockade his ancestor had worn at the ceremony of 1745, the imagination of the assembly was fired and there was a stir among the press photographers, both British and American. They crowded round him, photographing him at every conceivable distance, and at every conceivable angle. That white rosette, two hundred years and more old, had fired their imagination and, for the time being, was a bigger thing than the atomic bomb which had a few days before wiped out Hiroshima in a holocaust which could not have been conceived by the men who had assembled at Glen Finnan two hundred years before.

There is, I think, no contemporary account of the weather at the time of the unfurling of the Prince's standard. Was it a day of sunshine, with the hills clear and blue, or was the mist low upon Sgùrr nan Tarmachan and the rain driving down Loch Shiel? I think, from the fact that the approaching Camerons were seen first on the brow of the hill, the weather must have been clear. One would like to know whether the Prince, as he sailed down Loch Shiel, saw salmon and sea trout leaping, silvery, from the water. Presumably the loch held many of these fish, as it holds them now, and the season would have been right, for they enter the loch in shoals during the months of July and August. Did he hear tales of the Monster of Loch Shiel, which is well known in the district, but is not so celebrated as the Monster of Loch Ness? The "gentlemen of Skye" had presumably made their way from their landing place at Loch nan Cilltean at Arisaig, or Borodal on Loch nan Uamh, travelling by way of Kinlochailort and thence along the shore of Loch Eilt. Let us take the road westward from Glen Finnan and visit those places, rich in history and in romance.

CHAPTER III

LOCH MORAR AND LOCH HOURN

LOCH Eilt is celebrated for the size of its sea trout, which run up the river Ailort in May, June and July. The heaviest fish enter the river in May and June; the later run, although more numerous, are of smaller size. The small islands of Loch Eilt have pine trees planted thickly on them; there is a tradition that they were planted by the men who returned safe from Culloden as a memorial to those who fell. In winter and early spring whooper swans sometimes alight on Loch Eilt, spending some time there and swimming in stately manner in the sheltered bays, where they feed on the water weed: I have not seen the smaller Bewick's swan here, nor the large mute swan, which was very numerous on South Uist before it was shot to supply the black market in Glasgow.

After passing Loch Ailort and the small loch, Loch Dubh, the home, it is said, of a white *each uisge* or water horse, the road descends to Loch nan Uamh, where the first scenes on the Scottish mainland of the rising of 1745 took place. The Prince's vessel, the "Doutelle," sailed across from South Uist and anchored in Loch nan Uamh— Loch of the Caves—the boundary between the districts of Arisaig and Moidart. It is, even now, a wild and remote district and in those days, when no railway or road led through it eastward, it was still more so. Charles was depressed on the voyage across from the Outer Hebrides, because MacDonald of Boisdale had refused to support his cause. While the discussion between him and Boisdale was at its height two suspicious vessels were seen in the offing, and the "Doutelle" weighed anchor, towing astern of her the boat in which Boisdale had put off from the shore: she had proceeded several miles out to sea before Charles at length realised that even his persuasive powers were having no effect on the island chieftain, who then boarded his boat and set his course for the now receding shore. What a dramatic subject, this, for the brush of an artist, Boisdale embarking in his skiff while Prince Charlie, rebuffed and disappointed, watches him go. But when he had anchored in Loch nan Uamh and, sending messengers at once ashore, found a strong Jacobite atmosphere pervading the district, Charles's spirits revived. A tent was set up on the deck of the "Doutelle," and here the chiefs, chieftains and leading men of the district were entertained by him. MacDonald of Kinlochmoidart came aboard almost at once, and after a short interview was despatched with letters to Lochiel, the Duke of Perth, Murray of Broughton and others. Next day young Clanranald (nephew to Boisdale) accompanied by MacDonald of Glenalladale and MacDonald of Dalilea arrived, and were entertained with a variety of wine and spirits in the tent on deck, young Clanranald later remaining closeted with the Prince for the space of three hours. Young Clanranald and Allan MacDonald, a younger brother to Kinlochmoidart, were then sent across to the Isle of Skye to endeavour to persuade the Laird of Mac-Leod and Sir Alexander MacDonald of Sleat to join the Prince, but later returned with the unwelcome news that neither MacDonald nor MacLeod would agree to make cause with him seeing that the Prince had come without trained troops to form the nucleus of an army. On July 25, 1745, Prince Charles Edward, with his suite, landed on the north shore of Loch nan Uamh, and took up his quarters at Borodal, a farm belonging to Clanranald. Here he was attended by a bodyguard of about 100 MacDonalds. Lochiel now arrived at Borodal, meaning to point out to the Prince that his enterprise could not succeed, yet after conferring with him, seeing his resolution, and feeling his charm, he agreed to afford him all the help in his power, and to summon his clan, the Camerons, to arms. From Borodal, as I have mentioned earlier in this chapter, the Prince went by sea to Kinlochmoidart, where he remained some days before crossing to Loch Shiel and passing the night with MacDonald of Glenalladale before landing at Glenfinnan to raise his standard.

At that time the coast line northward from Arisaig was a comparatively populous district, as it is today. It has an atmosphere of the Outer Hebrides rather than of the mainland. The coast is sandy, with small shallow bays, often bird-haunted, and green machair extending to the edge of the sands. Indeed the White Sands of Morar, where the river Morar enters the sea, are proverbial for their beauty, their snow-whiteness being accentuated by the green foliage of the birches which grow to the edge of the shore here. Not only is the shore beautiful; the view seaward is also one of great charm, comprising as it does the islands of Eigg, and Rum of the lofty hills and, northward of these, the great island of Skye with its serrated range of mountains, the blue Cuillin, sung of in the song "Road to the Isles."

The new bridge, Dornie Ferry

The Morar river has a length of no more than a mile. It flows out of Loch Morar, the deepest fresh-water loch in Scotland. Sir Archibald Geikie, in his standard work, *The Scenery of Scotland*, states that a sounding in Loch Morar gave the depth of 180 fathoms, or 1,080 feet. This celebrated geologist was of opinion that Loch Morar was the deepest known hollow on any part of the European plateau with the exception of the submarine valley which skirts the southern part of Scandinavia. There is no known part of the Atlantic within fifty miles of the coast of Scotland with a depth as great as that of Loch Morar: the bed of that loch at its deepest part is actually over 1,000 feet below sea-level.* It might be expected that a loch of so great a depth might be the home of some unusual creature. If local tradition be credited, there is indeed a creature here, which appears only at long intervals. It is the Beast of Loch Morar, A' Mhorag, as it is familiarly named by the people of the country. It was said to appear before a death in the family of the MacDonalds of Morar; its appearances have been fewer than those of its cousin, the Loch Ness Monster, which it apparently resembles, both in appearance and habits. For the first time for a number of years it showed itself to a boat containing a number of persons, during the brief spell of intensely hot sunny weather at the end of July, 1948. It progresses, apparently, with the same undulating motion as the Loch Ness Monster, and, like it, has humps. If you believe in the existence of the Loch Ness Monster— and its appearances have been so frequent and so well attested that it is difficult to remain sceptical—you will probably agree that it is likely that other Highland lochs have similar creatures in their twilight depths. Actually there are at least four lochs, and probably more, which have their "beast." In three of these lochs the "monster" is so well known that it has a Gaelic name. Thus the Loch Ness Monster is Nisseag, that of Loch Shiel, Seilag, and that of Loch Morar, Mhorag. There may well have been a name for the Beast of Loch Arkaig, mentioned by Lord Malmesbury in his *Memoirs*. Loch Morar, or rather the neighbourhood of the Morar river, is the site of a hydro-electric station, the electricity being for the benefit of Morar and Mallaig.

Mallaig is the terminus of the West Highland Railway, now relegated to obscurity and absorbed in British Railways. Here is a fishing port of considerable importance at certain times of the year,

* The Admiralty have now found a greater depth off Raasay.

Loch Duich and, beyond, Loch Alsh

it is one of the ports from which steamers to Skye and the Outer Hebrides sail. During the years of the second world war, when all sorts of difficulties were placed in the way of the traveller, the Identity Card of each passenger was carefully scrutinised by the Security Officer on Mallaig pier before the owner was permitted to board the train. As the train passed through a Protected Area (between Mallaig and Fort William) different from that from which the passengers had come, they were handed cards to pass them through, the cards being taken from them by security officers and men who later boarded the train at Corpach. On one occasion I happened to be travelling on the foot-plate of the engine for a special purpose and was provided with a railway permit, from Mallaig to Glasgow. Foreseeing difficulties with my military card which passed me through the area, and fearing that if the card were not delivered up at Corpach I might find myself under arrest later on, I made myself as conspicuous as possible on the engine when we stopped at Corpach, but even then had difficulty in attracting the attention of the military. At last the sergeant saw me on the engine and, full of suspicions, hurried up. I gave him my cardboard ticket which passed me through the area, but he was still doubtful, and, to the amusement of the engine driver and the fireman, went off to consult his officer. The officer walked down the platform, saw me in the cab of the locomotive, and hesitated what next to do. He had plainly not been on an engine before, and the oil and smoke for a time deterred him. At last, summoning up his courage, he was on the point of swinging himself up on to the locomotive when the fireman, apparently innocently, released a jet of boiling water and steam about his feet, so that when he appeared, a little breathless, on the foot-plate, I thought I would further surprise him by shaking him warmly by the hand—my hands being by this time as black as those of an African. He was obliged, after a careful scrutiny, to confess that my papers were in order, and that I was not in fact travelling on the foot-plate in order to evade the regulations. As he was climbing down once more the driver, who had viewed the proceedings with mounting astonishment and disapproval, sent a second squirt of steam after him, which caused him to leap with fright several inches into the air. When he looked round, the fireman and driver were both engrossed in their several tasks.

There was a regulation at the time that no telescope or binocular could be carried without a special permit on the west coast, or in the

Hebrides. The deer controller was visiting on duty the island of Rum. On his return, he landed at Mallaig. Seeing his telescope, the military on duty at Mallaig pier ordered him, greatly protesting, into their hut for examination from which, somewhat shaken but a free man, he later emerged. An officer of Lovat's Scouts was on Mallaig pier, proceeding to the Isle of Skye on leave. The officers of the Scouts carry, or carried, as part of their uniform a stalking telescope. This caught the eye of the officer on duty on the pier, and he told the Scout that he had no business to be carrying a telescope in a protected area. "What am I then to do with it?" asked the Lovat Scout. The security officer thought for a while, then replied, "Put it in your suitcase."

The difficulty of movement in the west Highlands during the war years was great. As an example, if a minister from the Isle of Skye was asked to preach in one of the Outer Hebrides, perhaps only twenty miles across the Minch, he had to begin to make arrangements for his journey three weeks in advance, for, although he might be a native of Skye, he was not permitted, without a special permit, to cross the Minch. A distinguished officer on the retired list wished to take some sea trout fishing on a west coast loch, but before signing the lease wrote to the military authorities to ask whether he would be permitted to enter the area. He was refused permission. When people heard that I lived on the Isle of Skye they looked knowing, and hinted that most secret operations must be in progress in that island; when I assured them that they were wrong they looked at me in admiration, and murmured words to the effect that I was playing up well, and that they would not in fairness press me further on the subject, which nevertheless I could see intrigued them. They obviously did not believe me.

This was by no means the first time that government troops had been quartered in the district. They must have been still more in evidence after the battle of Culloden in the spring of 1746, and their design was then wholly hostile towards the people of the Highlands. They were searching especially for a noted character, Simon, Lord Lovat, who for a time was in hiding on one of the islands of Loch Morar: he was apprehended, and was found guilty of treason, losing his head at the Tower of London, where at the last ceremony of his full and exciting life he, an old man, displayed great bravery and composure.

The herring fishing brings innumerable sea gulls to Mallaig. They sail overhead in the teeth of the wind, and the air is filled with their clamour. In winter, as indeed at other seasons, herring gulls predominate: in spring they are joined by lesser black-backed gulls, birds which spend the stormy winter months off the coasts of Portugal, Spain and West Africa. Their food and habits resemble those of the herring gull; why the haunts of the two species should be in winter so far apart is a mystery. In winter at Mallaig among the hundreds of wheeling herring gulls may sometimes be seen a bird of creamy plumage, without the black wing tips of the herring gull. This is an Iceland gull, a winter straggler to the west coast of Scotland. Its name is inappropriate, for it nests not in Iceland but in Greenland. It may become very tame. A bird of this species in the very early spring of 1948 haunted the bay of Portree in Skye and, being fed on the pier several times daily, soon became fearless. On one occasion the cat which was supposed to keep the mice in check in the pier storehouse stalked and leaped upon the Iceland gull. The gull calmly seized the cat, and after a short scuffle puss retreated, tail between her legs. Mallaig looks out on to the Sound of Sleat, and on to the coast of Skye, some five miles distant. On a clear day Armadale Castle can be seen sheltering amid stately trees, the home of the MacDonalds of Sleat, descendants of the proud Lords of the Isles, who counted themselves as kings and ruled great territories, sailing in their galleys from island to island. Mallaig stands at the entrance to Loch Nevis, a sea loch of considerable length, which runs at first east, then south-east, and finally east-north-east into the hills. At the Kyles or Narrows of Knoydart the loch is in width only a few hundred yards, then broadens again to its lonely headwaters. From these headwaters, brackish by reason of the streams which flow into them, rises a hill of curious form, Sgor na h-Aide—Peak of the Hat. The hill recalls a witch's hat. This hat-like appearance is specially marked when the traveller is approaching Mallaig from the Outer Hebrides. If that approach is made in summer shortly after sunrise, and against the sunrise, or the sky made luminous by the sunrise, Sgor na h-Aide stands out on the eastern horizon. This hill is in height 2,800 feet; another, and a higher hill, Sgor na Ciche, 3,410 feet, rises to the north of it, and holds snow usually until late in the spring. The name Nevis is the same in Loch Nevis and Ben Nevis, though the two are far apart. Scholars are not agreed as to its meaning, neither is there agreement on the pronounciation of the name, some pronouncing it Neevis, others Nevvis. The present Gaelic form is Nimheas, but the older form was Neimheas.

Some six miles up the Sound of Sleat from Loch Nevis, another long sea loch, Loch Hourn, bites deep eastward into the hills. Its name has sometimes been translated as Loch of Hell, as opposed to the neighbouring Loch Nevis, which has been taken to mean Loch of Heaven. While there is uncertainty regarding the meaning of Loch Nevis, all the authorities are agreed that Loch Hourn is certainly not Loch of Hell. The correct Gaelic form is Loch Shubhairn, the "sh" and "bh" being mute. At the head of the loch are Coire Shubh and Loch Coire Shubh, place-names derived from *subh*, which may mean raspberry. At the head of Loch Hourn the hills rise very steeply, so that the voyager is reminded of a Norwegian fjord; in winter the sun is hidden here for months, and even at midsummer it scarcely tops the hills. The climate is mild, and eucalyptus trees flourish.

When Prince Charles Edward was a fugitive, with a price of £30,000 on his head, he must on one occasion have sailed past, or near to, the estuary of Loch Hourn, for in *The Lyon in Mourning* it is stated that the Prince sailed into Loch Nevis, when his boat was stopped by a small party of the militia of Sir Alexander MacDonald of Sleat. The royal fugitive may have thought that he was now at last to find himself a prisoner, but fortune still favoured him, for those who comprised the crew of the boat successfully answered the questions that were put to them, and they were permitted to proceed. On the shore of Loch Nevis the Prince landed and made his way to Clanranald's hut (his house having been burned down) at Morar.

In a side glen of Loch Hourn, Glen Barrisdale by name, are woods of old Scots pine. These old woods are interesting since it is sometimes said that the Scots pine will not flourish in a wet climate, yet here we have an annual rainfall of over 100 inches compared with a rainfall of less than half that amount in the Cairngorms, where the greatest area of the old pine forest in Scotland is found.

I have (pp. 187-188) described the floating of the pine timber down to the Spey and thence into the sea. In Glen Barrisdale in olden times the same procedure must have been followed, for the remains of the old dams are visible. It is said that much of the old forest was destroyed by a great fire which, beginning in Lochiel's country at Achnacarry, swept westward on an easterly gale, and destroyed great areas of wood. The stumps, and even the trunks of blackened pine are still to be seen in the peat on the Barrisdale "march." Irreparable damage was done to the old pine forest near the west shore of Loch Arkaig by fire during the years of the second world war. Although about the same time extensive hill fires were caused by German incendiary bombs, the conflagration which destroyed a great part of Lochiel's old pine forest was not caused by enemy action, but, I understand, by our own troops.

CHAPTER IV

GLEN ELG AND KYLERHEA NORTHWARD

GLEN Elg, like some other west mainland districts—as, for example, Morvern—is in character island rather than mainland. It has a daily motor boat service, carrying its mails, from Kyle of Lochalsh, and the mail steamer from Portree to Mallaig calls there, both morning and afternoon, on certain days of the week. The water is shallow in-shore, and there is no pier, but a ferry boat meets the steamer as she lies off the coast to land passengers and cargo. The only road to Glen Elg is over the high pass Mam Ratagan—Hill of the Small Forts—which climbs from sea-level to a height of 1,295 feet. If you cross the pass from the west, that is from Glen Elg, the gradient is moderate, but from the east, that is from Shiel Bridge at the head of Loch Duich, it is very steep, and care must be taken during the ascent: although the modern motor-car climbs the hill with comparative ease there are difficult and steep bends on which to pass a car. There are one or two places from which a view of the whole hill can be obtained, and I am happier when driving up the hill if I stop for a moment and satisfy myself that no car is descending. On the steep descent from the Lecht to Cock Bridge at the head of the Don there is a notice, "MOTORISTS: ENGAGE LOW GEAR." A notice of this sort might with advantage be placed at the summit of the pass of Mam Ratagan, for there is considerable risk in attempting to descend to Shiel Bridge and Loch Duich unless the car is engaged in second gear. But, as I have said, there is no necessity for the same precaution if the journey is being made in the opposite direction, that is from Shiel Bridge to Glen Elg.

It is known that Gaels from Ireland founded the kingdom of Dalriada, of which I have written earlier in this book. As the people gradually spread north, they named the districts they colonised after their mother country. Elg or Ealag was one of the poetical names of Ireland, and the distinguished Celtic scholar Professor W. J. Watson was of opinion that the name was given by the Irish settlers to commemorate their native country. The Gaels presumably found the Picts strongly entrenched in Glen Elg. There are at least three brochs in the district, a particularly fine one near Eileanriach.

247

Near Glen Elg is the strait of Kylerhea, across the strong tides of which rises the Isle of Skye, which here approaches the mainland of Scotland more nearly than at Kyleakin, where is the usual ferry to and from the mainland. At one time there was an inn at Kylerhea; until the Highland Railway was made to Kyle of Lochalsh this was the main ferry. In the early 1930s the experiment was made of running a ferry boat during the summer months across the strait of Kylerhea. As I have said, the hill pass between Shiel Bridge and Glen Elg is a steep one, and, when the strait has been crossed, an equally steep climb must be undertaken up to Bealach Udal, the Inhospitable Pass, before the motorist can find accommodation in the Isle of Skye. Because of these drawbacks, I must confess I was doubtful of the success of the ferry venture, but Mr. Lachlan MacInnes, by the efficiency of his service and his courtesy, was doing well when the advent of the second world war and the severe rationing of petrol (not to speak of the restrictions of a Protected Area against non-resident motorists) caused this ferry to be closed for the time being. In 1946 the ferry was re-opened, and plied during the summers 1946 and 1947, but, perhaps because they feared the two steep hills would make undue inroads on their meagre petrol rations, motorists did not support the ferry, and it was closed (as one hopes temporarily) during the summer of 1948. The distance to Skye from Inverness or Fort William by Kylerhea is six miles shorter than by way of Kyle of Lochalsh, and, even allowing for the two hills, I do not think the petrol consumption is much, if any, more than if the motorist travels by way of Kyle of Lochalsh.

The approach to Kylerhea by steamer is impressive. So narrow is the strait, it seems as if the ship is rapidly approaching the head of a sea loch, hemmed in by great hills: there is no appearance of an opening in those hills. The ship alters course, and, more quickly than it takes to relate, a narrow passage is seen ahead, through which the tide runs with great power, sometimes exceeding a speed of eight knots during a spring tide. Indeed coasters of low speed are obliged to anchor at the entrance to the strait if they find an adverse tide.

The strong ocean streams attract many sea birds, and there seems to be a spring migration route of kittiwakes northward through Kylerhea. In fine weather the sea passage is too land-locked for ocean birds to linger here, but in spring, after a succession of strong winds from a westerly quarter, I have seen gannets and puffins fishing.

The shearwaters keep usually to the more open water westward of Glen Elg, where they are almost always to be seen from April until August. Wild geese on migration pass over Kylerhea. I recall one autumn day, late in the afternoon, when the geese crossed high above me, the low sun, already hidden from the glen by the steep hills, shining on their plumage as they flew fast toward the south-east.

The strait of Kylerhea is perhaps a quarter of a mile broad. There is a tradition that it received its name after Reidh, one of the Fingalians lifting himself upon his spear, attempted to leap over it but fell into the swift stream because his spear broke, and was swept away and no more seen. It was from the Skye side of the strait that this leap is said to have been made. Fionn, Oscar, Caoilte, Diarmid and others of the Feinne were hunting the red deer in Skye. Their wives were living in a house on the mainland side of the strait. An enemy set fire to the house, and from Skye the Feinne saw dense smoke rising from the thatch. It was this sight that spurred them to vault Kylerhea, and they were all successful in that great jump, or vault, except Reidh.

An historic rock, marked by a beacon, stands a little way off-shore north of the north entrance to the strait, on the Skye side of it. It is marked on charts and maps as Sgeir na Cailliche, or the Carlin Stone, and obviously commemorates the same Cailleach or Hag whose hill, Beinn na Cailliche (there are two high hills of the same name less than eight miles apart) rises from the shore near the rock. The Carlin Rock is named in the Saga of King Haco, for it was here that his fleet of war galleys anchored on their voyage south in the summer of 1263. It is evident that they had reached the place when the tide in the strait was contrary, and had anchored there until the ebb tide should carry them through. At this time the west was under Norse rule, and the MacLeods, who claim a Norse descent, were even then in possession of the lands of Glen Elg. The ruins of their castle still stand. The family are said to have left it because a child fell to its death from one of the windows: the same story is told of Duntuilm Castle in Skye.

After the steamer on her way from Mallaig to Kyle of Lochalsh has battled (if the tide be contrary) through Kylerhea of the fierce currents and has entered the broader waters of Loch Alsh, the castle of Eilean Donnan in clear weather may be seen rising from the sea some five miles eastward. This old castle, stately and picturesque, stands where Loch Alsh divides to form, towards the south, Loch

Duich, and, toward the north, the narrow Loch Long. Here we are in MacRae country, and a MacRae is hereditary constable of the castle. It has more than once been besieged, as when, in the year 1539, Donald Gorm MacDonald of Sleat, as he was leading an assault upon it, was pierced in the thigh by an arrow. Donald Gorm with anger wrenched the arrow from the wound, and so bled to death. The old *Statistical Account* records that the oldest inhabitant of the parish remembers having seen the men of the district dancing reels on the leaden roof of the castle before setting out to take part in the rising of 1715, at which rising they suffered severely at the battle of Sheriff-muir. Four years later the castle was garrisoned by a Spanish regiment, under the command of William, fifth Earl of Seaforth. In this year was fought the battle of Glen Shiel, between a force of Seaforth's men and the Spaniards on the one side and government troops from Inverness under the command of General Wightman on the other. The victory lay with General Wightman's force. The graves of those killed in this engagement are to be seen below, and not far from, the main road near the head of Glen Shiel, and in or about the year 1942 I was sent a bullet that had been picked up in the gravel of the river bed. After the fight, His Majesty's Ship *Worcester* sailed up Loch Alsh, and bombarded the castle of Eilean Donnan, since it had sheltered rebels. For almost 200 years the castle remained a ruin, but a strong ruin, and then was restored by Colonel John MacRae-Gilstrap, whose grandfather seven times removed (the Reverend Farquhar MacRae, 1580-1662) had been appointed constable of Eilean Donnan by the Earl of Seaforth. It is probable that Eilean Donnan, Donnan's Island, commemorates St. Donnan of Eigg, who was murdered by pirates, together with his followers. St. Columba warned him against the risks of going as far north as Eigg, then in the kingdom of the Picts, but he persisted. Who the pirates were who slew the saint and his followers is not known; some authorities have suggested that they were Norsemen or Danes.

Near Eilean Donnan Castle the main road leading east from Skye by way of the ferry of Kyle of Lochalsh formerly crossed Loch Long by a ferry, but a bridge, named Dornie Bridge, has now been built across the sea loch, and the crossing is less picturesque, but also less subject to delay. The road along the shore of Loch Duich rises at first high above the loch, then drops almost to sea-level. As it rises brief views are had of Eilean Donnan Castle, the ancestral home of the Earls of Seaforth. No doubt when the chief was in residence (as, for example, in the year 1719 before the battle of Glen Shiel) the martial strains of the bagpipe might have been heard here, as the chief's piper played that celebrated pibroch, "Earl of Seaforth's Salute," a tune that is still played at competitions at Highland gatherings by the leading players of the day. There is a tradition that another well-known pibroch, the "Glen is Mine," was composed by Seaforth's piper as he marched up Glen Shiel, perhaps before the historic fight of 1719. Along the shore of Loch Duich, and high above it, large plantations of coniferous trees are seen: the climate suits them and they are growing fast and are transforming the hillsides here.

Chapter V

APPLECROSS TO LOCH MAREE

Let us sail back (if we are so fortunate as to have a passage in one of the few vessels that at the present time enter Loch Duich) to Kyle of Loch Alsh, which is less than half an hour's sail by the mail steamer, after she has cleared the strait of Kylerhea. Here, as I have said, is the main ferry, "over the sea to Skye," as the song has it. The sea strait is here half a mile in width, and the tides do not run strongly as they do in Kylerhea. On the Skye shore opposite is Kyleakin, a name which means Strait of Haco, and seems to have been given the strait after the passage of King Haco of Norway's fleet of war galleys through it. The railway, before being extended to Kyle of Lochalsh, had its terminus at Strome Ferry, a dozen miles eastward on the shore of Loch Carron, and the Skye steamer at one time used to embark passengers here.

Winter as in summer, Kyle of Lochalsh is, for its size, a busy port for, besides the Skye mail steamer, the steamer for Stornoway in Lewis each afternoon sails after the arrival of the mail train, and on certain days the Harris and Uist steamer arrives here, or sails early in the morning. As you stand on the pier at Kyle of Lochalsh, you see, rising across the sea strait, the ruin of Castle Maoil, an old Mac-Kinnon stronghold. There is a tradition that a Norse princess lived here, and that she levied tribute from each ship that sailed through the strait. A chain was stretched across the strait at its narrowest point and thus an effectual barrier was presented to shipping—one might say a boom defence in its most primitive form. There is a natural rock pillar on the Skye shore beneath Kyle House. It is perhaps 3 feet in height and has a "waist" which, says tradition, was worn by the end of the chain which was wound round it. The chain on the farther side of the strait was apparently secured on the small island, where the lighthouse now is. I have heard no record of a pillar having at one time been there, and indeed, if it had been present it would almost certainly have been destroyed during the building of the lighthouse. The small channels between the lighthouse island and the mainland shore would have been too narrow and dangerous for vessels to navigate. Old traditions die fast. Mrs. Harry MacDonald of Viewfield, Portree, who died in 1949, aged ninety years, told me that when she was a girl everyone at Kyleakin could point out the pillar below Kyle House round which the chain was supposed to have been wound. Now there are few people who know its whereabouts. Many strangers have settled both at Kyleakin and Kyle of Lochalsh, and thus the continuity of tradition has been largely broken. The shore near the lighthouse is a favourite haunt of the eider, and a compact flock of this species, containing both ducks and drakes, is almost daily seen during autumn and winter. During the final phase of the second world war Kyle of Lochalsh was, for a short time, a port of considerable importance, for German submarines were brought in under escort. Their crews, some of whom I saw, were being sent off in special trains, and looked unshaven and dejected, and many of them very youthful.

No one arriving at Kyle by road from the east on a clear day can fail to be impressed by the beauty of the view westward on the descent from the higher ground, especially toward sunset. Across the sea rise Beinn na Cailliche beyond Broadford, and behind that hill with its great cairn, reputed to be the burial place of a Norse princess and her treasure, the jagged range of the Cuillin, black or dark blue according to the light, but never smiling, and always stern, austere and majestic. The long, rugged outline of Raasay rises from the sea, and beyond it are some of the far-northern hills in Skye, Beinn Storr with its inaccessible pinnacle and, beyond it, spectre-haunted Beinn Eadarra. Kyle of Lochalsh may be said to be a broad promontory between two sea lochs, Loch Alsh and Loch Carron: Loch Carron again forms a promontory between its upper reaches and its northern branch, by name Loch Kishorn.

On the coast north of Loch Kishorn is Applecross, which is a "ghost-name," the original form of which is Aporcrosan. The church of Aporcrosan was founded by St. Maolrubha. There is an old record that he crossed from Ulster to Scotland in the year 671, and he seems to have founded the church of Aporcrosan in either 672 or 673; as abbot he presided here for fifty-one years. There is a curious tradition concerning the death of the saint, which took place in the Black Isle, on the eastern fringe of the eastern Highlands, far from Applecross of his love. The dying saint directed that "four red men of Aporcrosan" should carry his body over the hills to his western church, but the people of the Black Isle wished the remains of the holy man to lie in their own burial ground. When the body was placed on rests, to be carried to the local burial ground, the united efforts of all the people there assembled were unable to raise it. Realising from this that the last wishes of the saint must be respected, the people of the Black Isle then permitted the four red men to carry the body to Applecross. Like Glen Elg, Applecross, although on the mainland, resembles an island, in that its main communications are by sea. Each day the Stornoway steamer slows down off Applecross and, weather permitting, a ferry boat puts out to disembark passengers and mails. The communication by land is across a hill road which at its highest point, Bealach nam Bo (Pass of the Castle) is 2,100 feet abovet he sea. On the April day when I crossed the pass on foot a pair of ptarmigan were dozing at the roadside; the only other road on which I have seen ptarmigan is the Cairnwell, between Braemar and Perth, where the road reaches a height of 2,200 feet, but the actual ascent is less than in the Applecross road, which begins to climb at sea-level, whereas the base of the Cairnwell pass is at Braemar, 1,100 feet above the sea. The road to Applecross is usually impassable in winter for months at a time, because of snow.

The sanctuary of Applecross had a girth of six miles. The stone crosses set in the ground at long intervals marked the circumference of the sanctuary: once within it the fugitive was safe from pursuit, whatever crime he might have committed. No cross now remains, although in the memory of old people the last of the old crosses was still strong and upright. It was destroyed by a mason who, believing it to be a relic of popery, broke it with his big hammer. The sanctuary has gone; the monastery has gone, yet St. Maolrubha's grave remains. It is in the burial ground of the church, and, unlike the modern graves which lie north and south, lies east and west. The earth from the saint's grave held miraculous properties; no one with this earth carried on his person could be slain in battle. Two rounded stones mark the saint's grave. It is said that a more imposing memorial of red Norwegian granite, sent by a princess of Norway, was broken. The old monastery, and perhaps the saint himself, are commemorated in the green island which lies a little way off-shore. Its name is Eilean nan Naomh—Isle of Saints. The small community of Applecross are mostly crofters, and some of them supplement the work on the crofts with fishing. There was grave risk from the mine fields during the years of the second world war, and at least one fishing boat disappeared without trace between Kyle of Lochalsh and Applecross. The old Highland landowning family were the MacKenzies of Applecross; they are commemorated in a stately pibroch, "MacKenzie of Applecross's Salute."

The coast north of Applecross is moorland, with here and there a few crofts. There is no road, but a path, along which a bicycle or motor-bicycle might pass easily enough, but not a motor-car. When it reaches the estuary of that broad and deep sea loch, Loch Torridon, the path bends from north to east, and traverses the shore of this loch, joining the road at Shieldaig. The mountains which rise at the head of Loch Torridon are impressive in their beauty and dignity. They are of red, or rather chocolate-coloured sandstone, and at sunset in the summer months are transformed into veritable mountains of gold. Red sandstone is found in only one place in the Outer Hebrides, but is seen in Sleat of Skye and in the island of Rum. The hills of the Torridon Sandstone formation are massive and grand. Authorities agree on the extraordinary denudation to which this ancient sandstone has been subjected. The neighbour here of Torridon Sandstone is Hebridean Gneiss, of which Ben Alligin, that splendid peak above Loch Torridon, is formed.

From Loch Torridon to Gairloch no road leads along the rough coast. The MacKenzies of Gairloch were a branch of the ancient house of MacKenzie of Kintail. For centuries they were the leading family in the district, and still hold a part, at all events, of the old property. Their hereditary pipers were the MacKays, a long-lived race. It is said that during the lifetime of eight MacKenzies of Gairloch, who succeeded one another in direct succession from father to son, there were only four MacKay pipers. The MacKays were a Sutherland family, and the first of the pipers, Ruairidh MacKay, was born in the Reay country about the year 1592, and was as a lad piper to the chief of the MacKays. Because he cut off a man's hand he had to leave that district, and became piper to John Roy MacKenzie, fourth laird of Gairloch, about the year 1609. Rorie, who did not marry until he was over sixty, was piper to four of the MacKenzies of Gairloch in succession. He had one child, he who later became the celebrated Iain Dall (Blind John), or, as he was sometimes called, Am Piobaire Dall—the Blind Piper. As a young boy of seven he lost his sight after an attack of small-pox, but his blindness did not prevent his becoming a piper of great renown. He studied for seven years under the great MacCrimmon at his college of piping at Boreraig in Skye. His skill in piping aroused the jealousy of the other piping pupils at the college, and they decided (as they hoped) to make an end of their rival. They chased him over a rock which still bears the name Leum an Doill—Leap of the Blind Man. The height of the rock is between 20 and 30 feet, but the sightless piper fell on his feet, and apparently suffered no injury. Two hollows in the ground are said to be where his heels landed; I was shown them by an old man who had much lore of the district. Iain Dall, who combined the office of piper and bard, died at the great age of ninety-eight, in the year 1754. He is said to have composed twenty-four pibroch tunes, and composed also many songs and poems. His son, Angus, succeeded him as hereditary piper. There is a tale that when he went to play at a competition in Edinburgh, certain competing pipers, jealous of him, made several punctures in the sheepskin bag of his pipes. It looked as if he would be unable to compete, but a girl friend of his in some way obtained for him an undressed sheepskin, and he was able to make from it another bag—and carried off the first prize in the competition. It is said that the well-known pibroch, Moladh Mairi—Praise of Mary— was composed by him after this incident, in gratitude to the Mary who had helped him in his misfortune. These two stories of jealousy among pipers are an adverse commentary on the pipe players of the time. John, last of the MacKay hereditary pipers, was born in or about 1753, and emigrated to America, where he died in or about 1835.

Gareloch, or more correctly Gearr Loch, in English the Short Loch, has pink sands of Torridon sandstone, so that they seem to glow with hidden fires even on a dark day of mist and rain. This sea loch is separated by five miles of hilly land from Loch Maree, a long loch with many islands, from which the river Ewe, a river of only two miles in length, flows into Loch Ewe. It is almost certain that Loch Maree, which is only 29 feet above sea-level, was a continuation of Loch Ewe and was salt water at one time. The early name of Loch Maree was Loch Ewe, and this explains why the place-name Kinlochewe should be found at the head not of Loch Ewe but of Loch Maree. Timothy Pont writes about 1650 of the "fresch Loch of Ew," as opposed to "the salt Lochew." He puts it on record, perhaps for the first time, that the fresh Loch Ewe, "by sum it is cald Loch Mulruy." He says also that "this fair Loch is reported never to freze; it is compasd about

256

The Cuillin Hills from Balmacara

with many fair and tall woods as any in all the west of Scotland, in sum parts with hollyne, in sum places with fair and beautifull fyrrs of 60, 70, 80 foot of good and serviceable timmer for masts and raes, in other places ar great plentie of excellent great oakes, whair may be sawin out planks of 4 sumtyms 5 foot broad."

Loch Maree takes its present name from St. Maolrubha; its most celebrated island is Eilean Ma-rui, St. Maolrubha's Isle. There is a tradition that the saint for a time lived here. The island has religious associations extending over a very long period, and seems to have been associated with Druidic rites before the Christian era. There is, or was, a holy well on the island. The well, it is said, dried up after a man washed his mad dog in it. Here stands an oak tree, studded with nails. During the first world war the old tree, which had died, was carried away from the island, but was later brought back and set up in its former home. Into the old bleached tree many coins have been driven as offerings from the pilgrims who have through the centuries visited the isle and drunk of the waters of the sacred well. When Queen Victoria visited the island in 1877, she fixed her offering in the tree, the belief being that if a silent wish is wished by a person after having attached any metal article to the tree, that wish will be realised. It will be noticed that the procedure has been changed, for in earlier times the well, not the tree, possessed miraculous properties, and having drunk at the well the pilgrim placed his or her thank-offering in the tree. The sacrificing of bulls here, which continued until the year 1678 and perhaps even later, is believed to date back to the time of the Druids. In the seventeenth century the sacrifice of a bull on the isle was connected with the ceremonies for the cure of an insane person. The boat in which the afflicted person was placed was rowed thrice round the isle, and during these circuits the lunatic was thrice jerked (he or she was bound with ropes) into the water. This done, the party landed on the isle, and the afflicted one knelt before the altar, was later brought to the holy well to drink of it, and finally attached an offering to the tree.

On another island of Loch Maree, Eilean Suthainn, the osprey formerly nested, although at not so late a date as on either Loch an Eilein or Loch Arkaig. The osprey was here named by the people of the district Alan Iasgair—Alan the Fisherman. The firs of Loch Maree district, which were extolled by Timothy Pont in the seventeenth century, are still a feature of the shores of the loch, and have

Slioch and Loch Maree

thus far been spared by those who have felled so great a part of the old Caledonian Forest. They beautify the loch even on the wildest and most stormy day, as on a mid-September day when, after a night of heavy rain, I passed that way on a journey from Gairloch to Achnasheen. The weather for weeks that year had been wet and stormy, and the loch was high. The river Grudie, which rises in the corries of Beinn Eighe (3,300 feet), was in full spate, and it and its tributaries, leaping from the mist-cap in white cascades and flowing into the forest zone of the old pines, which were dark beneath a rainy, cloud-filled sky, recalled a scene in Norway rather in the Scottish Highlands.

Chief among the hills of the country of Loch Maree is Slioch. It rises from the east shore of Loch Maree to a height of 3,217 feet. Slioch stands alone, and its beauty and symmetry can the more easily be realised because of this. Especially striking does it appear when seen from the west; one of the best views of the hill that I know is across the sea from Flodigarry in the Isle of Skye when, in winter, it rises beyond the sea strait twenty miles wide and beyond the snowless shore in a white dome, with black lines and scars where the snow has failed to find lodgement on its precipitous slopes. A few minutes before sunset its virgin whiteness is changed to red and, at the moment of sunset, to violet before the shades of evening gradually rest upon it. John H. Dixon in his *Gairloch*, a book published in 1886 and giving much interesting information on the country, its history, legends and traditions, connects Slioch with Spear-head, for he says truly that the mountain resembles the form of a rather thick head of an ancient spear or lance, and still more closely that of an ancient flint arrow-head. Three miles down the shore of the loch from the base of Slioch is Letterewe, from which the beautiful Fionn Loch can be visited by a rough hill path.

At Kinlochewe (Head of Loch Ewe, where, as in Letterewe, we have the early name of Loch Maree) a road leads south-west to Loch Torridon, through magnificent scenery. Northward tower the peaks of Beinn Eighe and, four miles after leaving Kinlochewe, Loch Clair is seen. This beautiful loch is in the forest of Coulin. Where Coulin Lodge now stands the people of Kinlochewe long ago had their summer shielings, according to Professor Watson. The shores of both Loch Clair and Loch Coulin are clothed with old pines. The road now descends Glen Torridon and the vast bulk of Liathach rises almost sheer to the north. I recall one day late in May driving with a

friend down Glen Torridon. It was raining, but the weather had been
dry, and there was no water visible on the flanks of this hill. On our
return journey seven milk-white ribbons of streams appeared on
Liathach where no water had showed earlier in the day. The noise,
the murmur, of innumerable waterfalls grew loud, faded, again sounded
clearly, as gusts of wind struck the hillside, lifting the waterfalls and
blowing them back uphill as though they were mist. The waterfalls
swayed as the hill wind played upon them; they disappeared underground before they reached the glen. The upper slopes of the hill
were hidden in cloud, and this gave the illusion that the mountain
was even higher than it actually is. Great rolling vapours crossed
this formidable hill face, rocky and precipitous. It was not far from
here that the marks of a combat between a wild cat and a golden
eagle were visible one winter day in the snow. The road meets Loch
Torridon at its headwaters. On the loch side are various crofting
townships. Above the loch, in Torridon Forest, is the unusual place-
name Coire Mhic Nobuil—MacNoble's Corrie. At one time Mac-
Noble was a moderately common Highland surname, but it is now
rare, although the name Noble persists.

If you return to Kinlochewe, you join there the main road to the
railway at Achnasheen, well named Field of Storm, and by travelling
thence westward, either by road or by rail, reach Loch Carron and
Kyle of Lochalsh. From Kinlochewe the road climbs Glen Dochertie,
then traverses Loch Rosque (Loch a' Chroisg—Loch of the Crossing),
half a mile beyond which is Achnasheen. During the first world war
I was sent in my car by the Senior Naval Officer, Aultbea, with
dangerous explosives taken in a captured German submarine, to the
naval authorities in Inverness. In order that I might accomplish the
journey as speedily as possible I was given a very special permit,
called a z-permit, authorising me to burn full headlights in localities
where normally only side lamps were permitted. This was in the days
of acetyline head lamps, and on my return journey, when I had reached
Achnasheen and slowly made my way along the shore of Loch Maree
to Gairloch, not only had my headlights failed, but one paraffin side
lamp had also petered out. When passing through Gairloch I was
stopped by the local constable for travelling with only one side lamp.
When I showed him my z-permit, authorising me to carry full head-
lamps on the coastal area, he confessed that my case was beyond him,
and permitted me to proceed. That journey was a more adventurous

one than I realised at the time, for later it transpired that the explosive sticks should not have been carried loose in the car, as I had been ordered to carry them, for the jolting on the rough road might have touched them off, and car and driver might then have been liquidated —but the soothing word "liquidate" had not then been invented.

It is a wild and desolate country between Achnasheen and Achnachellach, but there are often whooper swans on Loch Sgamhain, and sometimes black-throated divers in their strikingly handsome breeding plumage are seen, although the bird does not breed here. As the road descends to Achnashellach, there is evidence that large areas of hillside have been recently planted with various conifer trees. Thriving plantations are seen, the work of the Forestry Commission. There is here the ever-present danger of fire from sparks from passing trains, and considerable areas of young plantations have been lost during recent years, despite the broad fire trenches dug near the railway to prevent fires on the railway embankment from spreading into the woods.

At Achnashellach is Loch Dughall, Dugall's Loch, a grand fishing loch; from it flows the river Carron. After Strathcarron the railway follows one side of Loch Carron, the road the other. On the road is the village of Lochcarron or Jeantown; the old name of the place is Torr-nan-Clar. At Stromeferry, where the road crosses Loch Carron, stand the ruins of the castle of Strome, an ancient seat of the family of the Lord of the Isles.

The first of the MacDonalds of Lochalsh was Celestine, second son of Alexander, Lord of the Isles. The House of Lochalsh held the lands of Lochalsh, Loch Carron and Loch Broom; they were superiors also of the lands of Lochiel in Lochaber. The Captain of Clanchameron was at one time appointed keeper or constable of the castle of Strome, which was captured and blown up by MacKenzie, Lord of Kintail, in 1603, and has thus been a ruin for nearly 350 years. After the ferry across Loch Carron the road no longer follows the coast, but climbs a steep pass, and descends to Loch Alsh near Balmacara; from the high ground there is a beautiful view in clear weather of Loch Duich and the old castle of Eilean Donnan, in its picturesque setting.

CHAPTER VI

THE COAST FROM GAIRLOCH
NORTHWARD

NORTHWARD of Gairloch is a broad promontory, washed on its west side by the Minch, and on its east by the less turbulent waters of Loch Ewe. At its most northerly point is a lighthouse, Rudha Reidh—the Smooth Point; its strong, sharp flashes of white light can be seen from far out on the Minch, and also from the north wing of the Isle of Skye. Near the lighthouse, crowding the tops of two rock stacks, a considerable colony of cormorants nest. This bird is not numerous along the west coast of Scotland during the nesting season, and I know of few colonies, although the green cormorant or shag, a smaller bird, nests on the coast wherever the rocks are suitable. When I passed that way one April day I noticed that the shags which were nesting on the lower ledges of the stacks already had eggs but the larger cormorants had not begun to lay. The difference in character between the two species is marked. The shag is a tame bird; the cormorant, at all events the cormorants which winter off the western coast and roost on the rocky islands, are wary and unapproachable, so that on the approach of a boat it is a common sight to see a single cormorant, which has been resting with a number of shags, take wing, whereas the shags remain, unafraid, on the ledges. Some county councils give protection to the shag, but none to the cormorant, which take a great number of smolts and sea trout at the river estuaries.

The road northward along the coast avoids Rudha Reidh, and crosses high ground, by way of Loch Tollie, to Poolewe, then approaching the river Ewe during the last mile of that river's course. Although its course is short, the Ewe is one of the strongest of the rivers of the north-west seaboard, and holds many salmon and sea trout, which enter it during the summer and early autumn months on passage to Loch Maree. Poolewe was the birth place of that well-known Highland artist in water colours, Finlay MacKinnon, a crofter's son, who made a name for himself because of the delicacy and accuracy of his work.

A mile north of Poolewe is Inverewe House, where one of the

most beautiful and remarkable gardens and grounds in the west Highlands is to be seen. Osgood MacKenzie of Inverewe was a well-known
Highlander, who, when he set about planting trees and shrubs in a
wind-swept country at the head of Loch Ewe, was told by his friends
that he was wasting both time and money. In his book, *A Hundred
Years in the Highlands*, he writes modestly enough of his efforts, and
the success which at last crowned them can be realised only by actually
visiting the place. Here I have seen mimosa in flower at Christmas:
eucalyptus trees grow and flourish, and semi-tropical plants find the
moist frost-free winters to their liking. The rainfall here is not so
great as in many west coast areas, for the hills rise some miles east of
the sea, and do not, as at Kinloch Hourn and other places, draw down
the rain in great quantities onto the coast. The annual rainfall at
Gairloch is less than half what it is at Kinloch Hourn, yet the eucalyptus flourishes at both places. Loch Ewe has seen stirring times during
two world wars. During the first war it was the base of the Tenth
Cruiser Squadron. The ships of the squadron were armed merchantmen, most of them great ocean liners. The vice-admiral in command
of the squadron was Admiral Tupper, and his ships sailed as far north
as the edge of the Arctic ice, to intercept possible surface raiders from
Germany. Little did those who then patrolled foresee that a second
war would come in their time, and that a German battleship would
be for a time at large in the North Atlantic.

Northward of Loch Ewe, across the promontory, is Gruinard Bay,
on the west shore of which are lesser, attractive bays, hidden on a
rocky coast. The small township of Mellan Udrigill stands beside the
most beautiful of these bays. On the clear September day when last I
visited it, the small burn which empties itself into the bay was in spate,
and its peaty waters flowed red-brown over the golden sands. Across
the blue sea rose, in clear sunlight, Ben More Coigeach and, beyond
it, the high hills of Sutherland, among which the long ridge of Foinne
Bheinn was prominent. An hour earlier, from the high ground above
Loch Ewe, I had looked westward across to Skye, and had seen the
summit of Beinn Eadarra rise to the blue sky, and had looked down
upon the deep Fionn Loch, the home of trout of fabulous size, which
are sometimes caught on a night-line baited with frogs. Westward
was the outline of Lewis, running northward towards the Butt. The
day was of that exceptional clearness which is sometimes a precursor
of rain, and when the moon rose that evening ragged clouds, driving

in at increasing speed from the south-west, soon filled the sky and brought with them rain and wind from the Atlantic. I remember Osgood MacKenzie, a patriarchal figure of distinguished bearing, with white, flowing beard and kindly eye, and dressed always in Highland garb, telling me that on the hill lochs behind Mellon Udrigill white-fronted geese had their home when he was young. He was glad when later I found the geese, for he feared that they had gone from the district since his young days. In winter and early spring the coast here is one of the haunts of the great northern diver, whose favourite fish, the flounder, is found in the sandy bays.

The shores of Loch Ewe and of Gruinard Bay support a considerable crofter population; the land that is worth cultivating is small in area, and it is all under crops. Here, as elsewhere in the west Highlands, the fuel burnt is peat. It is carried in creels from the peat mosses, where it has been cut in May and dried during the long June days, to the roadside, whence it is taken to the crofters' houses in creels, in carts, or in lorries. The crofters are, some of them, lobster fishers also; their boats can be seen moored in summer in sheltered bays, or drawn up on the shore. Here, as elsewhere along the western seaboard, Gaelic is the language spoken.

Beyond Gruinard, Little Loch Broom and Loch Broom bite deep into the land eastward. At the head of Little Loch Broom is Dundonnell Forest with its great hill An Teallach—The Forge—closely surrounded by lesser, attendant peaks. This is one of the hills of red sandstone; its high slopes are almost bare of vegetation, and it is unexpected to find here considerable areas of sea thrift, anchoring itself with strong roots deep in the ground to withstand the great winds of winter which so often blow here, day after day and week after week. At the mouth of Little Loch Broom is the crofting township of Scoraig, with a legitimate grievance: the houses have no road to them. The people might be on an island; they have all the disadvantages of island life, yet none of its advantages, for the isles, or at all events the larger isles, have regular steamer services, but here only an occasional boat calls, without passenger accommodation.

North of sheltered Dundonnell with its haunted wood the road for a time leaves the coast and climbs to a height of 1,060 feet. It passes near the hill loch, Lochaidh Bhroain, where the river Broom has its birth, then descends to Loch Broom by way of the north bank of the river. Far beneath the road, below Braemore House, is the tremendous chasm of Corryhalloch, in Gaelic Coire Shalach—the Ugly or Dirty Corrie—named because of its grim and intimidating aspect. The ravine is spanned by an attractive bridge. There is a high waterfall here, one of the sights of the district. The name of the waterfall, which is most impressive when the river is high, is Easan na Miasaich. Professor Watson writes that the name can be translated as Waterfalls of the Place of Platters, the Platters being the rounded hollows worn in the rocks by the action of the water. The name on the half-inch map is given as Falls of Measach. Below the great falls is a deep pool, black and seemingly bottomless even on a day of summer. Beneath this pool, the bed of the stream is comparatively shallow, with swift current and a few pools where salmon lie. I hooked a good salmon in one of these pools, and he took me two hundred yards down the river before I was able to beach him, just before we had arrived at an alder tree which jutted into the river and would have prevented my following the fish further. It was a clear morning of May, and where I landed the fish I could just see the cone of Sgùrr Mór Fannich rising, snow-capped and noble, on the southern horizon beyond the lesser intervening hills.

Before the road drops down to Strath Mór and the lower reaches of the river Broom there is a striking view of Loch Broom and the Minch beyond it, clear and blue as I saw it on a morning of early summer when the sun shone bright and the sky was clear. There were days I fished the Broom when the wind was rough and cold and summer seemed to be no nearer than it had been in March. That year had brought a spell of Arctic weather during the last days of April. The frost had blackened the young shoots of trees and shrubs; even the nettle shoots were blackened. At Inverbroom or Foy House is an avenue of lime trees, and I still remember clearly their shrivelled appearance. Fish were hard to move that year, but there was much besides fishing to interest the angler. Sandpipers haunted most of the pools, and when their young were hatched the parents showed signs of acute excitement and apprehension when their territory was invaded. One day—it was a cold, grey day with north-west wind—I saw a stoat running along the opposite bank of the river. I was almost motionless, and the small animal did not see me. He came, in his hunting or his wanderings, to a small bay. Instead of following the bank round the bay, as he might easily have done, he plunged without hesitation into the icy water, swam across the bay, and continued his course without a pause: he had chosen the water rather than make even a small detour, and I thought it remarkable behaviour on the part of a purely land animal. Kenny MacKenzie used to drive us up to the top beat each morning, and my admiration of him grew daily, when his front tyre, showing the red of the inner tube through a formidable gash, failed to burst and so precipitate us, as I fearfully expected, into the chasm of Corryhalloch. When a cold and rough May had given place to the warmer weather of June, wild hyacinths flowered on the sheltered banks of the river and after rain the young birch leaves scented the air. At its estuary, at the headwaters of Loch Broom, the river flows over a shingly shore and divides into several channels. In June the shore is coloured pink by the flowers of sea thrift.

The small town of Ullapool is seven miles from the head of Loch Broom, on its north shore. Ullapool is a Norse place-name, meaning Ulli's Homestead, and the place is Norse in appearance, and also in atmosphere. In 1788 the British Fishery Society built the town as a centre for herring and cod fishing, and during recent years it has again become a busy fishing port. The herring landed here are taken by lorry across Scotland, by way of Garve and Inverness, to Aberdeen and other large towns, the drivers making the long journey across the Dirrie More (in Gaelic An Diridh Mór—the Great Ascent) in wild winter weather, when on occasion they must force a passage through great drifts and perhaps of necessity abandon their lorries and struggle in the storm over an uninhabited country to the nearest house, many miles away. In summer Ullapool is an attractive place, and there is excellent sea fishing to be had here, the haddock fishing at certain times of the year being very good in the loch—better indeed than in any other west Highland loch. The salmon fishing in the Ullapool river is also good.

Looking south from the district of Ullapool, which, by the way, has one of the lowest rainfalls on the west coast, a multitude of hills are seen rising to the south. Most of them rise from the great deer forests of Fannich and Braemore. One of these high hills has the curious and pleasing name, Sgùrr Eideadh nan Clach Geala—Garment of White Stones Peak—from the white quartz blocks on it. At the march of Fannich Forest is another hill, with an almost similar name. This is Sgùrr nan Clach Geala—Peak of the White Stones. This is a lonely hill, with no house near; not far from its summit, on the early summer

265

day when I climbed the hill, I passed the large stones of snow-white quartz which give the hill its name. On that clear sunny day I could see the swell breaking white on the distant coast of Skye. Deer were feeding in the corries, which were fringed with great snow wreaths still unmelted from the storms of winter and spring. Here one was near the centre of the hill country, between the west coast and the east, and the view extended from Skye to Ben Nevis, which overlooks the Cromarty Firth. All that day I did not see a ptarmigan, nor red grouse, nor yet a golden plover nor a lapwing, for these high hills hold little bird life. Wheatears are on them, and a few meadow pipits, and perhaps a wandering eagle, but, as compared with the Cairngorms, their bird life is neither plentiful nor varied.

Somewhere near the head of Lochaidh Bhroain is a pass the name and site of which are in danger of being lost, for none knew of it when I made enquiries in the district. It is Bealach nam Brog—Pass of the Shoes. At the battle of Bealach nam Brog, " seaven score of the surname of Dingwall and eleven Monroes of the House of Foulls" were slain. The name, although lost on the map, lives in a very beautiful pibroch, of distinctive charm and melody.

Before the railway was built to Kyle of Lochalsh, Gairloch and Loch Broom were the two principal ports for the crossing to Stornoway in the Isle of Lewis. Dixon in his *Gairloch* mentions that the smack *North Britain* which carried the mails between Poolewe and Stornoway for eighteen years, struck a whale, running on to its back and cutting it to the backbone. When the smack ran on to the whale's back, her stern went under water to the companion. She made much water, but the Lewis coast was reached and the smack was run ashore at Stornoway.

One of the most beautiful and remote districts on the west coast lies north of Ullapool. It is Achiltibuie. There is no road to Achiltibuie along the coast; one must travel inland to Drumrunie, then northwestward, through the hill country, along a road where it is difficult to pass another car. From the road that imposing hill Cùl Bheag (2,525 feet) rises steeply, and one sees ahead Loch Lurgainn, Loch of the Legs or Shanks. It is said that Fionn and his mother had been fighting with giants in the east country near the foot of Ben Wyvis. Since they were outnumbered and were faring badly in the encounter, Fionn seized his mother by her legs, threw her over his shoulder, and fled westward. At Loch Lurgainn he halted to rest, and on laying his mother on the ground, found that her legs were all that was left of her; hence the place-name, Loch of the Shanks. Almost joined to Loch Lurgainn is Loch Bad a' Ghaill, in English the Loch of the Lowlander's Thicket, commemorating perhaps some stranger who hid here. The third loch of the chain is Loch Osgaig, a Norse name which is written on most maps in the outlandish and erroneous form Owskeich. This loch has a singular charm, and reminded me, on the summer day on which I saw it, of a lake of Iceland rather than a Highland loch; a strong, clear river issues from the loch and hurries foaming down to the sea at Garvie Bay.

During the drive past these three lonely lochs, along a road from which not a single house is to be seen, that great hill, or perhaps rather it should be said hill massif, Ben More Coigeach, rises to the west, high and rugged and, on the day when I passed by it, calling down the ocean clouds to its brow. The hill takes its name from the district of Coigeach—Place of Fifths. Professor Watson points out in his book, *Place-names of Ross and Cromarty*, that the division of land into fifths was a common and ancient Gaelic custom, the best known fifths being Cóig Cóigimh na h-Eirinn—the Five Fifths of Eire. He says that the Five Fifths of Coigeach were Achnahaird, Achlochan, Acheninver, Achabhraighe and Achduart. Ben More Coigeach, as I saw it on the April day when I climbed it, was a hill renewing its youth in bright sunshine after the long and severe winter storms. It was a June day in character, and one expected to find the birches in the gullies already in green foliage and not bare almost as at mid-winter. There were few birds seen on the hill that day, which was memorable because of the clearness of the air and the beauty of the view. As one climbed higher hill upon hill became visible. Even the white screes on Foinne Bheinn in the Reay Forest were plain and one half expected to be able to see North Rona almost 100 miles away. There was a casting of a golden eagle lying near the summit, on a rocky spur, but few birds were seen on that day. Sgùrr Mór Fannich rose nobly to the south-east, and the great massif of An Teallach in the Dundonnell Forest. Far to the south-west the Cuillin hills of Skye lay beneath a cloud of their own making. The plateau of Ben More Coigeach is of Torridon sandstone, and the rocks are in places curiously weathered. That April day will be remembered because of the piping of Great Music on the hill-top, and also because of the fragrance of the whins in the glen beneath, the golden flowers, motionless in the sun-heated air, exhaling an aroma of apricot. Later the Shiant Isles rose dark on the far horizon, and the Summer Isles were black against the afterglow. Such a day in April is rare, and because of its rarity is precious.

When the road reaches Rudha Mór—the Great Promontory—at Achnahaird Bay, it enters a country that has a Hebridean atmosphere. The hills are left behind, and there are low moors and a number of lochs to be seen. Achnahaird Bay has a considerable ebb; the sand at low tide is firm and glistening and above the mark of high tide are sand dunes and short grass, honeycombed with the burrows of rabbits which abound here. Across an arm of the sea Suilven—the Pillared Hill, sometimes called the Sugar Loaf—rises nobly. The road now bends southward, passing Loch Ra (Loch Ruadh—the Red Loch), and Loch Battachan or more correctly Loch nam Badachan—Loch of the Thickets—to the township of Achiltibuie with its hospitable hotel. Here one looks out over two miles of sea on to the Summer Islands, of which the largest and nearest is Tanera Mór with its sheltered harbour. Here the well-known naturalist Fraser Darling lived, his wife nobly sharing his seclusion, and tamed the seals and the barnacle geese. His books describe well their simple and happy life on their island. Professor Watson derives the place-name Tanera from the Norse, Harbour Island, and its harbour is well-known for its safety in heavy gales. From Achiltibuie the view southward across the entrance of Loch Broom embraces the great massif of An Teallach, a hill that, although a day's journey distant by road, is no more than fifteen miles from Achiltibuie as the eagle flies, or as the dark raven wings its way.

About six miles north of Achiltibuie, between Loch Osgaig and Loch Bad a' Ghail, the coast road to Lochinver leads north. For its distance, no more than fourteen miles, it passes through interesting and diverse scenery, winding now inland past moors and lochs, now along the sea coast, but almost always, on the April day I travelled that way, with gorse in blossom on its sides. There was a film of green on only a few of the birches in the sheltered glens, and the gorse blossom, the herald of summer, softened the austerity of the scene. The river Polly is passed not far from its mouth. This salmon river is slow-flowing and its name, Pollaidh, means a River of Pools. Farther north the river Kirkaig, the boundary between Ross and Sutherland, is crossed. Salmon are sometimes caught here in March, but June and

July are the best months for fishing. Rather more than two miles above the bridge are the Falls of Kirkaig, the river plunging into a pool that is black and apparently bottomless even in the fine weather of summer, when the river is clear and low. A gillie on the river dropped a stone into this pool with ninety feet of line attached to it, and did not reach the bottom. Here the salmon angler must fish with caution, and cannot, unaided, land a salmon. His companion must descend a ladder and, leaning over the black depths, one hand grasping the rope that is there for his support, like a climber on the Matterhorn, must gaff the fish with his free hand. Murdo Ross, head stalker on Glen Canisp Forest, told me that he rose a fish here which he estimated as being between 40 and 50 lb. It is doubtful if a fish of this weight could be landed in this pool; did the angler overbalance he might find himself swimming, like the salmon, in the foam-covered waters, which swirl and eddy in the spray of their making.

The noble dome of Suilven—the Pillar Hill—overlooks this region. Suilven for its size—it is no more than 2,400 feet in height—is the most impressive hill I have seen in the Highlands. It rises from a land of lochs and bogs, its upper reaches, from the Bealach Mór to the summit, the home of ptarmigan, golden eagle, and peregrine falcon. On the dark day of rain when I was on Suilven the view was impressive because of the many lochs which lay, dark as night, in the almost windless air. The great walls which drop almost sheer from the summit are named Caisteal Liath—Grey Castle. They are climbed by skilled mountaineers, but the more modest climber ascends the hill usually by way of the Bealach Mór—or Great Pass.

Lochinver is served by a road from Lairg and Invershin, passengers being transported by buses which run daily. At Lochinver trees, well-grown and with spreading branches, flourish to the tide. The houses are built along the sea front, and the place reminds me of a small Norwegian port. The sea communication is by the cargo boat from Glasgow which calls every ten days. Much could be done to improve sea communication along the west coast, for here the sea is the road and the sea passage from one port to another may be only a quarter of the distance covered by a car on the road.

The traveller has now entered a country with a strong Norse flavour, a country in some respects more remote than the Hebrides.

PART VI

THE COUNTRY OF DINGWALL AND THENCE TO SUTHERLAND AND THE NORTH-WEST SEABOARD

CHAPTER I

DINGWALL AND BEN WYVIS

DINGWALL, north-west of Inverness, stands at the gateway to the
north-west Highlands. It is a Norse word, Thing Völlr—Field of
Meeting—and here the Norse rulers held their "Thing" or Parliament. The word Thingvallir in Iceland, near Reykjavik, is the same.
The Norse meeting-place in Dingwall can still be traced, at the back
of Mill Street. Dingwall was created a Royal Burgh in 1226, and
the remains of its early royal castle stand within the present castle.

The great bulk of Ben Wyvis overshadows Dingwall. This hill—
it might be termed a hill-range—rises to a height of rather less than
3,500 feet. It holds snow until late in the year, and sometimes may be
seen as late as May rising in a coat of unbroken white from the low
country. Professor Watson gives the Gaelic name as Beinn Uais—
High Hill—from the root seen in *uas-al*, high, noble, and he mentions
that its height is best appreciated from Inverness and its neighbourhood.
Its spur which rises near Garve is named An Cabar—the Antler—
because of its sharpness. Pennant narrates that "Sir Henry Monro of
Foulis holds a forest from the Crown by a very whimsical tenure,
that of delivering a snowball on any day of the year that it is demanded;
and he seems in no danger of forfeiting his right by failure of the
quit-rent; for snow lies in the form of a *glaciere* in the chasms of
Benwewish, a neighbouring mountain, throughout the year." There
is good grass on Ben Wyvis, for sheep and red deer. A pilot in the
R.A.F. wrote an interesting article in the *Field* about his experiences,
when flying over Ben Wyvis, during the second world war, when the
hill was deep in snow. A stag, taking fright at the plane, floundered
into a drift, and was so deeply embedded that he was unable to extricate
himself. A pair of golden eagles saw the stag's predicament, and as the
airman circled overhead they, having designs on the helpless stag and
thinking that the aeroplane was also a bird of prey like themselves,
attacked it with bravery and ferocity; it took the pilot all his time to
avoid them.

I have mentioned the presence of swifts in summer on Lochnagar
and on the Cairngorms. One day in June when I was on Ben Wyvis

273   s

I was surprised at the number of swifts which were flying over the long ridge of the hill. On the west side the air was warm, for the sun was shining brightly, but when I had reached the high slopes near, and to the east of the summit, I found there a cold wind blowing in from the Cromarty Firth and the open sea beyond it. The warm sun had caused a great number of insects to appear on the hill, and the swifts were hawking them a short distance to the south-west of the ridges. In the evening, as I descended towards the Blackwater, above Loch Garve, the swifts came very near me, snapping up the insects which I had disturbed, and moving fast at a little height above the heather and grass. These birds perhaps nested in Dingwall, no more than a quarter of an hour's flight away. That evening I saw many house martins nesting beneath the eaves of the lonely cottage of the stalker at Garbat, beside the Blackwater, but these lesser birds I did not meet with on the high ground, nor do they usually wander far from their nesting place, but hunt for flies among the neighbouring birches.

Garbat cottage is on the Direadh Mór—the Great Ascent—across to the western seaboard at Loch Broom. It is in romantic Strath Garve, through which the Blackwater flows, sandpiper- and dipper-haunted, with birches that perfume the summer breeze. After rain the Blackwater deserves its name, for its waters, deeply peat-coloured, are black as the coat of the water horse in the deeper pools where the yellow froth eddies on the surface and the salmon lie unseen. The Blackwater is formed of three streams, the Glascarnoch River, the Strath Vaich River, and the smaller river which flows through Strath Rannoch. Their combined waters flow into, and through Loch Garve (which, despite the strong flow of water, readily freezes). A mile below Loch Garve are the Rogie Falls, picturesque amid white-stemmed birches, and especially worth visiting when the salmon are endeavouring to ascend them. The river now flows near woodcock-haunted Torrachilty and joins, a couple of miles lower down, the river Conon. The Conon flows down Strath Conon from the west —during a part of its course it is known as the river Meig. After their meeting, the Conon and the Blackwater are named the Conon, and the river, now of much greater volume, flows near Brahan Castle, ancestral home of the MacKenzies of Seaforth. In olden days, before the time of bridges, there were ferry boats on the Conon. In a description of the district in 1725 the writer, after mentioning Brahan Castle, "the principal mansion house of the Marques of Seafort, pleasantly situated on a rising ground adorned with gardins, parks and fine planting, and naturally beautifyed with woods," speaks of a ferry boat near the Kirk of Urray, and another nearer to Dingwall, called the ferry boat of Moy, both ferrying passengers over the Conon. From the south-west the Conon is joined by the river Orrin, which has come down from the high ground of Glen Orrin, and is a "spatey" river, and, when in flood, "very impetuous."

Loch Garve, through which the Blackwater flows and which, as I have mentioned, freezes quickly notwithstanding, is usually a haunt of whooper swans in winter and early spring. When the loch is hard-frozen these stately birds are compelled to frequent the small area of water which remains ice-free where the river leaves the loch; with them are usually seen goosanders, tufted duck and, sometimes, wigeon. Scarcely more than a mile west of Loch Garve, yet flowing into the Conon and not the Blackwater, is Loch Luichart, a long, narrow loch, a former haunt of the osprey. A mile west of the head of Loch Luichart the river Fannich flows down from the high ground, and joins the river Bran (which flows through Loch Luichart and, when it leaves the loch, is thereafter named the Conon). The Bran, which rises in Loch a' Chroisg, flows through Loch Achanalt, also a favourite haunt of wild swans, and Loch a' Chuilinn—Loch of the Holly. Loch Fannich, although a large loch, is invisible from the low ground. An impressive view of it is had from the summit of Sgùrr nan Clachan Geala (3,581 feet), to the north. At the head of Loch Fannich is The Nest—An Nead as it is known in Gaelic. This is perhaps the finest of the magnificent corries of Fannich deer forest. The name is unusual, and I have not heard it applied to a corrie else-where.

It will be seen that here are considerable rivers, bearing each more than one name; all, as the eagle flies, near one another and in sight at the same time from the air. It is not often that one is so fortunate as to witness the actual arrival of migrating birds. This experience I had one day in October when on high ground not many miles from Fan-nich. I saw a flock of birds descending from a great height, and as they were literally dropping into the heather I saw that they were fieldfares. They had come in from the north-east and, I have no doubt, had crossed the sea from Norway. In an earlier chapter I mentioned Sgùrr Mór Fannich, and its noble appearance when seen from the west. It is no less striking when viewed from the east. If one knows where to look for it, one can see it from the railway near Garve and I remember a winter day, when there was neither snow nor wind on the low ground, catching a glimpse of Scùrr Mór white and majestic, a pennon of drifted snow floating away to leeward from its cold summit into the blue of the sky.

CHAPTER II

SUTHERLAND: THE SHIN AND ASSYNT

SUTHERLAND, a great county, abounding in hills, includes three old divisions. The Reay Country, Duthaich Mhic Aoidh (MacKay's Country), is in the north, and extends eastward from Durness on the Atlantic to the border of Caithness. Assynt lies southward of Mac-Kay's Country, on the Atlantic seaboard. The third division was Sutherland, which now comprises all three. Sutherland proper (the word means South Land) was the name given by the Norsemen to the *south* part of their province of Caithness lying between the Ord of Caithness and the Kyle of Sutherland. That is the explanation why one of the most northerly of the counties of Scotland has the apparently absurd name South Land. The most northerly river of Sutherland is the Helmsdale, which forms the county boundary with Caithness. Ptolemy, writing about 120 A.D., mentions this river, which he names Ila, and of which the Gaelic name is still Ilidh. The name Helmsdale is much later, and is Norse. When the Norse occupied Sutherland and Caithness about the year 880 they found here a tribe named Catti, called, because of their ferocity, Wild Cats. The name of this tribe persists in Caithness, which is Katanes or Cat-promontory. These people were almost certainly Picts.

The two most celebrated salmon rivers of Sutherland, the Shin and the Helmsdale, flow into the North Sea or its approaches. The Shin reaches salt, or perhaps it might rather be said brackish, water at the Kyle of Sutherland, which in turn enters, by a comparatively narrow channel which resembles a broad river, the Dornoch Firth at Bonar Bridge. Although the Dornoch Firth is an arm of the North Sea, it resembles a sea loch of the west coast, at all events near its head. It is well sheltered, and trees grow to its shores; on its north shore in particular stately woods of oak are to be found.

The Shin, although a short river (it is not more than seven miles from its estuary to where it leaves Loch Shin), is, below the falls, one of the most excellent salmon rivers in the Scottish Highlands. It is, too, a beautiful river to fish. There is no wading; there are no long and tedious pools, such as are found in most rivers along their lower reaches, and each pool is entirely different from its fellows. A skilled angler can fish many of the pools from the same stance, by commencing with a short line, and gradually lengthening it until it almost reaches the far bank, to bring the fly, the only lure permitted on the Shin, over any salmon which may be disposed to take it. It is a joy to watch Angus MacPherson of the Inveran Hotel, he who is as skilled a fisherman as he is a piper, fishing a pool of the Shin. He has fished the river for many years and knows the water better than any man now living. See him, with no apparent effort, throw a line right across the river. Each cast is perfectly straight; each time the fly drops lightly on to the water. He is a grand fisherman and one of the kindest-hearted men I know. His hospitality, and that of his wife, who has been his strong support throughout his life, is one of the things which remain unchanging with the years. I never pass Inveran, at any hour of the day or the evening, without receiving a welcome such as I receive nowhere else, and I am glad to have this opportunity of paying this tribute to two people whose friendship has been one of the abiding pleasant things in my life. I hope he may recall, if he reads this, the April evening when, after darkness, he was called away in the midst of his piping to help an angler who was struggling unseen in the gloom with a monster salmon.

What of the Shin salmon? They are heavy fish, and thirty pounders are not uncommon. One February, Angus hooked one of the heaviest salmon he has seen in the Shin. The river was in spate, and anyone who knows what that means will not be surprised to hear that he had difficulty in keeping up with it (although he can follow a fish faster than any man I know), as it rushed from the pool in which it was hooked and down the stream in the heaviest water. As angler and salmon approached, at breathless speed, the bridge which spans the river 100 yards above the inn at Inveran the fish turned for a moment on its side, and Angus saw that it was "as big as a pig." That was the last he saw of the great fish, for, do what he might, he was unable to draw it close enough to the shore to steer it beneath the arch of the bridge through which he could have followed it. The salmon went through the middle arch, and of course broke the line. On another occasion, when he was playing a thirty pounder (which he landed) in the Home Pool there was an exciting incident when an otter took part in the hunt, and sent the great salmon away in a mad dash which looked as though it might spell disaster for the angler. Old writers have recorded the fact that the Shin, like the Ness, never freezes for, like the Ness, it flows from a great loch. I have fished the Shin in February when the frost on the river, or rather above the river, was so intense that my line froze to the rings of the rod, yet no film of ice formed even on the quiet edges of the Shin, although its waters were low and clear and the Kyle of Sutherland itself was frozen. During prolonged frost the Dee and the Spey, although their waters may have too swift a current to permit the actual rivers to freeze, have considerable quantities of grue or pancake ice floating seaward on the surface. The grue is water-saturated, and resembles half-melted snow. I have never seen even a small cake of floating ice come down the Shin.

The Falls of Shin, some three miles from the river estuary, are below the road, from which they are invisible. There is a fascination in watching the salmon, in early summer, endeavouring to pass over this formidable barrier. Many of them fail, leaping time after time and falling back heavily into the deep pool below, or perhaps striking the rock and falling back half-stunned, although I have not heard of one being killed. At the beginning of the fishing season they do not seek to pass above the falls, and it is not until May that they are seen leaping in any numbers. Angus MacPherson tells me that he believes most of the salmon ultimately pass this obstacle, but I have personally seen few succeed. They must envy the buoyant flight of the pair of water ousels which usually nest beside the falls, and must pass through the spray each time they bring food to their young.

Sir Robert Gordon writes of the Shin about the year 1650, and mentions the fishing of salmon at that time at the Falls. Here is his translated description:

> In the River Shin there is a huge and steep rock, from which the waters, flowing and meeting with a great rush and a loud noise, create a deep whirlpool. Here there is a profitable fishery of very large salmon.

Elsewhere the same writer puts on record the fact that:

> Shin is noted for its Falls, in struggling to ascend which the salmon slip into wicker nets and become a prey.

Although the Shin is on comparatively low ground throughout its course spring comes late here, and it is usually mid-May before the birches are filmed in green above its dark pools. The valley, or glen, or strath, is rather a deep one below the falls, but above them is broader, and the river less impetuous. At Lairg the Shin leaves Loch Shin, and salmon, which take freely in the river, are rarely caught in the loch.

The Cassley river and the Oykell river, which meet at Rosehall, flow through Strath Oykell and meet the Shin at its estuary. Lord Grey of Fallodon when Sir Edward Grey regularly fished the Cassley. George Ross, who used to gillie for him, told me that on one occasion Edward Grey was fishing a pool, one of the best on his beat, when he noticed that a pair of wagtails had begun to make their nest in a rock. He said to Ross, "We cannot fish this pool again, as we may disturb the wagtails and cause them to desert." George Ross told me that the incident impressed him greatly, for Sir Edward Grey would have almost certainly caught several salmon in that pool. Yet his love for birds was such that he cheerfully was willing to forgo that pleasure. It was fitting that, in the last year of his life, when he had almost lost his eyesight, he should have been given supreme pleasure by a robin which, after having fed from his hand, flew on to his head to sing a song of thanks before flying away. This the robin did habitually, and I was able to take a photograph of it in song on Sir Edward Grey's hat.

Near the headwaters of the Cassley that fine hill, Ben More Assynt, rises. It stands at the watershed between east and west, and from its summit is a view of great extent. The north coast of Skye is visible on a clear day, and so are the Outer Hebrides and also, far to the south, the Cairngorms. Below it, to the south-west, are Inchnadamff and Loch Assynt; around it are other great hills, Cuinneag or Quinag, Glas Bheinn and Ben Leoid. Beneath it, too, are lochs, set high in the hills—Fionn Loch Mór and Fionn Loch Beag, Gorm Loch Mór and others. From Gorm Loch Mór to the west coast is no more than three miles. Salt water is reached at Loch Glencoul, a loch lonely even for the west Highlands. Here is no house, nor even a path, until the township of Unapol four miles down the loch is reached, and, a short distance beyond Unapol, the ferry at Kylestrome. It is at Kylestrome that Loch Carn Bàn, its waters flowing in from the open sea, divides and forms as its north branch Loch Glendhu and, as its south, Loch Glencoul.

In a previous chapter I have brought the reader as far as Loch Inver. From that place, with its attractive salmon river, the traveller has the choice of two roads leading north. He may either keep to the coast, by way of Clashnessie and Oldany, or may travel at first north-

Gruinard Bay and the heights of An Teallach
Near Second Coast, Ross-shire

east to Loch Assynt and, skirting the north shore of that loch, cross high ground and descend to Unapol, and thus reach Kylestrome ferry.

The coast road northward from Loch Inver passes a number of crofting townships. That near the small bay of Clachtoll is particularly attractive. The houses in a picturesque group stand near a green, closely-grazed area of short turf, beyond which is the sand, firm and golden. It is worth while to deviate from the main road, and visit the lonely ocean promontory known as Rudha Storr. It receives its name from the Storr or Stake, now usually known as the Old Man of Storr, which rises from the sea. Rudha Storr is 300 feet above the sea, and the lighthouse is 100 feet above sea-level. It is one of the most wild places on the west mainland coast; here, more even that at Ardna-murchan Point, broods the spirit of ocean. On the headland the peats are celebrated for the excellence of their quality, and people travel some miles to cut them. Thus in early summer blue smoke is seen to rise from a number of places within sight of no house, as the people boil their tea on the peat fires which are easy to kindle at this, usually the driest season of the year. On the grassy lands, where the bog cotton waves, the crofters' horses pasture in herds, free almost as their wild ancestors of the East. The sea cliff is high, and here the waves almost always break, for the Atlantic swell which curves round the Butt of Lewis is rarely at rest.

That silent-flying ocean bird, the fulmar, has for some time now colonised the cliffs of Storr, and seems to embody the restless spirit of ocean: in the air it is tireless, sailing with supreme ease along the face of the great cliff; it is still abroad when dusk deepens and the white beams of the Storr light rest ghostly on land and sea until sunrise. The fulmars of Storr have greatly increased during the past twenty years, and when I visited that headland in April, 1949, I estimated that at least 500 pairs of these birds had their nesting stations here. The old Dutch explorers gave the name Mad Gnat to the fulmar, and I thought, as I watched these birds gliding backwards and forwards across the cliffs and above the sunlit sea, that they recalled gnats in a mazy dance. On that mid-April day I saw a migration of ravens northward. There was a fresh south-west breeze blowing and the birds were travelling high and at a great speed. The local ravens had long begun their nesting, and these were perhaps far northern birds. If the wind had held they would have reached Norway before evening. That day I saw, too, a peregrine falcon and a small company of golden

281

Ullapool, Ross-shire
Loch Lurgainn and An Stac, Ross-shire

plovers resting on Rudha Storr on migration. The wheatears had arrived, and there were pied wagtails and perhaps white wagtails from Iceland among them, but it is rather later in April before the white wagtail flights north.

On the shore of Loch Assynt is Ardvreck Castle, the ancient home of the MacLeods of Assynt, whose misfortunes are, so it is said, linked with their betrayal of Montrose—an accusation which as a family they have always denied. Their castle is a ruin, which 100 years and less ago was the nesting place of the osprey: the osprey too has gone.

It seems to bird lovers of the present age remarkable, even inexplicable, that good naturalists in the past should have apparently taken pleasure in killing our rare birds, notably the osprey. Charles St. John, as he shot an osprey on the nest and afterwards took her richly-marked eggs, seems at times to have been half-sorry and ashamed at his conduct. He was not alone in his killing of rare birds—indeed most of the naturalists of his day seem to have been equally guilty. John Colquhoun, who died in 1885, admits that he shot the female and trapped the male of the last pair of ospreys which nested on Loch Lomond, on the old Castle of Galbraith. He writes:

> They were a beautiful pair—the female, as in most birds of prey, being considerably the larger. The eggs of these ospreys had been regularly taken every year, and yet they never forsook their eyrie. It was a beautiful sight to see them sail into our bay on a calm summer night, and after flying round it several times, strike down upon a good-sized pike, and bear it away as if it had been a minnow.

And yet he shot them both! Colquhoun records the interesting fact that in his time the osprey nested on the island of the Lake of Menteith, or as he calls it, Loch Menteith. He says that the female was killed on that nest and also "that the ospreys which yearly hatched on Loch an Eilein have been wantonly destroyed within recent years." The curious thing is that both St. John and Colquhoun wrote of other collectors "wantonly destroying" the osprey, yet they did the very same thing themselves. What would not the present generation of nature lovers give to see the osprey on Loch Assynt, on Loch Lomond, on Loch an Eilein, and the white-tailed eagle sitting on that birch tree on Loch Baa, in the words of Colquhoun, "her white tail shining like the silver moon."

Loch Assynt, as I have said, was the home of the MacLeods of Assynt, who were the lords of the remote district of Assynt, at one time distinct from Sutherland, from the year 1314 or thereabouts, when Torquil MacLeod of Lewis married the heiress of MacNicol of Assynt, and thus became the ruler of the district. They held their lands by a charter from the Thane of Sutherland, "so long as wave beats upon the rock." Until the latter half of the seventeenth century the MacLeods held the territory, the last of that line being Niall MacLeod, who was deprived of it by the MacKenzies of Seaforth. The story is that Niall MacLeod sold the Great Montrose, who, starving and hunted, had thrown himself upon MacLeod for protection—that the Covenanters had paid him £20,000 for the valuable captive and 400 bolls of meal "and that sour," and that after the Restoration he was so greatly hated that he lost the estate.*

The family of the MacLeods of Assynt have always denied the story of their downfall, but if there had been no truth in it, it is the most remarkable fabrication, and most historians have agreed that there is some foundation for the tradition. John Buchan the historian describes how Montrose had thrown away in his flight his sword-belt and coat with the star of the Garter that he might escape recognition, and bought or borrowed rough Highland clothes. He was making north, for the friendly Reay country in the north-west, but he and his two companions missed their way. One of Niall MacLeod's men found Montrose and brought him to the castle of Ardvreck. Here he was imprisoned. I cannot do better than quote John Buchan's masterly words in describing what followed:

The name of the laird of Assynt lives in Scottish history with that of Sir John Menteith, who sold Wallace. It is remembered as the solitary case of a Gael who betrayed a suppliant for gold. Iain Lom, the bard of Keppoch, has left bitter verses on the "stripped tree of the false apples, Niall's son of woeful Assynt." He made little of his infamy. His lands were raided by Glengarry, the Mac-Leods, and the penitent MacKenzies. After the Restoration he was a good deal in gaol, and was twice tried for his life. His castle was burned, and no children survived to bear his name. He was awarded 25,000 pounds Scots for his services, of which 20,000 were to be paid in coin and the rest in oatmeal. It does not appear

* There is a curious story that the Castle of Ardvreck was burnt after a dance which continued until dawn on a Sunday, the tongues being cut from the mouths of the neighbouring cocks in order that the birds should not be able to herald the Sabbath day, and that curtains were drawn across the windows to keep out the light of Sunday.

that he ever got the money, but the receips for the meal were long extant, and Highland tradition is positive that two-thirds of it were sour.

The castle of Ardvreck became a ruin, and the osprey became its tenant. The osprey latterly met with a reception no better than that given to Montrose, and now the castle is inhabited neither by man nor bird. There is, at Lochmore Lodge, a striking picture of the osprey at the Castle of Ardvreck; it makes one realise how great an attraction that bird added to the ruins.

Quinag or, more correctly Cuinneag, is, nowadays at least, the name given to a hill massif. That massif consists of Sail Ghorm—Blue Peak, Sail Gharbh—Rough Peak—and, between the latter and Spidean Coinnich, the highest peak, Cuinneag—the Milk Stoup—which rises to a height of 2,653 feet. The peak of Spidean Coinnich is that nearest to Loch Assynt, and is most easily climbed from the highest point of the road between Loch Assynt and Kylestrome. On the day of late May when my wife and I climbed that hill the air was clear and the sun bright, but the view toward the north was partly obscured by cloud. The Cuinneag massif is a wild one, and Loch Assynt, far below, seems almost to belong to another world. Cuinneag is a massif of gneiss which is capped by Torridon sandstone and conglomerate. Sir Archibald Geikie, describing the vast age of the gneiss, states that it was as gnarled and venerable-looking when the dome of Torridon sandstone was laid down upon it as it is now. So sharp is the line of demarcation between the two rocks that, says Geikie, their respective areas may be accurately followed by the eye even at a distance of several miles; the tumbled sea of bare gneiss rolls, as it were, under the red sandstones, which, in nearly horizontal beds, rise into isolated and strangely-shaped mountains. There is a good view of the Outer Hebrides and the Isle of Skye from Cuinneag and its surrounding peaks. It is the view, rather than the bird life, that is the attraction in these rugged hills. A distant view of a golden eagle rewarded us that day on the high ground, the dark bird sailing majestically across the blue vault of the sky and disappearing behind a far hill, beside a cloud bank that grew on the breath of the north wind.

After the ferry at Kyleskue is crossed the road to Scourie continues along the coast. It is winding and devious, and the motorist or cyclist must allow ample time for the journey. The country is one of lochs and bogs, with the sea stretching away to the west towards the hazy outline of Lewis. Between Rudha Storr and Scourie is the broad and island-studded Eddrachillis Bay. This curious name is more correctly Eadarrachaolais (for Eadar dà Chaolas) and the meaning is Between two Straits. There are many islands in the bay. Calbha Mór and Calbha Beag lie near the mainland shore; farther out to sea are Meall Mór and Meall Beag. An arm of the main, very broad bay is Badcall Bay and it, too, has many islands lying at the mouth, sheltering the shore from the ocean swell.

Scourie, its hotel well known to anglers, is situated on the shore of Scourie Bay. Scourie is the usual base for Handa, an island that is rather less than a mile from the mainland at its nearest point, across the Sound of Handa. The name is Norse, and is the aspirated form of Sanda—Sandy Island. From the mainland one can see the fulmars sailing buoyantly across their island nesting ledges. There are many legends concerning Handa, now without a population. Rather more than a century ago seven families lived here. Like the people of St. Kilda, they had their queen, and, again like the St. Kilda folk, their Parliament, which met daily to decide the affairs of the day. It was after the potato famine in 1845 that the people of Handa emigrated to America, and now the island is the home of thousands of sea fowl. The landing places are on the east and south-east sides of the island, and the visitor who steps ashore finds himself upon a sandy beach, fringed with short, green turf—the machair of the Hebrides. On the west and north, the isle has a high rocky coast where, among blossoming sea thrift, many birds nest. Between the sandy beaches and the rocky coast an area of moorland is to be found, and small lochs. From one of the lochs the kittiwakes which nest in great colonies on the cliffs gather most of their nesting materials. One day when the kittiwakes were constructing their nests I happened to be on Handa, and watched a fascinating and delightful scene. Above the loch circled a white cloud of kittiwakes. They glided in an almost continuous stream down to the water, bathed with abandon, then, rising and shaking, while in flight, the water from their snowy plumage, they alighted at the edge of the loch, and pulled up billfuls of moss and grass. When a bird had gathered sufficient nesting material it rose into the sunlit air and flew away to the edge of the cliff, where it dropped out of sight to alight on its nesting ledge beneath. In the afternoon the kittiwakes were using as a bathing place another loch, almost half a mile distant from that which had been in use in the morning.

The Stack of Handa, a remarkable feature, rests upon three great pillars. It is only a few yards from the parent island, but is divided from it by a drop of 500 feet. At one time fearless men crossed this chasm in search of the eggs and the young of sea-fowl; it is said that the last persons to make that dangerous crossing were a fishing crew from the island of Lewis. According to the old *Statistical Account*, one of the MacLeods of Assynt lived on Handa. He was known as Iain Beag—Wee John—and although a small man had great strength and great skill in the wielding of arms. His galley of twelve oars he kept on Handa, and he became celebrated because of his slaying of the hated Judge Morrison of Lewis, the representative of James VI in the Outer Hebrides. Iain Beag afterwards married the judge's widow.

The best time to visit Handa is June or early July. By the end of July the bird population are beginning to leave for the Atlantic, which will be their home until the following spring. On a very clear day I have seen Handa from the hills in the north of Skye.

CHAPTER III

THROUGH THE HEART OF SUTHERLAND

IF we leave Scourie, beside the Atlantic, and travel east, we can cross Scotland by car in two hours. We travel through the great forest— here the word is used in the sense of deer forest—of Dirriemore, Direadh Mór—the Great Ascent—which, at the time Sir Robert Gordon wrote his *History of the Earl of Sutherland*, in the year 1639, was held of the Earl of Sutherland by the Great MacKay, who, eleven years before, had been created Lord Reay. It may have been on the death of this chief of the MacKays that the beautiful pibroch, "Lament for Donald Duachal MacKay," was composed. He is throughout Sir Robert Gordon's book named "MacKay" and not "Lord Reay," for "MacKay" was the higher title of the two. This wild country, which retains its wildness even at the present time, was part of that territory named Duthaich Mhic Aoidh—MacKay's Country.

The origin of the MacKays is lost in the mists of antiquity. Skene in his *Highlanders of Scotland* believes they were descended from the old Maormors or rulers of Caithness. The first chief of whom there is a record is Angus Dow (Dubh), Black Angus, towards the beginning of the fifteenth century; from him the later chiefs can all be traced. Their territories were confirmed by Donald, Lord of the Isles, after he had married the Countess of Ross. When Angus Dow was arrested by James I at Inverness he was said to be the leader of 4,000 men. Angus married a daughter of Donald of the Isles; their son was later known as Niall Wasse, because he was for a time imprisoned in the Bass Rock, "Wasse" being the phonetic spelling of the genitive of "Bass." MacKay was raised to the peerage by Charles I, with the title of Lord Reay, after having the preceding year been created a Baronet of Nova Scotia. With varying fortunes the chiefs held their lands until the nineteenth century. An interesting light is shed on the affairs of the family by Sir Walter Scott, who sailed round the coasts of Scotland in 1814 as the guest of the Northern Lighthouse Commissioners in their yacht. They paid a visit to Cape Wrath, in order that the Commissioners might decide the site of the lighthouse to be erected there. In his diary of the voyage, Sir Walter Scott writes:

Lord Reay's estate, containing 150,000 acres, and measuring eighty miles by sixty, was, before the commencement of the last leases, rented at £1,200 a year. It is now worth £5,000, and Mr. Anderson says that he may let it this ensuing year, when the leases expire, for about £15,000. But then he must resolve to part with his people, for these rents can only be given upon the supposition that sheep are generally to be introduced on the property. In an economical, and perhaps in a political point of view, it might be best that every part of a country were dedicated to that sort of occupation for which nature has best fitted it. But to effect this reform, in the present instance, Lord Reay must turn out several hundred families who have lived under him and his fathers for many generations, and the swords of whose fathers probably won the lands from which he is now expelling them. He is a good-natured man, I suppose, for Mr. A. says he is hesitating whether he shall not take a more moderate rise (£7,000 or £8,000), and keep his Highland tenantry.

It is perhaps fortunate for the name and honour of MacKay that he shortly afterwards disposed of these estates to the Earl of Sutherland, who ordered the great Sutherland clearance, of which so much has been written, and about which so much controversy has waged.

The road running east from Scourie joins, at Laxford Bridge, the road from Durness in the extreme north of the county; the combined tracks then travel east, or rather south-east, to Lairg. At Laxford Bridge heavy salmon may in times of low water be seen in the Bridge Pool. The road follows the course of the river eastward, sometimes in sight of it, and soon reaches Loch Stack, from which the river flows. Sir Robert Gordon of Gordonstoun writes, *circa* 1650, "MacKay hath a summer dwelling in an iland with Loch Stalk, in the Diri-More." The Laxford river takes its name from the sea loch into which it wanders; it is a Norse name and means Salmon Fjord, or Salmon Loch. Its reputation has been maintained through the centuries, and the Laxford is still celebrated among Scottish salmon rivers. It is in character a typical west coast river, the main run of fish entering it not in early spring, as in east coast rivers, but in summer. There are heavy fish in it, and the Duke of Westminster once played a salmon without seeing it for nearly two hours; he estimated its weight as at least 40 lb. Loch Stack produces large sea trout. One of the largest was caught by Sir Philip Egerton on a small "Dunkeld" fly, No. 12, on August 17, 1943, and weighed 18½ lb. It is believed to

Suilven, Cul Mor and Cul Beag, Sutherland

be the largest sea trout caught with rod and fly in Britain. The girth
of this great fish was 19¾ inches, the length 33 inches, the tail 9 inches
and the small of the tail 7¾ inches.

The angler on Loch Stack has at times to contend against winds
of tremendous force that strike the loch in violent squalls from the
heights of Ben Stack westward. These cause whirlpools, and one
September morning when I fished the loch the play of the westerly
gale was awe-inspiring on the open waters. John Scobie and his son
were both at the oars, yet it took them all their time to keep the boat
in a fishing position. We could fish only in the comparative shelter of
the bay above which John Scobie's house stands on Airdachuilinn—
Point of the Holly. A very old holly tree grows beside the house and
it, or its predecessor, may have given the place its name. That September gale blasted the nasturtiums on John Scobie's house, as I saw,
when I called there after abandoning fishing early in the afternoon.
It was a memorable sight when a violent gust lifted the surface waters
beyond the bay high, perhaps 100 feet, into the air, and carried them
at speed far to leeward. A transient sunbeam lighting one of these
columns of spindrift turned it to rose colour; at its base were lovely sea-
green hues of the storm-spirit that held sway on Loch Stack that day
when, as I heard later from guests who arrived at Lochmore that
afternoon, fine summer weather without noticeable wind had been
experienced in Inverness.

Another day on Loch Stack with John Scobie I recall. It was midsummer, and during the second world war, when double summer
time was the official time at this season of the year. That meant in
the west, where the time of sunset is approximately half an hour later
than at Greenwich, that you were two and a half hours ahead of the
clock. For example, when your clocks marked noon, the sun's time
was in reality half past nine in the morning, and when your clocks
untruthfully and perhaps reluctantly (since it is the duty of clocks to
be truthful) told you that it was eleven o'clock at night, and bed-time,
the sun's time was half past eight. Double summer time was an excellent thing for getting people up in the morning, but it was all wrong
for the fisherman. It is well known that there is a period from one to
three in the afternoon when fish do not take well, since, like those of
us who are wise, or have leisure, this is the time of their mid-day rest.
If you kept double summer time, you stopped for lunch at half past ten
by the salmon's time, which is one of the best periods of the day for

Sandwood Bay, Sutherland, looking towards Cape Wrath

taking fish. The artificial time made evening fishing also difficult, for the salmon might take until half past ten, which by double summer time was 1 a.m., when all good anglers should be in bed and asleep.

The salmon run into Loch Stack before the main run of sea trout, and on this evening of midsummer there was more likelihood of catching a salmon than a sea trout. It was indeed of considerable importance that we should catch a salmon, as my host was leaving for the south the next morning, and he was anxious to take a fish with him. He himself was fishing his old love, the Laxford, but the river ran low and clear, and there was little hope of a fish there, or rather a taking fish, for the pools were full of salmon, fish of burnished silver which leaped derisively high into the warm birch-perfumed air, in full view of the patient angler, who, hoping against hope, tried one fly after another (I wonder if he would have had more success with the natural-dyed salmon flies of the old Highland chiefs; they were rather large in size, and, according to an old fisherman who had long ago seen one of the Duke of Gordon's flies, were dyed crotal, which is a rich brown and yellow). That summer evening, therefore, when John Scobie rowed me out into the loch after dinner, we knew that on us depended the success or failure of that evening's fishing. It had been a day of great heat, the sky blue and cloudless, the hills, Arcuil and Foinne Bheinn, rising clear and sharp, and so arid that it seemed no cloud could rest upon them. There was little hope of a salmon until the sun set behind the hills, and for that we must continue to fish on the loch until after midnight. Before that hour the easterly breeze freshened, and we saw with dissatisfaction that an easterly haar or white mist was beginning to form on the high hills to the east of the loch. The most likely place for a salmon was the mouth of the Lòn burn. Lòn is the Gaelic word for a slow-flowing stream, and this burn meanders through bogs before entering the loch. We hopefully tried this part of the loch, John Scobie working the boat skilfully along the edge of the shoal of gravel brought down by the river. If my memory serves me right we twice rose a salmon, but he came short. After midnight (so called) the east wind had brought with it a woolly white cloud layer, which rolled down the sun-heated slopes of Arcuil and over the rounded summit of Meall a' Chuirn—Hill of the Cairn. The wind became cold on the loch, and although we continued to fish till the small hours, we achieved no success. At the lodge, when at last I reached it, I found that I was, as indeed I had expected, the last hope, for the river had yielded nothing, and I felt that I had failed to live up to the unjustified angling reputation I had gained when, after arriving at the lodge on a previous occasion at nine in the evening, I had gone down after a late supper to the Laxford and had in half an hour landed a sixteen pound salmon.

I think it was that summer, or perhaps the summer following, that a solitary whooper swan remained on the loch. It had no mate, and was often feeding on the short grass some little distance from the water. In Iceland I have seen a pair of whoopers feeding on grass beyond sight of any loch, and it would therefore seem that these fine birds are more at home on the land than is the mute swan. They sometimes winter on Loch Stack, but during that Arctic spell in February, 1947, were driven from it, as they were driven from almost every Highland loch, by the ice. In the Isle of Skye we had unusual frost, but no snow, and heather fires, often out of control, were burning daily; in Suther-- land there was deep snow in addition to keen frost, and John Scobie was able to walk on the ice the whole of the three miles and more which separate his house from Stack Lodge at the west end of the loch.

The black-throated divers which nest on some of the Reay Forest lochs often lose their eggs because of flooding. The diver lays where she can dive from her eggs into the water, and these lochs, being fed by a number of streams, are subject to frequent and considerable rises. During recent years the divers have only exceptionally been able to hatch their eggs, although they have usually laid a second clutch to replace those lost through the rise in the level of the loch. John Scobie has evidence that one year the diver transported her eggs from a small island almost submerged to a larger, neighbouring island: she had been sitting for some time when the isle was submerged, and she could not, he is sure, have laid a second clutch by the time he saw her two days later brooding on another islet near. That reminds me that Thomas Pennant, who wrote his *British Zoology* about 1770, records the fact, as told him, he says cautiously, that the great northern diver hatches her eggs beneath her wings when swimming on the water (the eggs of the great northern diver, a bird which nests in Greenland, in Spitsbergen, and other far northern countries, had at that time not been found).

One season—it was, if I remember rightly, 1942—the divers were flooded out as usual, and as late as June 22 (this is very late for a black-throated diver, for it lays early in May and is a month earlier in nesting than the red-throated diver) I watched the actual nesting operations of the divers. The loch was rising fast, and one of the divers landed on an island and began to build up with rushes the side of her new nest, already threatened by the rising water. She sat on the nest and with swift movements laid the rushes by her side. On a friend appearing she first crouched flat on the nest, then dived into the loch. She was soon back, and continued to add rushes to the threatened nest. After a time, as she literally lay awash in shallow water, she pulled up rushes which were submerged. This was not easy work, and she attempted unsuccessfully to pull up, or cut with her sharp bill, some of the young green rushes, without result. Finally, as she swam, she broke off higher rushes that projected above the rising water, throwing them over her shoulder so that they floated toward the nest. Could she have had in her mind the vague idea of utilising the on-shore breeze, to drift the rushes against the nest and there form a break-water? Her efforts were in vain, for next day when we rowed out to the island, we found the single egg lying in water and deserted. I gathered the rushes the diver had collected, and found that they weighed 3 lb.; most of them were cut cleanly, as if with a knife, the line of cut being diagonal.

I have had many walks in the Reay Forest. Let me describe one of them, from the lodge at Gualann, high above the river Dionard, across the low shoulder of Foinne Bheinn to Ardachuilinn and thence on to Loch More, a walk, as one wanders through the peat haggs, of perhaps fifteen to twenty miles. During the whole of that walk Dara the collie and I were out of sight of any house, or track. The day was fair, but the sun was soon obscured by cloud, and mist rested lightly on the high tops. From Gualann we climbed to the shoulder of Foinne Bheinn, passing lochans where dunlin gnomishly called, and knolls where golden plover, following us on sharp wings, piped mournfully. On this occasion we did not climb as high as the country of the ptarmigan, but high enough to look down upon the maze of great boulders that lie above that hill loch of many bays, long and devious, named Mathair Gharbh Uilt—Mother of the Rough Stream. The burn, Garbh Allt—the Rough Burn—flows from it into another narrow loch, and thence into the west sea at Rhiconich.

Farther on we crossed Loch an Tigh Sheilg—Loch of the Hunting House—of which the ruins can be seen on an island. It was used by the chiefs of MacKay in olden days, when on hunting expeditions.

It was a rough hut of turf and stones, roofed with branches of trees, earth "divots" and bent thatch. Beyond the land of lochs and peat bogs rose the cone of Ben Stack; nearer were the great rocks and precipices of Arcuil. There are many districts of the Highlands from which the people were cleared during the middle part of the nine-teenth century, when sheep were found to pay a more substantial dividend than men, but this wide country over which I now looked had never been inhabited, although there may have been summer shielings here and there. Sir Robert Gordon writes of Arcuil in the middle of the seventeenth century, and states that "in the Diri-more there is a hill called Arkill; all the deir that ar bred therin, or hant within the bounds of that hill, have forked taills, thrie inches long, wherby they are easailie knowne and decerned from all other deir. In these forrests, and in all this province, ther is great store of partriges, pluivers, capercalegs, blackwaks, murefowls, heth-hens, swanes, also the lair-igigh or knag, a foull lyk unto a paroket, or parret, which maks place for her nest with her beck, in the oak trie." There is now no trace of the fork-tailed stags of Arcuil, but Gordon was a sound writer and he must have had good grounds for his statement. I saw only one pair of grouse all that day, and no eagle nor raven.

After I had come on a stalking path, and had found easier walking there, I reached a loch that is named Loch Airidh a' Bhaird—Loch of the Bard's Shieling. Tradition in the district makes the bard Rob Donn, who was a celebrated hunter, besides being a celebrated poet. It may have been here that he composed his most celebrated love song, "S'trom Leam an Airidh." There were sandpipers on this loch, and, anxious for their young, they accompanied us for some distance until we were again wandering slowly over the peat haggs, where the "going" was wearisome towards the close of a long walk. Ahead of us the blue waters of Loch Stack softened the austerity of the scene. On a grassy terrace a little distance from the water a swan was standing, and as we approached I could see through my glass that it was the solitary whooper which had frequented the loch that summer: it was a lonely white figure, without mate or brood. When I reached Air-dachuilinn I received there the Highland welcome which is still given in lonely places. John Scobie had been rowing Jack Leslie on the loch; when they returned it was with the news that a 12 lb. sea trout had been caught, despite adverse fishing conditions. Jack thus retained his reputation of being a successful angler for sea trout on Loch Stack.

I need not stress the welcome which was given me at Lochmore, for I have so many pleasant associations with that lodge that it occupies a special place in my mind. I remember Neville Chamberlain, wrapped in a veil as a protection against midges, setting out from the lodge to look for a golden eagle, a bird which he had not seen until that day, and which obliged him shortly afterwards by rising quite close to him and his host, and flying lazily away with that rather laboured wing action which characterises a golden eagle's flight on low ground on a calm day. Neville Chamberlain was an exceptionally keen fisherman, with an almost boyish enthusiasm. I think that his visit to Lochmore and the Laxford in August, 1939, gave him great happiness; the last I saw of him, then or later, was examining with care the post which records the different heights of the river, and perhaps hoping for a rise in the water, for the river at that time, after an exceptionally fine August, was low. A week later he had been recalled to London, and he, and all of us, lived in those twilight days, through which, as it seemed, the sun shone ironically, which preceded the second world war.

CHAPTER IV

LOCH MORE AND THE DIONARD

TEN years later, in the same month of August, Loch More was visited by a cloud-burst which must have been terrifying to those who experienced it. There was nothing to warn John MacAulay and his wife, whose home is on the east shore of the loch, of the tremendous event that was soon to come to them—nothing, that is, except the behaviour of the cows. In summer the cows are accustomed to come of their own accord from the hill pasture to the byre to be milked of a morning. On the morning of August 1 they did not arrive, and when search was made for them they refused to be driven to the byre. To their fore-knowledge they owed their lives.

The weather for four days had been intensely hot (although the rest of that summer, before and after, was cold and wet, with little sun). At daybreak on August 1 heavy rain fell, and distant thunder was heard. The thunder was almost overhead, and the rain torrential, by eight o'clock, summer time. Shortly after eight, a wall of water was seen descending the bed of the almost dried up burn which flows near the house of the MacAulays. At this time the pet lamb was awaiting its morning drink of milk warm from the cows: the hens also were waiting to be fed. Neither the hens nor the lamb had the second-sight—call it what you will—of the cows. With terrifying swiftness the wall of turgid water, with a noise more tremendous than the reverberations of the thunder, reached the house. The lamb and the hens were swept to their doom; the MacAulays sought refuge in their house, which is eighty years old, and of such sound construction that it withstood the fierce onset of the flood. The family saw their motor-car swept away. It was carried a distance of perhaps fifty yards, then buried beneath earth and stones. A month later, when I visited the scene of destruction, the only part of the car visible was a small portion of the roof. It was estimated that 7 feet of stones and rubble covered the vehicle, and the insurance company, after inspecting it, had come to the conclusion that its excavation and removal would cost more than the car was worth.

The cloud-burst was seen from the farther shore of the loch, and a boat put out to the rescue, but the torrent entering the loch set up so strong a current in the neighbourhood that the two men rowing the boat were unable for a considerable time to beach their craft in the neighbourhood of the house. The MacAulays were taken across the loch and spent that night with friends. Next day they returned and scarcely recognised their old home. Great boulders had been carried down the bed of the burn. One of them, which I saw, was estimated to be thirty tons in weight. It had been carried down a considerable distance—perhaps half a mile. Stones and gravel had been piled against the MacAulays' house to a depth of 3 feet. Their most fertile grazing field was unrecognisable under stones and earth. Birch trees, uprooted and battered by boulders, lay around the house. I saw the stump of one tree which had been broken clean across a couple of feet from its base —presumably by one of the great boulders during its descent.

From the opposite shore of Loch More, along which the public road passes, the extent and severity of the damage was not evident, and that shore entirely escaped the cloud-burst, which struck the high ground above the east shore. That thunderstorm, following four days of heat, was widespread. From the Isle of Rum, in the Hebrides, a correspondent wrote that he had been ringing shearwaters, and had been guided down from the high hills by the vivid flashes of lightning, which had rendered his torch unnecessary.

Lochmore has long been celebrated as a deer forest. Times have changed; deer now share the ground with a considerable stock of sheep, and deer stalkers have now turned shepherds. On the steep rocky slope opposite the lodge, the screes show above the heather in such a manner that they form a picture of a gigantic bird—a fabulous golden eagle—with outspread wings. The late Lord Desborough, who used often to go to Lochmore in the old days, asked me in a letter whether his old friend the stone eagle was still there, and was glad when I was able to assure him that it remained on guard. He was a tremendous walker and tales are still told of the speed at which, when stalking, he climbed those high hills, steep and formidable even to an athlete such as he was. He lit his pipe at the foot of Foinne Bheinn and reached the top before it was finished.

There is here hard walking even for the angler, unless indeed he rides on one of the hill ponies which are provided for him by his host. The waters of Loch Dionard, a hill loch which is shared by Lochmore, Gualann and Gobernuisgach, are more than seven miles from Lochmore Lodge, and it is a long day's expedition to fish the loch. There is a path across the hills, beginning near Lòn and crossing the shoulder of Meall a' Chuirn, a climb of rather less than 2,000 feet. At the top of the Bealach or pass it is unexpected to see the pink flowers of sea thrift carpet the ground, dark beneath thick cloud on the day I crossed. When I had descended a little way below the mist I saw ahead of me a view of exceptional wildness—hill upon hill rising in gloomy austerity beneath the cloud-filled sky. The path descends near a clear, strong stream, known as Allt an Easain Ghil—Burn of the White Waterfall —which has its source in An Dubh Loch—the Black Loch. It is not until Loch Dionard has been almost reached that its lonely waters can be seen. It is perhaps the wildest of all lochs in the Highlands to hold salmon and sea trout. West, precipices and very steep slopes rise to the clouds, and as you fish the loch you see swaying waterfalls emerge from the mist-cap and hear the sound of their falling, now loud, now subdued as the wind snatches the sound from the corries. There is no sign of any human dwelling, and indeed the nearest one is many miles away. Were the loch more accessible it would be more often fished, for great catches of sea trout and salmon have on occasion been taken in it. A south wind here is the best fishing wind. It blew cold and damp from the north-east on that day when I crossed the pass, and we caught only one sea trout, a good fish of 5 lb.

Edmund Fergusson of Gualann, a keen and skilled fisherman, frequently walked to the loch. He told me of his experience one day when he saw a whooper swan fly in over the high hills at a great altitude and plane down to the loch at tremendous speed and with supreme grace. The swan alighted on the water, and the rush of those great wings through the air was at once stilled. He said that the arrival of that wild swan, upon the waters of that remote loch, was one of the most beautiful and striking things he had seen in his life, the snowy wings bearing their owner past the dark precipice with its white, swaying waterfall and then coming to rest, beneath a blue sky, on the blue waters of Loch Dionard. This waterfall, which has its birth usually in the clouds, becomes a fast-flowing burn at the foot of the cliff. It then flows underground, and enters the loch unseen. A dipper nests in the falls, or near their base, and when it has finished feeding in the loch may be seen to rise into the air and follow faithfully the unseen course of the burn; indeed this is one of the very few places where a dipper can be seen flying across heather, with no stream visible near it. This dipper perhaps follows the course of its ancestors, which then flew above a visible stream before cloud-bursts had brought down so much earth, stones and gravel that the burn had been obliged to make for itself an underground passage, as the Dee has done high on Ben MacDhui before reappearing near the watershed of Lairig Ghru as the Pools of Dee.

This high waterfall is only one of the many side streams which flow into the loch; the main stream, which may be said to be the young Dionard river (as it is named when it leaves the loch and flows through Strath Dionard) enters the loch from the south. In this stream, for a distance of nearly a mile above the loch, are gravelly pools and "runs," where the salmon spawn. What makes salmon spawn early? In the year 1942 they were so early that when George Ross, the keeper, and I visited the loch toward the close of October to try for a late sea trout (I had caught one in the river with sea lice on it that week) we found that most of the salmon had finished spawning and were already in the kelt stage; indeed we actually caught a male kelt salmon at the mouth of the loch that day and saw no signs of a clean-run sea trout. When I asked those experts, James Munro and Robert MacAulay at Lochmore, the reason for this early spawning, which George Ross assured me was earlier than he had ever known, they said it was due to the heavy and almost continuous rains which had kept the river above its usual height throughout the late summer and autumn. This explanation seemed satisfactory until I heard that the spawning season on the Tweed was also unusually early, yet the Tweed, since the wind that brings rain to the Dionard is usually a dry one in the Tweed valley, was that autumn at an unusually low level. Why had the fish, both on the Tweed and on the Dionard far removed from it, spawned earlier than had been recorded? Even the breed of salmon in those two rivers is different. The Tweed fish, or at all events the early spawners, run in during January and February; those of the Dionard do not appear until June and the main run is during the first fortnight of July: yet both races of salmon that year were spawning before October was out.

Since I have taken the reader across the hills from Lochmore and deposited him, perhaps stiff and tired, at Loch Dionard, I may here give some account of the Dionard river. It flows from the loch where the country is treeless, or almost so, yet there is evidence that this district was at one time wooded. On the day when I walked across the hills and caught one sea trout of 5 lb. I passed, in the peat haggs near the head of the loch, the stump and roots of a very large and obviously very old Scots pine, and have little doubt that at one time a pine forest, burnt perhaps to drive out the wolves, grew here. The tree may have been here perhaps in 1650 when an old writer speaks of many wolves being in the district.

I have my friend Edmund Fergusson to thank for many good days on the Dionard: he and Marjory, his wife, are very keen fishers, and after they bought the property of Gualann, made a good path from that place almost to Dugall's Pool, a distance of over five miles. The procedure usually is to start from the lodge of Gualann on a push bike. Although the path is good it is narrow, with sudden bends and curves, and the rider must be skilled in order to keep his (or her) seat. The bicycle is useful, as the salmon can be tied to it at the end of the day. I have seen John George MacKay carrying 70 lb. of salmon in this way, and believe that on occasion he has pushed his bicycle (for under those conditions there is no room for a rider) with over 100 lb. of salmon slung and tied to it. Gualann, as its name tells, is the Shoulder: it was built as a hotel by the Duke of Sutherland in the middle of the nineteenth century, and stands actually at the highest part of the whole road from Durness to Lairg. This means that the angler must descend each morning from a height of 600 feet to one of less than 200 feet, not that this is of importance at the beginning of the day, but it is a different matter after a long day's fishing, for the last mile is a steep ascent, so steep that even if no salmon have been caught the angler must dismount and laboriously push his bicycle, seeing all the time the main road high above him and making slow progress towards it and the lodge.

The Dionard has not the reputation of the Laxford, yet I think its salmon rise to the fly more freely, and when the river is right in July it is no uncommon thing to see twelve to fifteen salmon brought home to the lodge in the evening. There are many good pools on the Dionard. I think that, were I asked which was my favourite pool, I would name Heather Point where, if conditions are right, the angler is almost certain to hook a salmon. There is a beautiful "run" at the head of the pool, and a peaty bank, in which a pair of water ousels sometimes build their nest, where the angler can make himself inconspicuous. The "run" flows into deep water, and at its middle the pool is, for the Dionard, a wide one. From halfway across to the opposite bank there is a backwater, which almost resembles a miniature loch. Lower down the pool, the river narrows and bends sharply, with a rather quiet and deep stream. Fish are caught throughout the pool, but the "run" at the head is the most likely cast. The loch-like backwater is a place where salmon are often seen cruising and rising, but a strong wind and good ripple are essential to fish it, and a long line has to be thrown. Dionard salmon are not as a rule heavy fish, but I had a great battle with a big fish in Heather Point. The river was high, and I could not get the fish close to the bank near me. At last the fly came away. The fish was exhausted and rested, in the normal position although without movement, in about 18 inches of water for over half an hour. I put on my largest salmon fly and tried to foul-hook it, but the fly scraped its silvery sides and did not take hold. John George MacKay, who was higher up the river with Major Carmichael, then arrived, saw the fish, and very cautiously waded in (although he had no waders on), got out his gaff and was just about to strike the salmon when it came to life, realised its danger, and swam slowly away into the peaty depths. Later in the summer the fish was hooked again on two occasions, and broke the fly, and George Ross saw it several times on the spawning beds and estimated its weight at 40 lb. Just to see what would happen, I returned to the middle of the pool after the great fish had swum away, made one cast with my huge fly, and immediately hooked another large salmon. This shows that the size of the fly is not so important as some people would have us believe, for no one would have thought of using a fly of half that size at midsummer.

Another attractive pool is Dugall's Run, which ends in Dugall's Pool. Dugall's Run is one of the few pools that I know where the salmon in moderately low water can actually be seen as they lie, near to the farther bank. For some reason they are less wary here than in most pools and a salmon may be seen coming up, "nosing" the fly, and perhaps taking it. Dugall's Pool is sluggish, and very deep; I have never been able to see, even in low water, its peaty floor. I got a good salmon of 24 lb. here one July day, and saw a curious fish landed. It was apparently a kelt, for it had the large head of a kelt, with the "beak" that is characteristic of the male kelt salmon, yet this fish had sea lice on it, showing that it was fresh-run. It was seen that this salmon had been badly injured, perhaps by an otter or a seal, and this may have prevented it shedding its "beak" and putting on condition

during its stay in the sea. Since it is thought by experts that less than
1 per cent. of male kelts ever return to fresh water after spawning,
this "mended" kelt in the livery of a clean fish in midsummer was
strange, to say the least of it.

Who is this Dugall who is commemorated in place-names in the
district? On Foinne Bheinn are Coire Dhughaill—Dugall's Corrie,
Cnoc Dhughaill—Dugall's Knoll, and Allt Dhughaill—Dugall's
Burn. Across Foinne Bheinn westward, rather beyond its neighbour
Arcuill, is Coire Mhic Dhughaill—the Corrie of Dugall's Son. On
the Stack beat of the forest is Loch Pollan Dhughaill. This name is
said locally to be more correctly Loch Puill Eoin Dhughaill. All
these, and other place-names of the district, are said to commemorate
Donald Dughall MacKay. The Gaelic scholar Neil Ross told me that
the name here ought more correctly to be written Duachal, an old
Gaelic word meaning Dauntless. If so, it is a fine name for one of the
most renowned of the MacKay chiefs. For the list of place-names I
am indebted to John George MacKay, whose knowledge of old
matters is considerable.

Do salmon always return to the river in which they have been
hatched? The general belief is that they do, but it would be remarkable
if errors in this homing instinct did not occur. A number of years ago,
spawn from Shin salmon was introduced to the Laxford, and not only
have a heavier race of fish appeared in the Laxford, but in the Dionard,
too, some heavy salmon have been caught. Until then the Dionard
fish, although numerous, had been small, and it is possible that some
of the homing Laxford fish have entered the Dionard by mistake.

Those days by the Dionard in summer were pleasant ones, and the
interest was heightened because of the effort necessary to reach the
river and return from it, salmon-laden, up-hill at night. Loch Dionard
is rather far, either from Lochmore or from Gualann, unless the walk
comes first and the fishing second. On a clear sunny day the walk is
a pleasant one, but that is not the day when fish rise in the loch, and
more often than not the angler trudges through bog and long, wet
grass (after leaving the path) and, arriving wet and weary at the loch,
sits in a boat, perhaps catching nothing, until it is time for him to
begin the eight-miles return journey, either to Gualann, or, it may be,
over the hill to Lochmore.

The Dionard enters the ocean at the Kyle of Durness, where, at
ebb-tide, large areas of golden sand are exposed. The lower reaches of

the river are usually fished from Cape Wrath Hotel; in that district there are one or two lochs with particularly heavy brown trout in them.

The whole country of the Dionard is dominated by Foinne Bheinn, a great hill, or perhaps rather, as with Quinag, a hill massif, of which I write more fully in the next chapter.

CHAPTER V

FOINNE BHEINN AND CAPE WRATH

On days of extreme visibility, especially in early spring, I sometimes see, from the north coast of the Isle of Skye, the long ridge of a distant hill rising across the Minch far to the north-east. In early spring that hill is usually covered deep in snow, and when the sun shines on it, Foinne Bheinn, then of Arctic appearance, seventy-five miles distant, is brilliantly white against the blue of the horizon. Seen thus, Foinne Bheinn—Hill of Warts—seems a hill range rather than a single hill, for the summit ridge extends a matter of five miles and is deeply cut, near the centre, by a narrow defile, named Cadha na Beucaich—Defile of the Roaring. The highest ground on Foinne Bheinn is rather less than 3,000 feet above sea-level. It is thus 1,300 feet lower than Ben MacDhui, yet there are few Highland hills wilder or grander than Foinne Bheinn. The climb from Gualann to the north top is easy, and the climb from Lochmore to the south top is also a comparatively simple walk, but the traverse of the hill, or hill range, is arduous, as I found when I did the walk from Lochmore on a fine sunny day of midsummer. Dara the collie and I climbed from Loch Stack, where a noisy greenshank flew excitedly backwards and forwards over us: I heard later that its mate had been found dead below the telegraph wires beside the road, having perhaps failed to see them when excited by some passer-by. It was one of those rare days in the north-west Highlands when the sky was cloudless, and Loch Stack, lying beneath the unclouded, deep blue of the sky, reflected and intensified that blue. There was no ripple on that radiant blue water, upon which the patrolling greenshank's wings traced a small, transient shadow. The birches that grow on Airdachuilinn did not stir; their aroma scented the morning air. We climbed beside Allt a' Chuirn, the water falling over white cascades, birch-shadowed, below us. Near the watershed between Loch Stack and Loch Dionard, where marsh marigolds, their flowers wide open to the noon sun, grew beside ice-cold, foaming springs, we left the path and climbed the grassy slopes of Creag Dionard, which is the south spur of Foinne Bheinn. There were hinds grazing on these slopes, and Dara barked once—a short, rather high bark of warning. We walked across an arid plateau, where the shaly gneiss lay exposed on the ground and only here and there were to be seen alpine plants and hill grasses. The defile of Cadha na Beucaich is more formidable than it appears, and must be traversed—there is no way round. The screes are unstable, and care must be taken not to displace them. At the foot of the defile is a deer track, apparently little used: it is likely that the stags cross it chiefly in the autumn, when the rut is on; this may have been the origin of the name—Defile of the Roaring. The ascent from this defile is rather easier than the descent, but there is still some distance to walk to the north top of the hill. To the east is Cir Ghorm—the Blue Comb—a wild rocky ridge, serrated and toothed, whence its name. The sun shone with great power and there was no spring at which to slake one's thirst. Far beneath, the waters of Loch a' Bhlar and Loch na Tuaidh sparkled tantalisingly in the breeze which had arisen.

Among the many hills one saw that memorable day was Ben Leod or Beinn Leoid. This hill is named after one of the MacLeods of Assynt who used to hunt there. He drove the deer from here to Ben More Assynt, to a great deer trap at Mòthar an Fèidh. All his clansmen took part in this great deer drive, usually when harvest was over.

It was eight o'clock in the evening when we reached the north cairn, and two hours later when Gualann welcomed us. There is no night at this time of year in the north-west, and a fishing expedition to one of the hill lochs was just starting from the lodge. I recalled that ninety years earlier Charles Richard Weld passed that way also on foot. Gualann was then an inn, and a sportsman had shot 10-12 brace of ptarmigan on Foinne Bheinn that day. The birds were lying on the floor of the passage. All this, and much more, is recorded in his book, *Two Months in the Highlands*.

On another occasion I was spying from the summit of Foinne Bheinn. The view was very clear towards the north and north-west, and I had just found Suleskerry Stack in the field of my telescope when a golden eagle soared into the field. The eagle was perhaps four miles distant; Suleskerry Stack was perhaps forty miles distant. It was remarkable to see the dark form of the eagle and, far beyond it, the ocean stack, whitened by the great colony of gannets which breed here.

Both those expeditions were in summer. One day on the threshold of winter, when George Ross and I climbed the hill we waited for

304

Smoo Cave, Durness, Sutherland

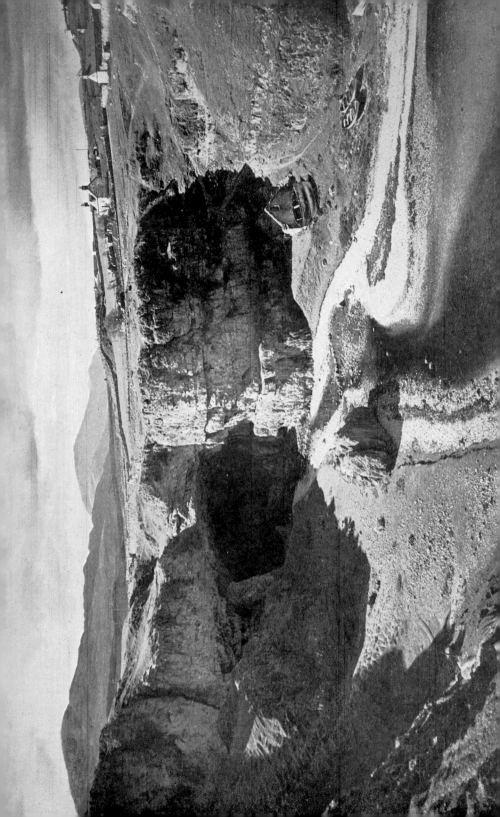

what seemed a very long time on the top, hoping that the mist would clear. There was a covering of snow, soft and powdery, and ice crystals were forming on the mist-laden wind. From time to time the sky showed blue for a moment at the zenith—this happens so often when the cloud thins, but does not entirely leave a hill-top. From a short distance below the summit, while we were still below the cloud, we had seen Ben Hope, rounded and massive, and Ben Loyal beyond it. That is the only day on which I remember having smelt the smell of salmon. The fish were on the spawning beds of the Dionard when we made our way along the path beside the river that evening, and the smell of them was strong. It was a smell of a herring-like character— and indeed the herring is of the salmon tribe—yet was less powerful and quite distinctive. It may have come from the ova as well as the spawning fish.

Accidents to aircraft during the second world war on the Highland hills were singularly few: on the opposite side of Strath Dionard to Foinne Bheinn a Mosquito crashed, flying at high speed, on a day of tempest and close mist on the hill-face; another met its fate on Ben More Assynt, while a third, a Flying Fortress, crashed on Beinn Eadarra in the north of Skye. More than one aircraft crashed also on the Cairngorm range. Considering the number of aircraft out daily over the Highland hills, more disasters might have been expected.

From Foinne Bheinn the view extends from Handa to Cape Wrath, and from Cape Wrath, where the coast bends eastward, through Durness along the shore to the boundary between Sutherland and Caithness. On the horizon eastward, Morven, a distinctive, conical hill in Langwell deer forest in Caithness, is easily identified in clear weather. Ben Hope, as I have said, is plain, and John George MacKay told me that on one occasion when he was on Foinne Bheinn sheep-gathering he was spying Ben Hope. The visibility was exceptional, and he was looking at stags lying or feeding near the summit of Ben Hope when he distinctly saw a golden eagle soar low above them across the ridge. The distance between Ben Hope and Foinne Bheinn is ten miles as the eagle flies, a very long way to see a bird even of the wing-span of the golden eagle.

As seen from Foinne Bheinn, the stretch of coast between Handa and Cape Wrath looks comparatively short, and easy to traverse. The walk is much longer and harder than it looks. It may be begun at Rhiconich, where the osprey formerly nested, at the head of Loch

305   U

The Avenue to Dunrobin Castle, Sutherland

Inchard. By the summer of 1948 this sea loch had become an important fishing base, and white fish and herrings caught in the northern waters of the Minch and in the Atlantic beyond were landed here, and were taken across Scotland in lorries. Along the north shore of Loch Inchard are a number of townships—Achriesgill, Badcall, Kinloch Bervie and others. At Kinloch Bervie MacBrayne's cargo steamer from Glasgow makes its last call along the west coast before returning south. The crofts are small here, and the harvest often is late, for the summers are cold and the soil, being peaty, does not favour rapid growth. Beyond Kinloch Bervie the road passes more townships— Oldshore Mór and Oldshore Beag, Blarmor and Sheigra. From Sheigra the coast is a wild one to Sandwood Bay and Sandwood Loch.

Sandwood is a place of exceptional beauty, and a place, too, of great loneliness such as is akin to Polar lands, rather than Scotland. Lying almost buried in the sand here are the wrecks of many vessels. These wrecks are of great age, for no ship has come ashore here since the lighthouse was built on Cape Wrath, and that is more than a hundred years ago. These ancient wrecks give the traveller a strange impression—he feels that the shore is haunted by the spirits of ships which lie here, slowly, very slowly, disintegrating. Sandwood is from Sand-vatn—Sand-water—a name given it by the Norsemen during their time in this northern country. Almost linked to Sandwood Bay is Sandwood Loch, where a small river flows a hundred yards from loch to ocean. One August day when I passed that way a salmon was attempting to make its way up the shallow stream: when the fish saw me it turned tail and literally fled, splashing to the safety of salt water. The salmon passed near some of the wrecks, which are buried in sand above the reach of the highest tide; it is evident that when the wrecks occurred the sea-level was higher than it is at the present day, and Sandwood Loch was a sea loch. It may even be that the vessels were making for the shelter of the sea loch, and were wrecked at the stormy bar.

From Sandwood to Cape Wrath is a distance of seven or eight miles, along a coast that is entirely without human habitations. A couple of miles before Cape Wrath is reached is the site of the ship-wreck of one of the vessels of the fleet of the Norse King Haco—he who is commemorated in Kyleakin and fought the battle of Largs in 1263. The tradition is that all the crew of the war galley were lost, with the exception of two men who, with great daring, scaled the high cliff. One of the men had a hatchet in his belt, and in order that he might be more free for the precipitous climb left the hatchet on a ledge of the rock, where, it is said, the rusted remains can still be seen.

Cape Wrath takes its name from a Norse name, Hvarf, meaning a turning-point. In Gaelic the name is written Am Parbh. The name is given because the coast, which has hitherto run northward, now turns toward the east. In an old description of Sutherland given in vol. iii, p. 100 of MacFarlane's *Geographical Collections*, the writer puts it on record that:

> there is an excellent and delectable place for hunting called the Parve, where they hunt the red Deer in abundance and sometimes they drive them into the Ocean Sea (Atlantic) at the Pharohead (Cape Wrath) where they take them in Boats as they list.

The lighthouse on Cape Wrath is built at a height of 363 feet above the sea, and the light itself is 400 feet above sea-level—so high that its rays are often obscured from passing ships by the ocean clouds which rest upon the headland. With winds from a westerly or north-westerly point, the sea is often heavy and dangerous here, and vessels keep well off-shore when passing.

Cape Wrath is one of the best places on the Scottish coast from which to watch the passing gannets. From March until autumn, and at certain times in winter, these ocean birds are seen to pass in an almost continuous stream. It is possible that here are seen the gannet population of St. Kilda, Sùla Sgeir and Suleskerry Stack, flying to or from their fishing grounds. An almost equally good observation post for the study of these birds in flight is the lighthouse on the Butt of Lewis. On the April day when I stood on Cape Wrath the wind was north and the gannets were, almost all of them, flying south. They arrived a little way off-shore, having followed the north coast of Scotland from the direction of the Pentland Firth. When they had rounded Cape Wrath they flew, with easy, gliding flight, towards the distant coast of Lewis. They may have been St. Kilda birds returning after fishing in the North Sea; that flight would not be nearly so far as the journeys the shearwaters of Skokholm in the Irish Sea make when flying thence to feed in the waters of the Bay of Biscay. The stacks of St. Kilda, where the gannets nest, stand at an approximate distance of 160 miles south-west of Cape Wrath.

There is a narrow road to the lighthouse at Cape Wrath from the Kyle of Durness. It is a disappointing walk, for there is little or no view the whole distance of eight miles; yet, because of this, the sudden view, as one approaches the lighthouse, of blue sea and high cliffs is the more inspiring. Here, a little way out to sea, are two low rocks, over which the Atlantic swells cream. The names of these rocks are Am Bodach—the Old Man, and A' Chailleach—the Old Woman. One sees, too, a slender stack which rises near Sandwood Bay, and is named Am Buachaille—the Herdsman.

At the Kyle of Durness we have reached again the estuary of the Dionard river. This Kyle of golden sands broadens out into Balnacille Bay. The name means Township of the Cell or Church. At Balnacille was the site of one of the oldest Culdee settlements in Sutherland. The Culdees were early missionaries from Iona. In the old church of Balnacille is buried one who was a remarkable character. His full name, as we should now spell it, is Donald MacMurrach Mac Iain Mhoir. He was a native of Lewis and was compelled to leave that island. He was sheltered for some time by MacLeod of Assynt before the great MacKay, father of the first Lord Reay, conferred upon him the life rent of the lands of Westmoin. He is said to have been a man ruthless and powerful. One of his crimes is said to have been committed near Scourie, at a loch named Bhaidarach. A man named James MacLeod had incurred the enmity of the MacKays and the Morrisons (perhaps this refers to Judge Morrison, the hated king's representative in Lewis), and Donald MacMurrach was engaged to kill him. James MacLeod, realising his danger, was at the time living in a straw-thatched hut on the island of Loch Bhaidarach, and perhaps felt safe, but Donald fired arrows with burning grass bound to them at the hut, and soon set it alight. When the owner appeared in view he was shot dead. His son attempted to swim ashore and escape, but Donald shot him also. It is said that he had been promised the half of Eddrachillis for this crime.

In a recess in the wall of the old church at Balnacille Donald's stone coffin can be seen. The inscription on it is as follows:

> DONALD MAC MURCHON
> HIER LYIS LO:
> VAS ILL TO HIS FREEND
> VAR TO HIS FO:
> TRUE TO HIS MAISTER
> IN WEIRD OR WO:
>
> 1623.

On the gravestone are skull and crossbones, and a figure, supposed to be Diarmid slaying the wild boar on Ben Loyal. It is said that, to prevent his enemies desecrating his grave, Donald MacMurrach gave 1,000 merks to the Master of Reay, who was then building the church, to reserve a burial place for him in its wall, in order that the people he had wronged should not be able to walk over him. It is said, too, that he is buried in an upright position. In this churchyard is the grave of Rob Donn, the Reay bard.

There are grounds for believing that the monastic settlement of Balnacille was founded by Saint Maolrubha of Applecross. In various districts of the west and north-west coast there are traditions of a Sagart Ruadh, or Red Priest, who, some people think, was Maolrubha; his time was the late seventh century. Durness is one of the places where he is still spoken of, or was by the old people. I have elsewhere in this book noted that Maolrubha gave directions that "four red men" of Aporerosan were to carry his body from the Black Isle to Applecross. Can it be that in the titles Red Priest, and Red Men, we have the contemporary designation of a certain order of the early Celtic Church?

There is a burial ground also on Eilean Hoan, off the mainland shore. It would seem from one of the poems by Rob Donn that islands were sometimes chosen for burial places because of the wolves which roamed the countryside; in the district of Cape Wrath, according to an old account, "verie great plentie of wolves do hunt in this desert place."

Balnacille house stands very near the sea. It is an old house, and was the home of the eldest son of the Lord Reay of the time for several generations, the eldest son having the courtesy title Master of Reay.

Running north from Balnacille is a rather narrow, sandy promontory, the haunt of many rabbits, which ends at Fair Ard, anglicised as Far Out Head. Buzzards have their home on the promontory, no doubt attracted by the rabbit population. One looks from here across the sea to Orkney, the cliffs of Hoy rising on the horizon.

Near Balnacille and Durness, with fertile lands and large crofts, is the Cave of Smoo, consisting of three immense caverns. A boat is necessary to visit the two inner caverns, and to enter the last of them the occupants of the boat have to lie flat. Lights are also necessary. The cave is covered with stalactites and stalagmites. Sir Walter Scott, on the cruise during which he visited Cape Wrath, was impressed by the Cave of Smoo. He wrote in his diary: "A water kelpie or an evil spirit of aquatic propensities could not have chosen a fitter abode; and, to say the truth, I believe at our first entrance, and when all our feelings were afloat at the novelty of the scene, the unexpected splashing of a seal would have routed the whole dozen of us." The Smoo burn falls into the cave from a height of 80 feet.

Durness is the starting point of the daily bus to the railway at Lairg, over sixty miles distant. Jimmy the bus driver has been for many years a popular figure. Even in summer the run is a long one; in winter the conditions are sometimes Arctic. Shovels are then carried, but on occasion the bus is snowed up on the high slopes of the Gualann, and the passengers must be prepared to make themselves as comfortable as possible until they are dug out.

CHAPTER VI

ERIBOLL AND TONGUE

THE people of the north coast of Sutherland are strong and virile; from early times they had the reputation of being of unusual intelligence. It is said that one reason for this was that, Lord Reay's eldest son having his home at Balnacille, the district was in contact with the outside world, and that noted men stayed there, and noted preachers officiated at the local church. Gaelic is still spoken by the older people, but it is doubtful whether, as a living language, it will survive when the present generation have passed away. The surnames of most of the inhabitants are, as might be expected from the associations of the district, MacKay.

On the coast four miles east of Durness Loch Eriboll bites deep into the land. Eriboll is a Norse name; it is from bol, a farm, and eyrr, a beach. When Haco's fleet of war galleys was anchored in the loch in October of the year 1263, there was an eclipse of the sun which alarmed the Vikings considerably. They sent a party of men ashore for water, and they were set upon by the people of the district: only one man lived to return to the fleet. If one reads the *Haco Saga*, one is given the impression that this was an instance of "unprovoked aggression," but the tradition of the country is that the Norsemen were raiding cattle and sheep when they were intercepted. The graves of Vikings who were slain are still pointed out on the shore of the loch.

The distance between Loch Eriboll and the Kyle of Tongue is, in a straight line, no more than six miles, but very much farther by road. At the head of the loch is fine scenery, where Strath Beag winds among the hills. Here one is not far from Foinne Bheinn, and the strath is in one place less that two miles from Loch Dionard. One of the corries which rise from the glen is named Uruisg Choire. There is, as I have elsewhere recorded, Coire nan Uruisgean in the Trossachs. The Uruisg was a supernatural being, and only a wild and grim corrie would bear that name.

The road leads along the east shore of Loch Eriboll, then turns inland and crosses the river Hope where it leaves Loch Hope, a long

311

and narrow loch. The river Hope is, for its length, among the best salmon rivers in Scotland. The road to Tongue from the Hope river rises quickly and crosses a wild stretch of moorland named A' Mhoine —the Moss. When it reaches the Kyle of Tongue it forks, one branch leading to Melness, the other to the head of the Kyle and thence to Tongue on the farther shore. As one drives or walks up the kyle there is a particularly striking view of Ben Loyal, a mighty hill, which rises to a height of just over 2,500 feet. At the approaches to Tongue is, or rather was, for they are now being felled, one of the rare woods of the Sutherland coast. Tongue House was the home of the chiefs of the MacKays—they who latterly bore the title Lord Reay. The Duke of Sutherland, who now owns the House of Tongue, tells me that in 1829 Lord Reay sold the Reay Country to his ancestor for £300,000. The following is an excerpt from Sir Wm. Fraser's *Sutherland Book* (vol. i, pp. 36-7):

ACQUISITION OF THE REAY COUNTRY.

During the lifetime of the Duchess-Countess of Sutherland large acquisitions of territory were added to the ancient earldom. After her marriage to Lord Gower, who afterwards became Marquis of Stafford and first Duke of Sutherland, he in 1829 purchased from Eric, Lord Reay, the whole of the Reay country, at a cost of £300,000. He also at different times acquired the following lands: The estate of Bighouse, from Major Colin MacKay; the barony of Skelbo, in the parish of Creich; the lands of Armadale and Strathy, in the barony of Farr; the barony of Torboll; the lands of Uppat near Dunrobin; the estate of Carrol in the parish of Clyne; that of Ardross, with fishings on the Shin; part of the Kyles of Oykel and the Dornoch Firth; the lands of Inveran, from MacLeod of Cadboll; with the superiority of the burgh of Wick and certain properties in Dornoch. Besides these purchased by the first Duke, his son, the second Duke, prior to 1835 purchased the lands of Creich, also the lands of Langwell, being part of the Skibo estate, another part of the same estate, Sandycroft or Captain's Park, being acquired by an excambion with Mr. Dempster of Skibo; likewise the lands of Teabreck, near Tain, and the lands of Embo, with various properties in the burghs of Tain, Wick, and Dornoch.

These acquisitions of lands by the first and second Dukes were of great value and extent, and consolidated by far the greater portion of Sutherland in their possession. Originally the Sutherland interest lay on the east coast, stretching northwards from the Dornoch Firth, and the acquisition of the western portion of the country gave them a continuous stretch from Dornoch on the east to Tongue and Cape Wrath on the west.

There is a legend that Sir Donald MacKay, the first Lord Reay, was most learned, and studied the black art. It is said that, like a ghost, he cast no shadow as he walked, and on one occasion overcame the Devil in a hand-to-hand fight. The old heroes of the Gael made use of the magic art. We read of the beardless Cuchulainn providing himself with a magic beard by pronouncing a spell over a handful of grass. Tongue House is a pleasant building, sheltered by trees. The garden is a singularly beautiful one, and when I visited it in mid-September was a blaze of colour. In the garden is an attractive sun-dial of unusual design; it bears the date 1714. The House of Tongue, although close to the sea, is sheltered from the winds of ocean.

A few miles down the Kyle is a wind-swept and bare island named Eilean nan Ron—Isle of Seals—or Roan Island. The human population left this island during recent years, for the people found it too lonely, and there was considerable difficulty in launching and securing a boat, since there is no proper harbour. The old people were reluctant to leave, but they could not continue to live on the island without the help of the younger generation. The same thing happened on St. Kilda, the young people more or less forcing the older generation to leave that island. The houses on Roan Island remain and, as viewed from the sea, appear to be still (1949) in a good state of repair. As we circled the island in a motor-launch an escort of fulmars took up their station astern; they nest on the island cliffs.

After the strong winds and ocean swell of the Kyle of Tongue it was a pleasant contrast to stand on the green, sheltered lawn of the House of Tongue and to hear on the evening air the clear notes of that old pibroch, "Lament for Donald Dugall MacKay," sometimes called "Lord Reay's Lament." It is an old tune, with sea sorrow in it, and is exceedingly musical and beautiful. The tune ended as the night wind rustled the fading leaves of the trees.

The motto of the MacKays is *Manu Forti*: it appears on one of the three pediments which are built into the wall of the dining room of the House of Tongue. That over the mantelpiece bears an ornamental shield charged with the MacKay arms. On the sloping side of the pediment is the motto: the MacKays are said to have adopted it when

Queen Mary, being at Inverness, summoned the chief of the clan to appear before her. He, since he was doubtful of his reception, and even of his head, did not obey the summons. Later, when the Earl of Sutherland by the queen's command visited him, and asked him by what right he held his lands, he clasped his dagger and laid his hand, holding it, on the table, exclaiming, "Lamh laidir"—by my strong hand. These significant words, in Latin, have been the motto of the MacKays since that day.

The road along the coast passes Bettyhill, at the estuary of the river Naver, where there is a pleasant beach on which the Atlantic waves break slowly. The Naver is the Nabaros mentioned by Ptolemy among the rivers of Scotland. From Bettyhill the road continues along the coast to Melvich and shortly afterwards crosses the county boundary to Caithness. The village of Reay, from which Lord Reay takes his title, is actually just inside Caithness. There is a road south through Strath Halladale, thence over the watershed to Strath Kildonan and the Helmsdale river, celebrated for its salmon fishing. In the Suisgill burn, a tributary of the Helmsdale, gold has been found, and its discovery a century ago occasioned a gold rush. It is said that the total value of the gold discovered in the district then was £12,000.

The east coast is reached at Helmsdale, and the road along that coast, to Golspie and the south, does not come within the province of this book, but it is worth recording that the fulmar has very recently bred on Dunrobin Castle, after frequenting the seaward face of the castle in the summers of 1947, 1948 and 1949. Pennant makes two interesting observations on Dunrobin Castle and its district. He says that the crocus has been cultivated at Dunrobin, showing that this spring flower was then much rarer than it now is, and he notes a particularly fine field of ripening wheat when he passed that way. Sir Robert Gordon records that tobacco was grown at Dunrobin in the seventeenth century.

If we return to Tongue, we find there a good road leading almost due south to Lairg, across the moors and beneath the hills. It traverses Loch Loyal and passes close to Ben Loyal and, at Altnaharra, is close to another loch of considerable size, Loch Naver. Ben Klibreck here dominates the scene, a noble hill which is visible from great distances, even from the Cairngorms. The road from Bettyhill through Strath Naver joins the Tongue road at Altnaharra. Strath Naver, once a populous glen with good land, suffered during the evictions perhaps more than any other Highland strath.

Some four miles up the strath is a small loch, on the opposite side of the river from the road. The name of the loch is Loch mo Naire, and its waters are said to have miraculous healing properties, for all persons except those bearing the surname Gordon. The tradition is that a woman, carrying with her certain pebbles which effected miraculous cures when dipped in water, was chased down the strath by a man of the name of Gordon, who wished to take the stones from her. When she reached the loch, she threw the pebbles into the water, calling out "Mo Nàire, Mo Nàire"—shame, shame. The pebbles are supposed to give the water of the loch its healing properties. It is necessary in order to be cured to reach the loch on the first Monday of May, or the first Monday of August (presumably Old Style) at midnight. The sufferer awaits the dawn, strips himself or herself with no spoken word, and before entering the loch, throws in a coin. He or she wades far in, and allows the water to close over the head three times. During each total immersion the sufferer must wish fervently to be cured. After dressing, and walking sunwise round the loch, the pilgrim must walk beyond sight of the loch before sunrise.

After passing Altnaharra the road slowly climbs to a height of 828 feet at the Crask (An Crasg—the Crossing), where there is often considerable drifting in winter and early spring. It is a lonely crossing of the watershed, with no house in sight. To the north-west Ben Hee (2,864 feet) rises beyond lesser hills; east is the Ben Klibreck massif. From the Crask southward is a long and gentle slope to Loch Shin and Lairg.

Among the most remote districts of Sutherland are the deer forests of Ben Armine, or what Sir Robert Gordon terms "the two hills called Bin-Ormin," and Loch Choire. Ben Armine lodge is sixteen miles from the nearest telegraph office, at Rogart, and the delivery of a telegram here is an expensive business, as I found to my cost. Ben Armine—the Hill of the Hero—rises beyond the lodge, and there is a track through the hills to Loch Choire Lodge, which stands beside Loch Choire and beneath Ben Klibreck. The stalker at Ben Armine may be snowed up for weeks at a time.

Caithness not being generally considered a Highland county, I shall have little to say of it. Langwell deer forest, which is just beyond the Sutherland boundary, is the site of one of the most distinctive hills in Scotland, Morven or the Great Hill. There are several Morvens; one of which, rising near Dinnet on Deeside, was thus written of by Byron:

> When I roved a young Highlander over the heath
> Or climbed thy dark summit, oh Morven of snow.

The view from Morven on a clear day is unusually wide. South rise the Cairngorms; north is to be seen Orkney; west are the great Sutherland hills, often under cloud when Morven itself is clear. Indeed Morven is singularly free of mist, perhaps because it rises to the east of the watershed, and has no high hills near it to call down the clouds. Beneath Morven is the source of the Langwell water. This small river was for some weeks during a recent year haunted by an osprey, which was often watched diving for fish in the pools. It may have been a young bird of the year, on its way south from Lapland or Sweden. It disappeared during a flood, when the river was too muddy for fish to be visible.

I have taken the reader through Sutherland, across the hills and along its stern and lonely shores, with their Viking associations. I have described the grandeur of Foinne Bheinn, and the gannet-haunted coast of Cape Wrath. I have said nothing of a comparatively small hill between Foinne Bheinn and Cape Wrath, but the book may be fittingly closed with an account of a summer sunset which I had from this hill, Farraval by name, and when I see that hill, as I occasionally do from my home in the north of Skye, just, and only just, emerging from the distant ocean horizon, I recall that midsummer evening when I had what was one of the most memorable experiences of my days and nights on the Highland hills.

I was staying at Gualann at the time. The day had been hot, and the river, low and clear, did not encourage fishing. It was after supper that two friends and I set out to climb the hill—an easy walk from the Gualann—for it was evident that a sunset of unusual beauty might be expected that night. Farraval is a hill with a broad brow. It is no more than 1,600 feet in height, but is unusually wind-swept, and the junipers which grow on these upper slopes—these plants are here more common than usual—creep prostrate over the ground, and their growth, because of the prevailing west winds and gales, is almost entirely to the east of the main root. It was half past ten by summer time when we reached the small cairn on the hill-top. The glowing orb of the sun was still above the horizon. The distant horizon was hazy and it was not possible to tell where the sky ended and the sea began. The sun revealed this mystery for us, for as the orb reached the horizon its spherical shape was apparently changed. A stalk seemed to grow from it, a glowing stalk which held a mushroom-shaped suin. Slowly that stalk of red fire was quenched in the waters of the Atlantc; slowly the sun dipped. At eighteen minutes to eleven, or 9.42 by the sun's time, the upper rim at last vanished, and a pool of deep red formed upon that distant sea, perhaps seventy miles distant, beneath which it had set. Foinne Bheinn for a few seconds continued to glow with purple light, then his summit, cone-shaped as seen from Farraval, became cold and grey. The sea wind died; like a jewel Loch Dionard lay amethystine. A golden plover rose and flew on swift wings eastward. There was no darkness that night, and very early the sun climbed again above the horizon, this time from the direction of Hoy in Orkney.

Could one expect one such day, one such evening, in each year, all the storms, the bitter gales, the might of the elements hurled, as it were, against the face of puny man, would be worth enduring for the sake of a beauty that is scarcely of earth, but is rather of Tir nan Og— the Land of Immortals.

INDEX

324